JAMS
AND
JELLIES

May Byron

JAMS
AND
JELLIES

543 Recipes

Dover Publications, Inc., New York

International Standard Book Number: 0-486-23130-5
Library of Congress Catalog Card Number: 74-83766

Manufactured in the United States of America
Dover Publications, Inc.
180 Varick Street
New York, N.Y. 10014

NOTE FOR THE
AMERICAN READER

BOTH THE LIQUID AND DRY MEASURES used in this book are British imperial measures. The *liquid* measures—pints, quarts and gallons—are a little more than 20% larger than the corresponding American ones; one British imperial gallon, for example, is approximately equivalent to *five* American quarts. The difference between British and American *dry* measures—pints, quarts, pecks and bushels—is only 5% and may be disregarded for the purposes of this book.

Granulated sugar may be substituted for *loaf sugar*, which is not available in the United States. *Caster sugar* is a very fine granulated sugar. *Demerara sugar* is a type of brown sugar, and *icing sugar* is confectioners' sugar.

Some of the fruits mentioned which are not commercially grown in the United States may only be available in specialty shops or not at all. It is not advised that Rowan jelly be made because the berries of the Mountain Ash in the United States may be poisonous.

While the great value of this book lies in its unique recipes, the methods given for preserving jam and jellies are somewhat outdated. The following methods for making and storing jellied fruit products are those approved by the United States Department of Agriculture.

Jelly glasses or canning jars may be used as containers for jellied fruit products. Be sure all jars and closures are perfect. Discard any with cracks or chips; defects prevent airtight seals.

For jellies and for fruit products firm enough to be sealed with paraffin, use glasses or straight-sided containers that will make an attractive mold.

For preserves and soft jams, use canning jars with lids that can be tightly sealed. (Paraffin tends to loosen and break the seal on such products.) In warm, humid climates, put all jams, conserves, and marmalades in canning jars with lids that can be sealed tightly.

Get glasses or jars ready before you start to make the jellied product. Wash containers in warm, soapy water and rinse with hot water. Keep them hot—either in a slow oven or in hot water—until they are used. This will prevent containers from breaking when filled with hot jelly or jam.

Wash and rinse all lids and bands. Metal lids with sealing compound may need boiling or holding in boiling water for a few minutes—follow the manufacturer's directions.

If you use porcelain-lined zinc caps, have clean, new rings of the right size for jars. Wash rings in hot, soapy water. Rinse well.

To seal with lids. — Use only standard home canning jars and lids. For jars with two-piece lids: Fill hot jars to ⅛ inch of top with hot jelly or fruit mixture. Wipe jar rim clean, place hot metal lid on jar with sealing compound next to glass, screw metal band down firmly, and stand jar upright to cool. For jars with porcelain-lined zinc caps: Place wet rubber ring on shoulder of empty jar. Fill jar to ⅛ inch of top, screw cap down tight to complete seal, and stand jar upright to cool.

Work quickly when packing and sealing jars. To keep fruit from floating to the top, gently shake jars of jam occasionally as they cool.

To seal with paraffin. — Use this method only with mixtures that make fairly firm products. Use only enough paraffin to make a layer ⅛ inch thick. A single thin layer—which can expand or contract readily—gives a better seal than one thick layer or two thin layers. Prick air bubbles in paraffin. Bubbles cause holes as paraffin hardens; they may prevent a good seal. A double boiler is best for melting paraffin and keeping it hot without reaching smoking temperature.

For jelly, pour hot mixture immediately into hot glass containers to within ½ inch of top and cover with hot paraffin.

For jam, conserves, and marmalades, remove from heat and stir gently at frequent intervals for 5 minutes. This will help prevent floating fruit in the finished product. Before each stirring, skim off all foam that appears on the surface. Pour into hot glass containers to within ½ inch of top. Cover immediately with hot paraffin.

Storing jellied fruit products. — Let products stand overnight to avoid breaking gel. Cover glasses with metal or paper lids. Label with name, date, and lot number if you make more than one lot a day. Store in cool, dry place; the shorter the storage time, the better the eating quality of the product.

Uncooked jams may be held up to 3 weeks in a refrigerator; for longer storage, they should be placed in a freezer.

CONTENTS

CHAPTER I

REMARKS IN GENERAL

CHAPTER II

JAMS, JELLIES, MARMALADES, ETC.

APPLE

CONTENTS

CONTENTS

CRANBERRY

CURRANTS, BLACK

CURRANTS, RED AND WHITE

DATE

ELDER

FIG

GOOSEBERRY

GRAPE

GRAPEFRUIT OR POMELO

GUAVA

LEMON

CONTENTS ix

CONTENTS

CONTENTS

xi

RASPBERRY, LOGANBERRY, WINEBERRY

RHUBARB

ROWAN OR MOUNTAIN ASH

STRAWBERRY

CONTENTS

CHAPTER III

PRESERVES OF MIXED FRUITS

CONTENTS

CONTENTS

CHAPTER IV

FRUITS PRESERVED WHOLE IN SYRUP OR SUGAR

CHAPTER V

FRUIT CHEESES AND PASTES

CONTENTS

CHAPTER VI

FRUIT BUTTERS

CHAPTER VII

CANDIED, CRYSTALLISED, AND BRANDIED FRUITS

CONTENTS

CHAPTER VIII
SPICED FRUITS

CHAPTER IX
VARIOUS

CHAPTER X

FRUITS BOTTLED WITHOUT SUGAR

CHAPTER XI

DRIED FRUITS, WITH AND WITHOUT SUGAR

CONTENTS

CHAPTER I

REMARKS IN GENERAL

I HAVE entitled this, comprehensively, the *Jam Book*; because when we think of preserved fruit, we mostly think of it as jam—*i.e.* fruit preserved in a heavy solution of sugar. But it is really designed to cover the preservation of fruit in all branches of that culinary art: jams, jellies, marmalades, preserves, conserves, cheeses ; pastes, butters, chips ; fruit crystallised, candied, and brandied ; fruit dried and fruit bottled, with or without sugar, every possible means by which one can keep for a long while those fruits which are naturally shortlived things.

The object of preserving fruit is to ward off, exclude, or neutralise those bacilli which otherwise would cause its almost immediate decay. A heavy solution of sugar ; a strong acid, like vinegar ; or storage in sterilised jars (which is usually termed "bottling," or "canning") in which the fruit is externally heated to boiling-point—these are the three most popular methods. The preservation of fruit in syrup is sometimes, but not always, a blend of Nos. 1 and 3. The drying of fruit is but little practised in Britain.

It has been well said by an eminent authority on
diet, that preserved fruit is an essential both as
food and to health : not a luxury, but " one of the
most useful and economical foods in existence."
Preserved fruit conveys the acids, mineral salts, and
other medicinal properties of the fruit in question,
plus its concentrated food value, with or without
the very important item of sugar. It is extremely
palatable and pleasant, and it provides a means of
saving illimitable quantities of perishable material.

This is one of the most important branches of
human industry—and one of the most neglected,
since people took to purchasing instead of preserving.
The purchasable commodity has, hitherto, been
very little dearer, and sometimes much cheaper, than
what one could provide for one's self. Yet in no
possible respect can the former compare with the
latter, where inherent value is concerned. The
constituents of bought jam are not the constituents
of home-made jam, and the chemical preservatives
employed in the making of the one, are happily unknown in the concoction of the other. But, by
some means or other, it is certain that jam must
be procurable. We cannot do without preserved
fruit in some form.

The present volume is intended to deal, not only
with the ordinary domestic methods of fruit-pre-
serving, which, to a greater or less extent, are to be
found in all cookery books, but with those means
which do not necessitate the use of sugar, and
which, therefore, are specially to be invoked at the
present time. It is imperative that we should
waste nothing—that fruits hitherto allowed to fall

should be harvested, that fruits hitherto largely ignored or neglected should contribute their quota towards the help of human needs. The reader will probably be surprised to find how many fruits, whether singly or in combination, may be preserved by economic methods and with satisfactory results. She would probably be far more surprised, could she realise the appalling wastage, to be reckoned probably in thousands of tons, which goes on yearly throughout this kingdom, owing to inertia, lack of knowledge, sparsity of enterprise, and want of co-operation.

If the possessors of good preserving-pans shared these utensils with less fortunate neighbours, and if country people well supplied with tree fruit combined in the joint purchase of a "steriliser" for bottling, or an "evaporator" for desiccating, there would be no loss, but vast profit, to everybody concerned ; and the "kindly fruits of the earth" would not be thrown away upon us as they so long have been. We import enormous quantities of dried foreign fruit ; we might utilise our own, with a minimum of trouble and expenditure. There is no apple on earth, for instance, to beat the English apple ; yet it is left to rot upon a million trees, whilst our more frugal Transatlantic kinsfolk turn their apples into dried rings and so forth, and—sell them to us—at a very good price !

The same remarks apply to fruit-pulp—of which a vast amount is annually imported from the Continent by our jam factories, which could be chiefly well supplied by English fruit-growers. All that is needed is common sense, knowledge,

and collaboration. There are fortunes to be made
over fruit-pulp by those who have a fraction of
" push-and-go."

However, this book is mainly intended for the
individual housewife, who will, it is hoped and
believed, be able to avail herself with ease and
economy of the very large number of recipes for
preserving fruit.

NECESSARY UTENSILS

(Indispensable for preserving on a small scale)

Copper, bell-metal, or enamel-lined preserving-
pan.

Double-boiler.

Small enamelled pans.

Coarse and fine sieves.

Jelly-bags of flannel and of butter-muslin.

Earthen or crockery bowls (deep).

Earthen jar with lid.

Wooden spoons (also termed spaddles and
spatulas).

Colander.

Scales.

Parchment, waxed paper, bladder, labels, string.

Glass jars or bottles, and white pots, of various
sizes.

Perforated skimmer.

Large fish-kettle or boiler.

(Indispensable for preserving on a larger scale)

Orange cutter.

Cherry stoner.

Fruit corer.

The rest consists of passages of imitation between bass and treble, and of good modulation, all couched in beautiful and melodious forms, and ending with a very graceful passage in double counterpoint over a pedal of ten bars' length on A, resolving into the tonic on the first note of the *Allegro con brio*:

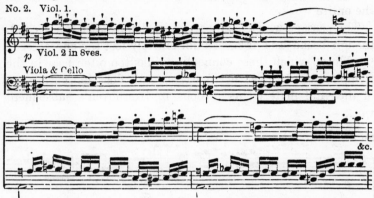

It is strange at this early date to meet with the arpeggio of the chord of D minor, in a shape which almost textually anticipates the Ninth Symphony—

The opening of the principal theme of the *Allegro* is one of the passages just alluded to as belonging to the old school in the distinct definition and regularity of its construction—

But though square in cut it is by no means wanting in
spirit; and the fiery flash of the fiddles in the interval between
the two sections of the subject (bar 4 of the quotation) is
splendid, and gives a good specimen of the extraordinary
energy which imbues that seraphic instrument throughout
the entire work.

The passage which connects this theme with the second,
though broad and free, has not entirely lost the character of
' padding,' which these connecting links too often bear in the
Symphonies of the earlier masters ; and does not spring out
of the vital material as it does in Beethoven's subsequent
work—

No. 5.

The second theme itself—

No. 6.

has a certain precise military air about it, but is full of vivacity,
and is wonderfully set off by the energetic brilliancy of the
violins, which here (bar 8), as in the first theme, rush in
between the strains of the subject.

On the repetition of the subject in the flutes, clarinets,
horns, and bassoons, it is accompanied by the strings in a

delightful tremolo, a figure which is quite a characteristic of this Symphony—

The passage which follows the second subject is cast in a quasi-canonical form—

smacking strongly of the old school, and not founded on the materials already quoted.   It is after eight bars of this connecting matter that the capricious passage occurs, to which allusion has been already made, and which is the more interesting because it seems to act as a warrant for something similarly wilful in others of the Symphonies.   Beethoven is about to close in the key of A, is, in fact, within one chord of so doing, (*) when it occurs to him suddenly to interrupt the close by the intrusion of ten bars—

made up from a characteristic figure in the first theme (see No. 4), and of excellent effect, but still absolutely capricious in their introduction here, and doubtless a great puzzle to the hearers of 1803.

The working-out is masterly, not only for its contrivances —canon, double counterpoint, modulations, &c.—but also for its effects of instrumentation, beautiful solo use of the wind, brilliant figures for the violins, and new accompaniments to the subjects—witness especially the triplets which accompany the second subject in a passage shortly before the *reprise*. In the *reprise* itself a good deal of condensation occurs. The *Coda*, though brilliant and effective, contains no new or very striking features.

II. The *Larghetto*, in its elegant, indolent beauty—which is seriously impaired if the movement is taken too fast—is an absolute contrast to the sharp, definite, somewhat peremptory tone of the *Allegro*. Its repetitions are endless, but who ever wished them curtailed ?

That strain again—it had a dying fall.

It is in A, the dominant of the original key, and is couched in the ordinary ' first movement ' form. Its principal theme is in two strains of eight bars each, each strain given out by the strings and then repeated by the wind, with exquisite enrichments in the violins—

In a book of sketches in the Bibliothek at Berlin, Mr. Shedlock has recently discovered the following fragment, apparently a very early draft of this beautiful melody (the signature of A major must be understood)—

No. 12.

That given by Thayer, in his *Thematisches Verzeichniss* (No. 103), and by Nottebohm, in his publication of the Sketch Book of 1802 (p. 11), already spoken of, would seem to be rather aimed at the slow movement of Symphony No. 5—

No. 13. *Andante Sinfonia.*

Corni soli.   &c.

It may have been intended for this Symphony, but can hardly be a sketch for the present *Larghetto*.

After the repetition of the strain quoted as No. 11, a continuation is afforded by the following melody, alternating between wind and string—

No. 14.

Upon this follows the second theme proper of the movement, in the orthodox key of E major; a theme which maintains the same character as the foregoing, with a certain pleasant, lazy grace inherent in its syncopations, both of melody and bass, which will be noticed in the *Adagio* of the Ninth Symphony. It is given first plain—

No. 15.   Viol. 1.

Bassi *p*   *cres.*

and then in a florid form.   And this leads to a short passage
of close harmony (the origin of which may perhaps be traced
in a Quartet of Haydn's—No. 9 in Peters's Collection, ' 15 '—
as follows) :—

No. 16.

though Beethoven has added a point in the cross accents.
He gives the passage first with the strings alone—

No. 17.

and then with the full band.   Eight bars of fanciful drollery
(anticipating the demisemiquavers of the next quotation)
lead into the key of E, and to the following beautiful passage,
which is worthy to be the second chief theme of the movement, though technically it is merely the development of the
ordinary coda-figure.   This is given out by the cellos, with
second violins in octaves—

No. 18.

Its quaint grace, the contrast of *legato* and *staccato*,
and the air of quasi-mystery that pervades it—as if the

cellos were communicating some *segreto d' importanza* in a stage-whisper——are full of inimitable though quiet humour.

This ends the first section of the *Larghetto* and completes the materials of the movement. But Beethoven (with a curious contrast to the rough bluntness of his manners) seems bent on showing us with what minute refinement he can set off, adorn, and elaborate the lovely ideas which he has thus laid before us in their simple form. The labour and pains involved in the process must have been immense; but, here as elsewhere, he never spared himself, and never relinquished a passage till it was as good as he could make it; and hence one great part of the secret of the immortality of his music.

The working-out section begins at once with a modification of the initial theme (No. 10) in the minor, thus deliciously introduced—

No. 19.

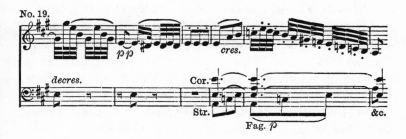

and developed for some considerable time with consummate skill, great beauty of modulation, and continual variety of *nuance*.

As the working-out proceeds the ornamentation grows more and more rich, delicate, melodious, and fanciful. Here is a specimen of imitation, bar by bar, between the oboes in octaves, with bassoon a further octave lower, and the basses, with an elegant figure in the first violin, and an exciting iteration in the violas and cellos—

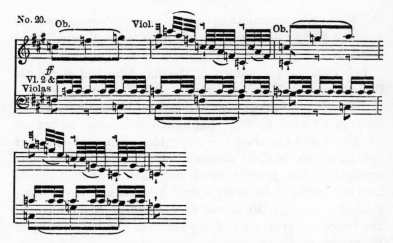

The figures are so clearly and craftily designed, and the instrumentation is so thin and so nicely calculated, that there is no difficulty in following it all in performance. These airy and refined ornaments may well have been Schubert's models for the similar enrichments which so greatly adorn the *Andante* of his great Symphony in C. We know, at any rate, that the movement now before us was especially dear to him, from the fact that he has followed it (down even to details) in the slow movement of his Grand Duo (Op. 140) for the pianoforte in C major.* And doubtless he 'heard the angels singing' in the *Larghetto* of Beethoven's Second Symphony, as we know that he did in the *Trio* of Mozart's G minor.

So flowing and vocal throughout is this beautiful movement in its subjects, their developments and ornaments, that it is not surprising that it has been frequently arranged for voices and for instrumental chamber music. Of the former, one, which still commands a certain sale, dates from as early as the year 1831, and is a duet for two sopranos, with piano accompaniment, arranged by Professor Edward Taylor, and

---

* Instrumented by Joachim, and played at the Crystal Palace on March 4, 1876. 'Sinfonie von Franz Schubert. Nach Op. 140 instrumentirt von Joseph Joachim.' Vienna : F. Schreiber.

inscribed to Mr. Thos. Attwood, one of the leading musicians of the day. Another, published in Germany, is for soprano solo, to words by Silcher, of equal significance.

III. The *Scherzo*, in D, is more individual and original than either of the preceding movements—though still below the level of the Beethoven whom we know. Its picturesqueness and force, the humorous alternations of soft and loud, and of dashes and dots (too much neglected in the recent editions), and the directness of the means for producing them, are remarkable. It opens thus—

and after sixteen bars comes the double bar, and then the following piquant tune, and wild solution (again with the rushing fiddles)—

This is worked for some little time with a kind of obstinate monotony, and then repeated, till at length the first tune returns, this time in oboe and bassoon, heralded in the most saucy manner by the alternate play of the two violins—

Nothing more picturesque and seizing can well be imagined.

The *Trio*—still in D, and wanting no subtle change of key to make it interesting—begins with the following melody harmonized in four parts for oboes and bassoons, reinforced at the sixth bar by the horns—

No. 24.

This is repeated, making sixteen bars in all. We are then, without an instant's warning, plunged head over ears into F sharp major, and, as it were, held there till the water runs into our eyes and ears—

No. 25.

then as suddenly back again into D, *fortissimo*—

No. 26.

The spirit and vigour of these two little movements are really astonishing. The music seems sometimes almost to fly at your throat. Note the constant sudden contrasts both in amount and quality of sound. In amount we find *f*, *p*, *ff*, *pp* alternately almost throughout. In quality we have first the full orchestra, then a single violin, then two horns, then two violins, then the full orchestra again, all within the space of half-a-dozen bars. But the end is chiefly gained by all kinds of unexpected changes of key, not mere senseless freaks, but changes both sudden and suitable, such as at once to rouse the attention, and, with all their oddity, to convince the reason and satisfy the taste. We start in D; then in a moment are in B flat, then in A, then in D, then in F. Then there is the change already noticed in the *Trio*, into F sharp, and back at a blow into D! Such changes of key and tone were too abrupt for the older composers. The musicians of the eighteenth century were too commonly the domestic servants of archbishops and princes, wore powder, and pigtails, and swords, and court dresses, and gold lace, passed their time bowing and waiting in ante-rooms, dined at the servants' table,* and could be abused and even kicked out of the room, as Mozart actually was, and discharged at a moment's notice like ordinary lackeys. Being thus forced to regulate their conduct by etiquette, and habitually to keep down their emotions under decorous rules and forms, they could not suddenly change all their habits when they came to make their music, or give their thoughts and feelings the free and natural vent which they would have had, but for the habits engendered by the perpetual curb and restraint of their social position. In this light one can understand the jovial life of Mozart, the skittles and the suppers, and all the rest. It was his only outlet, and must have been necessary to him—vital. But Beethoven had set such social rules and restrictions at naught. It was his nature, one of the most characteristic things in him, to be free and unrestrained. Almost with his first appearance in Vienna he behaved as the equal of everyone he met, and after he had begun to feel his own way, as he had in this Symphony, his music is constantly showing the independence of his mind.

It is remarkable that nearly twenty years later, in the composition of the *Trio* of the Ninth Symphony, Beethoven should have returned to so early a work as this. The

---

* This fact is specially mentioned in one of Mozart's Letters.

following sketch, however, probably of 1818, is quoted by Nottebohm*—

No. 27.
     Sinfonia 3tes Stück.

It shows, at any rate, that a moving bass, which forms so conspicuous a feature in the actual *Trio* of No. 9, was originally intended to be a feature of the movement.

IV. But to go back to the work itself, it possesses what the First Symphony did not exhibit to the same degree, but what is so eminently characteristic of all the other eight—individuality. It may be possible—if a mere amateur can be allowed the confession—to confound for a moment in recollection the first movement of the First Symphony with the Overture to 'Prometheus,' or its *Finale* with one of Haydn's *Finales.* But with the Second Symphony this is not possible. Each one of its four sections is perfectly distinct and individual in its own proper character, and cannot be confounded with any other movement in any Symphony or other composition, of Beethoven or of any one else. The very terms in which it is spoken of by the early critics show how astonishing it was to the public of that day. The first *Allegro* and the *Scherzo* were the favourite movements. The *Allegro* is constantly termed 'colossal' and 'grand,' words which now could scarcely be applied to it with propriety. The *Larghetto,* strange to say, is hardly mentioned; in fact, in Paris they had—so Berlioz tells† us—to substitute the *Allegretto* from the Seventh

---

* *Zweite Beethoveniana,* p. 165.
† *Voyage Musical,* &c., Paris. 1841, i., 265, 266.

Symphony in order to make the No. 2 go down at all.
But the *Finale* puzzled everybody; it was so harsh (*grell*),
wild, bizarre, and capricious. It was this oddity in the
Finale—this want of decorum, rather than any obscurity
arising from depth of thought—and the difficulty felt by the
performers in mastering the technique of the entire work
(which is always spoken of as extraordinarily hard to play),
that were the two main complaints in the notices of the early
performances. We may be thankful that we now feel neither
of these drawbacks, and that our only sentiment is amusement at the humour and personality of the music, delight at
its grace, and astonishment at its energy and fire. Beside
the *Finales* to Beethoven's Fourth, Fifth, Seventh, and
Eighth Symphonies, with which we are all so familiar, that
of No. 2 finds a lower level; but at that date those great
works were non-existent. The *Finale* to Mozart's G minor
was the most fiery thing in that line that the world then
possessed. But the *Finale* of Beethoven's No. 2 has got
all the fire of *that*, with an amount of force, humour, and
abruptness that even Mozart never evinced, and that must
have taken everyone by surprise in 1803, and have compelled them into listening to it, against their will, against
their æsthetic judgment and sense of propriety, and everything else.

It is in the form called a Rondo (though not strictly that)
and starts in the most abrupt fashion and very fast (*Allegro
molto*)—

No. 28. *Allegro molto.*

Then comes a passage which can hardly be called a subject
or episode—

No. 29.

but its high spirits are in excellent keeping with that which
precedes it, and it leads well into the second subject, which,
though not extraordinary in itself, is most spontaneous, and
very pleasant in sound, with its vocal passages for oboe and
bassoon, and would be well calculated to allay the fever with
which its predecessor started if its lively accompaniment were
not too full of motion (notice here again especially the fiery
intrusions of the violins)—

No. 30.

Long as this subsidiary theme is—unusually long for
Beethoven—it is immediately repeated in the minor; and
then, after a passage of padding, comes the repetition of the
opening subject, led up to by a phrase formed out of its two
initial notes, and accompanied by the bassoon in arpeggios.
This leads into a working-out, with a great deal of humorous
play, before the *reprise* of the original material is reached. In
the *reprise* the second subject (No. 30) is repeated in D, and
this again is followed by a long and very original *Coda*.
This begins with the opening subject (No. 28), but soon

comes to a pause, first on the chord of A, with the dominant seventh on C sharp, and then on the chord of F sharp upon A sharp. And now begins the most individual and Beethovenish part of the entire work. It is as if, after the chord of F sharp, we had passed through a door and were in a new, enchanted world. All that we have heard before vanishes. Earth is forgotten, and we are in Heaven. The rhythm changes; the bass goes down octave after octave *pianissimo*, distinctly heard through the thin scoring—

No. 31. (skeleton)

a fresh subject comes in in the wind; the opening theme is once more alluded to, but only to lead into an entirely new thought —a magic shimmering, impressive as the evening sun shining broad and low on the ocean; a lovely flowing melody in the oboe and bassoon, accompanied in notes of equal value by the basses, and with a pedal D through three octaves in the horns and violins. The beauty of this passage words cannot describe; it is pure Beethoven, a region full of magic and mystery, into which no one before ever led the hearers of music. After further working we arrive at another pause, this time on F sharp itself; a short resumption of the former new rhythm follows, intensified by the bass being *pizzicato;* but it does not last; a rapid ending, and the whole is over !

Such is this beautiful work as it was given us by its author ninety years ago, at his concert on the Tuesday in Holy Week, 1803. And even now, after nearly a century of progress in music, of infinitely greater progress than that in any other art—after Beethoven's own enormous advance, after Schumann, Brahms, Wagner—even now, what can be newer or pleasanter to hear than the whole Symphony? What more delicious than the alternate lazy grace and mysterious humour of the slow movement, the caprice and fire and enchantment of the *Finale*? To this very day the whole work is as fresh as ever in its indomitable fiery flash and its irresistible strength. Were ever fiddles more brilliant than they are here? more rampant in their freaks and vagaries, bursting out like flames in the pauses of the wind, exulting in their strength and beauty—say between the sections of the opening theme in the first *Allegro*—

or between those of the second theme in the same movement—

or in a similar position in the *Finale*—

or in the *Larghetto*—

Had ever the bassoon and oboe such parts before? and so on throughout. Listen to it, and see if it is not so.

In connection with the violins, I may be pardoned
for mentioning a fact which, remembering Beethoven's
minute attention to such points, must surely have some
intentional significance—I mean the prominent occurrence in
every movement of a *tremolo* figure—

in the fiddles. It is found in the *Allegro con brio*, in the
brilliant passages accompanying the first subject, in the
equally brilliant figures accompanying the second subject, and
in the working-out of the same movement. In the *Larghetto*
it frequently occurs ; also in the F sharp passage in the *Trio :*
and in the most characteristic part of the *Coda* of the *Finale*
it is peculiarly effective. It might almost be taken as a motto
for the work. We shall encounter it again in the Fourth
Symphony.

In some respects the Second Symphony is, though not
the greatest, the most interesting of the nine. It shows
with peculiar clearness how firmly Beethoven grasped the
structural forms which had been impressed on instrumental
music when he began to practise it ; while it contains more
than a promise of the strong individuality which possessed
him, and in his works caused him to stretch those forms here
and there, without breaking the bounds which seem to be
indispensable for really coherent and satisfactory composition.
' The same structure,' says Wagner,* ' can be traced in his
last sonatas, quartets, and symphonies as unmistakably as in
his first. But compare these works one with another, place
the Eighth Symphony beside the Second, and wonder at
the entirely new world in almost precisely the same form.'
It has been well said that

> Two worlds at once they view
> Who stand upon the confines of the new ;

---

* Wagner's *Beethoven*—Dannreuther's translation (Reeves, 1880), p. 42.

and taking our stand in the beautiful work which we have just been endeavouring to trace, or rather perhaps in the *Coda* of its *Finale*, we can survey at a glance the region which lies behind—the music of the eighteenth century, at once strong, orderly, elegant, humorous, if perhaps somewhat demure ; and that more ideal region of deeper feeling, loftier imagination, and keener thrill, radiant with ' the light that never was on sea or land,' a region which was opened by Beethoven, and has since been explored by his noble disciples, not unworthy of so great a master.

The Symphony was first performed on the Tuesday in Holy Week ('*Char-Dinstag*'), 5th April, 1803, at a concert given by Beethoven in the ' Theater-an-der-Wien,' Vienna, when the programme included also the Oratorio 'The Mount of Olives,' the First Symphony, and the Piano Concerto in C minor.* The date of the earliest edition is March, 1804—that is, the parts; the score does not appear to have been published till 1820, by Simrock, of Bonn. The work was dedicated to Beethoven's very good friend Prince Charles Lichnowsky. It was arranged by the composer himself as a Trio for pianoforte and strings, which is published in Breitkopf's complete edition, No. 90.

The orchestra is the ordinary Haydn-Mozart one—without trombones, but with the addition of clarinets, and the orchestral effects are often strikingly like those in Mozart's operas, that of ' Figaro,' for instance.

We have now endeavoured to trace the two first steps in Beethoven's Symphonic career.   The next we shall find to be a prodigious stride.

He was always on the advance.   Even in 1800, in forwarding ' Adelaide ' to Mathison the poet, he says: ' I send the song not without anxiety.   You yourself know what change a few years make when one is always advancing.   The greater one's progress in Art, the less is one satisfied with

---

* Thayer, ii., 222.   The report in the *A. m. Z.* mentions the Oratorio only.

one's earlier works.' And he put this maxim into practice with characteristic energy. The famous Septet, which at its first performance in April, 1800, when Haydn's oratorio was all the fashion, he jokingly called his ' Creation,' and which is now a greater favourite than ever with musicians and amateurs alike, he afterwards detested, and would have annihilated if he could. ' What is that? ' he said, on one occasion in his later life to the daughter of his friend Madame Streicher, as she was playing the well-known ever green Thirty-two Variations in C minor, so beloved by Mendelssohn in his late years. ' What is that? Why your own! ' ' Mine? That piece of folly mine?' was the rejoinder; ' Oh, Beethoven, what an ass you must have been! ' In 1822 a conversation is recorded with a Madame Cibbini, very touching when one thinks of this great master, whose artistic life had been one upward progress since the days when he began to compose. The lady said that he was ' the only composer who had never written anything weak or trivial.' ' The devil I am! ' was the retort; 'many and many of my works would I suppress if I could.'

Bearing this in mind, it is easy to appreciate the story of his biographer, Schindler, who informs us that in the year 1816, after the performance of the Seventh and Eighth Symphonies, a proposal was made to Beethoven by a resident* in Vienna to write two Symphonies in the style of his first two. No wonder that the suggestion made him furious. Translate the story into a literary form, and imagine Shakespeare being asked, after he had produced 'Othello' and 'Hamlet,' to write a play in the style of the 'Two Gentlemen of Verona' or ' Love's Labour's Lost,' and the absurdity of this well-meaning amateur will be apparent to everyone.

---

* This is stated by Schindler (ii., 367) to have been General Ham, an Englishman. The fact of the proposal may be true, but I have ascertained, by the courtesy of the authorities at the War Office, the Record Office, and the Foreign Office, that no such name is to be found in the English Army Lists or other official documents of that day. The name is sometimes given as Alexander Kyd. (Hueffer, *Italian Sketches*, 141.)

A still more curious instance of the same mistake is afforded by a writer in the *Musical World* of May 6, 1836 (p. 118), a musician, and an eminent one too, who, in his anxiety to make the Ninth Symphony better known, seriously proposes that a Symphony of ordinary length should be made by taking the first and third movements of No. 9 and combining them with the last movement of No. 2 as a *Finale*! Absurd indeed; but we may be thankful that, owing to the lapse of time, such a mistake is not possible for us. On its first performance at Leipzig the work evidently caused much agitation. It was received by the *Zeitung für die elegante *Welt* 'as a gross enormity, an immense wounded snake, unwilling to die, but writhing in its last agonies, and bleeding to death (in the *Finale*).' Such, however, was not the general opinion, though the work is always spoken of more or less with hesitation, and as not so *safe* as No. 1.

In France it had to be considerably reduced before it could be put into the programme of the Concerts Spirituels of 1821, and, as already mentioned (p. 36), the *Allegretto* of No. 7 was substituted for its own slow movement. The *Allegretto* was encored, but the rest of the work proved an absolute failure!

In England it seems to have formed part of the *répertoire* of the Philharmonic from its foundation in 1813, though, as the Symphonies were not at that time particularised on the programmes by their keys, it is impossible to be quite sure. In 1825 the *Harmonicon*, with a ridiculous tone of patronage, says that it was 'written when his mind was rich in new ideas, and had not to seek novelty in the regions of grotesque melody and harshly combined harmony' (p. 111). 'The *Larghetto* (encored) speaks a language infinitely more intelligible than the majority of vocal compositions.' Next year, however, the critic is so much excited by the music as to wish for 'a repose of at least a full half-hour' after it (1826, p. 129).

---

* See Reprint in the *Allg. mus. Zeitung*, July 23, 1828, p. 488.

The key of D major was employed by Beethoven for some
of his finest works : amongst them the Missa Solennis ; the
Violin Concerto ; the Trio for pianoforte, violin, and cello,
Op. 70, No. 1; a Quartet, No. 3 of the first set of six (Op. 18);
two remarkable Pianoforte Sonatas, Op. 10, No. 3, and
Op. 28, usually, though inaccurately, called 'Sonata Pas-
torale'; and also the noble *Andante Cantabile* of the great
Trio in B flat, Op. 97.

'TESTAMENT.' *

The following is the document mentioned on page 19
above. The italics are Beethoven's own.

FOR MY BROTHERS CARL AND †   BEETHOVEN.

O you my fellow-men, who take me or denounce me for
morose, crabbed, or misanthropical, how you do me wrong!
you know not the secret cause of what seems thus to you.
My heart and my disposition were from childhood up inclined
to the tender feeling of goodwill, I was always minded to
perform even great actions ; but only consider that for six
years past I have fallen into an incurable condition, aggra-
vated by senseless physicians, year after year deceived in the
hope of recovery, and in the end compelled to contemplate a *lasting malady*, the cure of which may take years or even prove
impossible.   Born with a fiery lively temperament, inclined
even for the amusements of society, I was early forced to
isolate myself, to lead a solitary life.   If now and again I tried
for once to give the go-by to all this, O how rudely was I

---

* I am indebted to my friend, the late Mr. R. W. MacLeod Fullarton, Q.C.,
for his help in the translation of this remarkable document.   The original
is given by Mr. Thayer in his Biography, ii., 193.

† I have seen no explanation of the singular fact that Beethoven has left out
the name of his brother Johann both here and farther down in the letter.
The change from 'you' to 'thou' in the P.S. would seem to indicate that Beethoven is there addressing a single person.   The original document, given to
Madame Lind-Goldschmidt and her husband by Ernst, and presented by Mr.
Goldschmidt after her death to the city of Hamburg, was in London before it
left this country, and a photograph of it is in possession of the writer.   It
covers three pages of a large folio sheet.

repulsed by the redoubled mournful experience of my defec-
tive hearing ; but not yet could I bring myself to say to people
' Speak louder, shout, for I am deaf.'   O how should I then
bring myself to admit the weakness of *a sense* which ought to
be more perfect in me than in others, a sense which I once
possessed in the greatest perfection, a perfection such as few
assuredly of my profession have yet possessed it in—O I
cannot do it! forgive me then, if you see me shrink away
when I would fain mingle among you.   Double pain does
my misfortune give me, in making me misunderstood.
Recreation in human society, the more delicate passages of
conversation, confidential outpourings, none of these are for
me ; all alone, almost only so much as the sheerest necessity
demands can I bring myself to venture into society ; I must
live like an exile ; if I venture into company a burning dread
falls on me, the dreadful risk of letting my condition be
perceived.   So it was these last six months which I passed in
the country, being ordered by my sensible physician to spare
my hearing as much as possible.   He fell in with what has now
become almost my natural disposition, though sometimes,
carried away by the craving for society, I let myself be misled
into it ; but what humiliation when someone stood by me
and heard a flute in the distance, and *I* heard *nothing*, or when
someone heard *the herd-boy singing*, and I again heard nothing.
Such occurrences brought me nigh to despair, a little more
and I had put an end to my own life—only it, *my art,*
held me back.   O it seemed to me impossible to quit the
world until I had produced all I felt it in me to produce ;
and so I reprieved this wretched life—truly wretched, a
body so sensitive that a change of any rapidity may alter
my state from very good to very bad.   Patience—that's the
word, she it is I must take for my guide ; I have done
so—lasting I hope shall be my resolve to endure, till it
please the inexorable Parcæ to sever the thread.   It may be
things will go better. may be not ; I am prepared—already

in my twenty-eighth* year forced—to turn philosopher: it is not easy, for an artist harder than for anyone. O God, Thou seest into my inward part, Thou art acquainted with it, Thou knowest that love to man and the inclination to beneficence dwell therein. O my fellow-men, when hereafter you read this, think that you have done me wrong; and the unfortunate, let him console himself by finding a companion in misfortune, who, despite all natural obstacles, has yet done everything in his power to take rank amongst good artists and good men.— You, my brothers Carl and   , as soon as I am dead, if Professor Schmidt is still alive, beg him in my name to describe my illness, and append this present document to his account in order that the world may at least as far as possible be reconciled with me after my death.—At the same time I appoint you both heirs to my little fortune (if so it may be styled); divide it fairly, and agree and help one another; what you have done against me has been, you well know, long since forgiven. You, brother Carl, I especially thank for the attachment you have shown me in this latter time. My wish is that you may have a better life with fewer cares than I have had; exhort your children to *virtue*, that alone can give happiness—not money, I speak from experience; that it was which upheld me even in misery, to that and to my art my thanks are due, that I did not end my life by suicide.—Farewell, and love each other. I send thanks to all my friends, especially *Prince Lichnowski* and *Professor Schmidt.* I want Prince L.'s instruments to remain in the safe keeping of one of you, but don't let there be any strife between you about it; only whenever they can help you to something more useful, sell them by all means. How glad am I if even under the sod I can be of use to you—so

---

* Beethoven was born on Dec. 16, 1770, and was therefore at this date nearly at the end of his thirty-second year. It was one of his little weaknesses to wish to be taken for younger than he was ; and he occasionally spoke of himself accordingly.

may it prove ! With joy I hasten to meet death face to face.
If he come before I have had opportunity to unfold all my
artistic capabilities, he will, despite my hard fate, yet come
too soon, and I no doubt should wish him later; but even
then I am content; does he not free me from a state of cease-
less suffering ? Come when thou wilt, I shall face thee with
courage. Farewell, and do not quite forget me in death, I
have deserved it of you, who in my life had often thought for
you, for your happiness ; may it be yours !

LUDWIG VAN BEETHOVEN.

Heiligenstadt,*
6th October, 1802.

(Seal.)

For my brothers
Carl and
to read and to execute after my death.

Heiligenstadt,* 10th October, 1802. So I take leave
of †thee—sad leave. Yes, the beloved hope that I
brought here with me—at least in some degree to be
cured—that hope must now altogether desert me.
As the autumn leaves fall withered, so this hope too
is for me withered up ; almost as I came here, I
go away. Even the lofty courage, which often in
the lovely summer days animated me, has
vanished. O Providence, let for once a pure day *of
joy* ‡ be mine—so long already is true joy's
inward resonance a stranger to me. O when,
O when, O God, can I in the temple of Nature
and of Humanity feel it once again. Never ? No
—O that were too cruel !

---

* Spelt Heiglnstadt by Beethoven, in both places.

† Is it sure that this P.S. is addressed to his brothers? May it not be to Countess
Theresa Brunswick, to whom he was betrothed in 1806, or some other lady ?

‡ *Der Freude.* The italics are his own. This word acquires a deeper significance when we know from a letter of the time that Beethoven was, even
at that early date, meditating the composition of Schiller's ode *An die Freude,*
which he accomplished in the Ninth Symphony, in 1823. See Fischenich's
letter to Charlotte von Schiller, dated Bonn, Feb. 26, 1793, and quoted by
Thayer in his Biography, i., 237.

SYMPHONY No. 3 (EROICA), IN E FLAT (Op. 55).

Dedicated to Prince Lobkowitz.

'SINFONIA EROICA, composta per festeggiare il sovvenire di un grand' Uomo, e dedicata A Sua Altezza Serenissima il Principe di Lobkowitz da Luigi van Beethoven, Op. 55. No. III. delle Sinfonie.'

Allegro con brio (60—♩.). (E flat.)

Marcia funebre: Adagio assai (80—♪). (C minor.)

Scherzo and Trio: Allegro vivace (116—♩.). Alla breve (116—𝅗𝅥). (E flat.)

Finale: Allegro molto (76—♩), interrupted by Poco Andante, con espressione (108—♪), and ending Presto (116—♪). (E flat.)

SCORE.

2 Drums.	2 Clarinets.
2 Trumpets.	2 Bassoons.
3 Horns.	1st and 2nd Violins.
2 Flutes.	Viola.
2 Oboes.	Violoncello e Basso.

Probably the first appearance of three horns in the Orchestra.

The orchestral parts were published in October, 1806, Vienna, Contor delle arti e d'Industria. The score is an 8vo of 231 pages, uniform with those of Nos. 1 and 2, and was published in 1820. The title-page is in Italian, as given above. . . . 'Partizione. Prix 18 Fr. Bonna e Colonia presso N. Simrock. 1973.'

A special interest will always attach to the Eroica apart from its own merits, in the fact that it is Beethoven's first Symphony on the 'new road' which he announced to Krumpholz in 1802. 'I am not satisfied,' said he, 'with my works up to the present time. From to-day I mean to take *a new road*.' This was after the completion of the

Sonata in D (Op. 28), in 1801.* Great as is the advance in
the three Piano Sonatas of Op. 31, especially that in D minor,
and in the three Violin Sonatas of Op. 30, especially that in
C minor, over their predecessors, it must be confessed that the
leap from Symphony No. 2 to the Eroica is still greater.
The Symphonies in C and D, with all their breadth and spirit,
belong to the school of Mozart and Haydn. True, in the
Minuet of the one and the *Coda* to the *Finale* of the other,
as we have endeavoured to show, there are distinct invasions
of Beethoven's individuality, giving glimpses into the new
world. But these are only glimpses, and as a whole the two
earlier Symphonies belong to the old order. The Eroica
first shows us the methods which were so completely to
revolutionise that department of music—the continuous and
organic mode of connecting the second subject with the first,
the introduction of episodes into the working-out, the extraordinary importance of the *Coda*. These in the first
movement. In the second there is the title of 'March,' a
distinct innovation on previous custom. In the third there is the
title of ' Scherzo,' here used in the †Symphonies for the first
time, and also there are the breadth and proportions of the
piece, hitherto the smallest of the four, but now raised to a
level with the others; and in the *Finale*, the daring and
romance which pervade the movement under so much strict-
ness of form. All these are steps in Beethoven's advance of
the Symphony ; and, as the earliest example of these things,
the Eroica will always have a great historical claim to
distinction, entirely apart from the nobility and beauty of
its strains.

---

* See Thayer, ii., 186, 364.

† The first actual use of the term by Beethoven is in the third movement of
the Trio in E flat, Op. 1, No. 1. The term Minuet is employed for the *Scherzos*
of the Symphonies for many years both by German and English critics. It is
strange to hear the *Scherzo* of this very Symphony spoken of as 'an ill-suited
Minuet' (see page 92).

Another point of interest in the Symphony is the fact that it is the second of his complete instrumental works* which Beethoven himself allowed to be published with a title; the former one being the 'Sonate pathétique,' Op. 13. How the Symphony came by a title, and especially by its present title, is a remarkable story. The first suggestion seems to have been made to Beethoven by General Bernadotte† during his short residence in Vienna, in the spring of 1798, as ambassador from the French nation. The suggestion was that a Symphony should be written in honour of Napoleon Bonaparte. At that date Napoleon was known less as a soldier than as a public man, who had been the passionate champion of freedom, the saviour of his country, the

---

* The list of Beethoven's own titles, on his published works, is as follows :—

1. 'Sonate pathétique,' Op. 13.
2. 'La Malinconia.'　*Adagio* in String Quartet No. 6.
3. 'Marcia funebre sulla morte d'un Eroe.'　Third movement of Op. 26.
4. 'Sinfonia eroica, composta per festeggiare il sovvenire di un grand' Uomo,' &c.　Op. 55.
5. 'Sinfonia pastorale,' Op. 68.
6. 'Les Adieux, l'Absence et le Retour, Sonate,' Op. 81*a*.
7. 'Wellington's Sieg, oder die Schlacht bei Vittoria,' Op. 91.
8. 'Gratulations Menuett' (Nov., 1823).
9. 'Sinfonie mit Schluss-Chor über Schiller's Ode, An die Freude,' Op. 125.
10. 'Die Wuth über den verlornen Groschen, ausgetobt in einer Caprice,' for Pianoforte Solo.　Op. 129.
11. 'Canzona di ringraziamento in modo lidico, offerta alla divinità da un guarito,' and 'Sentendo nuova forza.'　*Molto Adagio* and *Andante* in String Quartet, Op. 132.
12. 'Der schwergefasste Entschluss.　Muss es sein ?　Es muss sein !'　*Finale* to String Quartet, Op. 135.
13. 'Lustig.　Traurig.　Zwei kleine Klavierstücke.'　Supplemental vol. to B. & H.'s great edition, p. 360.

'Moonlight,' Op. 27, No. 2 ; 'Pastorale,' Op. 28 ; 'Appassionata,' Op. 57 ; 'Emperor,' Op. 73—and if there be any others—are all fabrications.

† Schindler, Ed. 3, i., 101. A soldier like Bernadotte was not likely to know or care about music ; and it is therefore not improbable that the idea was due to Rudolph Kreutzer, the violin player, who filled the office of Secretary to the Legation. In this case the 'Kreutzer Sonata' (Op. 47), composed 1802-3, acquires a certain relationship to the Symphony, which is not invalidated by the fact (if it be a fact) that Kreutzer never played the great work dedicated to him. Bernadotte arrived in Vienna Feb. 8 and quitted it April 15, 1798.

restorer of order and prosperity, the great leader to whom
no difficulties were obstacles. He was not then the
tyrant, and the scourge of Austria and the rest of Europe,
which he afterwards became. He was the symbol and embodi-
ment of the new world of freedom and hope which the Revolution had held forth to mankind. Moreover, no De Remusat
or Chaptal had then revealed the unutterable selfishness
and meanness of his character. Beethoven always had
republican sympathies, and it is easy to understand that the
proposal would be grateful to him. We cannot suppose that
a man of Beethoven's intellect and susceptibility could grow
up with the French Revolution, and in such close proximity
to France as Bonn was, without being influenced by it. Much
of the fire and independence of the first two Symphonies are
to be traced to that source. The feeling was in the air.
Much also which distinguishes his course after he became a
resident in the Austrian capital, and was so unlike the
conduct of other musicians of the day—the general independence of his attitude ; the manner in which he asserted
his right to what his predecessors had taken as favours ; his
refusal to enter the service of any of the Austrian nobility ; his
neglect of etiquette and personal rudeness to his superiors in
rank—all these things were doubtless more or less due to the
influence of the Revolutionary ideas. But he had not yet openly
acknowledged this in his music. *Prometheus* was a not unsuitable hero for a work that may have been full of revolutionary
ideas, though invisible through the veil of the ballet.
Perhaps the melody which he employed in this *Finale*,
and elsewhere twice outside his ballet, may have had to
him some specially radical signification. At any rate, his
first overt expression of sympathy with the new order of
things was in the 'Eroica.' And a truly dignified expression it
was. We shall have an opportunity, in considering the Ninth
Symphony, of noticing how carefully he avoids the bad taste of
Schiller's wild escapades. Here we only notice the fact that the

'Eroica' was his first obviously revolutionary music. He was, however, in no* hurry with the work, and it seems not to have been till the summer of 1803 that he began the actual composition at Baden and Ober-Döbling, where he spent his holiday that year. On his return to his lodgings in the theatre 'an-der-Wien' for the winter, we hear of his having played the *Finale* of the Symphony to a friend.† Ries, in his *Biographische Notizen*, distinctly says that early in the spring of 1804 a fair copy of the score was made, and lay on Beethoven's worktable in full view, with the outside page containing the words —at the very top, 'Buonaparte,' and at the very bottom, 'Luigi van Beethoven,' thus :—

BUONAPARTE

LUIGI VAN BEETHOVEN

How the space between the two illustrious names was to be filled in no one knew, and probably no one dared to ask. Another copy it would appear had gone to the Embassy for transmission to the First Consul.‡

Meantime, however, a change was taking place in Napoleon, of which Beethoven knew nothing. On May 2nd, 1804, a

---

* The earliest sketches contained in the book published by Mr. Nottebohm (*Ein Skizzenbuch von Beethoven*, &c., Breitkopf und Härtel, 1880) date from 1802. An earlier book may, of course, be discovered.

† Mähler the painter. (Thayer, ii., 236.)

‡ Schindler, 3rd Ed., i., 107.

motion was passed in the Senate, asking him to take the title
of Emperor, and on May 18th the title was assumed by him.
When the news reached Vienna it was taken to Beethoven by
Ries,* and a tremendous explosion was the consequence.
'After all, then, he is nothing but an ordinary mortal!
He will trample all the rights of men under foot, to
indulge his ambition, and become a greater tyrant than any
one!' And with these words he seized his music, tore the
title-page in half, and threw it on the ground. After this
his admiration was turned into hatred, and he is said never
again to have referred to the connection between his work and
the Emperor till seventeen years afterwards, when the news
of Napoleon's death at St. Helena (May 5, 1821) reached
him. He then said: 'I have already composed the proper
music for that catastrophe,' meaning the Funeral March,
which forms the second movement of the work—if indeed
he did not mean the whole Symphony. In this light, how
touching is the term *sovvenire* in the title! The great man,
though emperor, is already dead, and the remembrance of his
greatness alone survives!

The copy of the Eroica which is preserved in the
Library of the 'Gesellschaft der Musikfreunde' in Vienna is
not an autograph, though it contains many notes and remarks
in Beethoven's own† hand; and it is not at all ‡impossible that
it may be the identical copy from which the title-page was

---

* *Biog. Notizen*, 2te Abth., p. 78.

† One of these is to erase the repeat of the first portion of the opening movement. This has been taken as evidence that at that time he thought such repetition
unnecessary. But nothing can be inferred from it until we know the circum-
stances under which he made the erasure. Beethoven must have been sometimes
very hard pressed in shortening his works for performance. Otto Jahn tells
us of a copy of the 'Leonora No. 2' Overture, in which he had been compelled
actually to cross out the first trumpet passage, and the eight bars connecting
it with the second!

‡ Mr. Thayer thinks it impossible (*Them. Verzeichniss*, p. 58).

torn off. It is an oblong volume, 12¾ inches by 9½, and has now the following title-page—

> SINFONIA GRANDE
> INTITULATA BONAPARTE
> 8̄0̄4 IM AUGUST
> DEL SIGR.
> LOUIS VAN BEETHOVEN
> GESCHRIEBEN
> AUF BONAPARTE
>
> Sinfonia 3   Op. 55

The original title would seem to have consisted of lines 1, 3, 4, 5, 8; lines 2, 6, 7 (all three in pencil) having been afterwards added, 6 and 7 certainly, 2 possibly, by Beethoven himself. Line 2 is now barely legible. The copy appears thus in the catalogue of the sale of Beethoven's effects: 'No. 144. Fremde Abschrift der Sinfonie Eroique in Partitur mit eigenhändigen Anmerkungen.' It is valued at 3 florins, and it fetched 3 fl. 10 kr. ; which, at the then currency, was worth about 3 francs. The copy then came into the possession of Joseph Dessauer, the composer, of Vienna, and is now in the Library of the ' Gesellschaft der Musikfreunde.'

The title just given is obviously an intermediate one between Beethoven's original and that prefixed to the edition of the Parts published in October, 1806, and to Simrock's edition of the Score, No. 1,973, published 1820.

But there is no reason to suppose that beyond the title-page the work was altered. It is still a portrait—and we may believe a favourable portrait—of Napoleon, and should be listened to in that sense. Not as a conqueror —that would not attract Beethoven's admiration; but for the general grandeur and loftiness of his course and of his public character. How far the portraiture extends, whether to the first movement only or through the entire work, there will probably be always a difference of opinion. The first movement is certain. The March is certain also, from Beethoven's own remark just quoted ; and the writer believes, after the best consideration he can give to the subject, that the other movements are also included in the picture, and that the *Poco Andante* at the end represents the apotheosis of the hero. But, in addition to any arguments based on consideration, there can be no doubt that it was the whole work, not any separate portion of it, that Beethoven twice inscribed with Bonaparte's name.* It has been well said that, though the Eroica was a portrait of Bonaparte, it is as much a portrait of Beethoven himself. But that is the case with everything that he wrote.

Certain accessories to the music seem to testify to some anxiety on Beethoven's part in regard to his new work. The long title and the two prefatory notices, without a parallel in his works for their length, all seem to have a significance. The title is given at the head of these remarks. The notices, affixed to the first editions of both parts and score, are as follows—he was quite aware of the unusual length of his work: 1. Questa Sinfonia essendo scritta apposta più lunga delle solite, si deve eseguire più vicino al principio ch' al fine di un Academia, e poco doppo un Overtura, un' Aria, ed un Concerto ; accioche, sentita troppo tardi, non perda per l' auditore, già faticato dalle precedenti produzioni, il suo proprio, proposto effetto.

---

* To the fact of the entire Symphony being a portrait of Bonaparte there is the following evidence:—

1. Beethoven's first inscription—' Buonaparte——Luigi van Beethoven.'

2. His second ditto—' Geschrieben auf Bonaparte.'

3. The statement of Ries.

4. The fact of the inscriptions being written not over the movements, but on the outside cover of both copies of the complete work.

soft enough to pass through a fine sieve which will
retain all the seeds. They can be mashed and
bruised in the pan. Measure and reheat the juice ;
add twelve ounces of heated sugar per pint. Boil
until the jelly sets—about forty-five minutes.

33. BLACKBERRY JELLY, No. 3

Six pounds of blackberries, three pounds of sour
apples, wiped, cored, and sliced. Place these in the
preserving-pan, first covered with cold water.
When the fruit is quite pulped, drain the juice
through a muslin bag or hair sieve, and to every
pint of juice add three-quarters of a pound of
preserving sugar. Boil for an hour or so ; stir and
skim well.

34. BLACKBERRY JELLY, No. 4

Put the berries (not quite ripe) in a double-boiler,
or in a jar in a saucepan ; put cold water in the outer
receptacle, and let it heat gradually and boil slowly
till the fruit is soft. Strain through a muslin ; allow
one pound of sugar to every pint of juice. Boil the
juice for twenty-five minutes, heating the sugar
meanwhile; add the sugar, stir well till it is quite
dissolved, boil up quickly, and pour off into glasses.

35. UNRIPE BLACKBERRY JELLY

The advantage of this recipe is that you can use
the blackberries in their red unripe state, so long
as they are a good size. Put the fruit into a preserving-pan, cover it with water, and boil till it is

soft enough for the juice to come out freely. Strain
it through a fine sieve, and to each pint of juice
allow one pound of lump (not preserving) sugar.
Boil all together, stirring and skimming now and
then, until it will set—about an hour. This will
be a red jelly instead of black, and of excellent
taste.

CHERRY

NOTE.—Although we have wild cherries (and
neglect their fruit most unreasonably), the garden
cherry is supposed to have been introduced by the
Romans, who themselves acquired it from Asia
about 70 B.C. One of the prettiest and most attractive of fruits, " cherry-ripe " is not one of the most
suitable for jam. It is better preserved whole,
dried, candied, or brandied ; also, it is invaluable
for various liqueurs and beverages. If used for
jam, great care must be taken not to let it boil a
minute too long (or it becomes treacly). Only
" cooking " cherries should be used for this purpose.

36. CHERRY CONSERVE

Take sound cooking cherries, and weigh them
before stoning. To every pound allow eight ounces
of sugar ; to every six pounds, one pint of red
currant juice ; to every pint of juice, one pound of
sugar. Having stoned the cherries, place them in
a preserving-pan and let cook until the juice is
nearly evaporated ; add the currant juice and the
sugar crushed into powder ; mix well, and boil until
the conserve will set—about twenty-five minutes,

stirring and skimming well. The cherry stones should be cracked and some of the kernels added to the conserve shortly before you take it off the fire. The remaining kernels may be steeped in brandy, in a tightly corked bottle, for flavouring purposes.

37. CHERRY JAM, No. 1

Stalk and stone twelve pounds of fresh ripe cherries; put them in a preserving-pan with one pint of red currant juice and eight pounds of granulated sugar. Mix thoroughly, put pan on sharp fire, and cook for half an hour, stirring and mixing frequently. Pour into jars when thickened and set. Do not cover till cool.

38. CHERRY JAM, No. 2

Tart cherries are the best for this purpose. Stone and weigh the fruit, taking care not to waste any juice. To every four pounds of cherries add one pint of red currant juice. Simmer till the fruit is tender, then add sugar, pound for pound; boil up, and pour off so soon as the jam sets.

39. CHERRY JAM, No. 3

Take ripe, but not over-ripe, cherries; stone (over a bowl) and weigh them; add equal weight of sugar, and place in an earthen or china vessel overnight. Next day put into preserving-pan, and boil until the jam thickens and sets.

40. CHERRY JAM, No. 4

Take four pounds of cherries, and stone them carefully so as to save the juice. Place four pounds of sugar with three teacupfuls of water in a preserving-pan, and bring to boiling-point. When it has boiled ten minutes, put in the cherries, and let them boil for thirty minutes. As soon as the jam begins to set, remove it from stove.

41. CHERRY JAM, No. 5

Take sound cherries, under rather than over-ripe; weigh and then stone them. Set aside twelve ounces of sugar for every pound of fruit. Heat the cherries slowly in a preserving-pan, and bring to boiling-point, then let simmer for fifteen minutes; add the sugar, stir and skim well. Have ready the following flavouring : a handful of cherry stones, crushed and steeped in a little water for twenty-four hours, the liquid then strained off to add to the jam. Boil up until the jam will set.

42. CHERRY JELLY, No. 1

Take cherries not quite ripe ; stone and put them in an earthenware dish in a slow oven till all the juice is extracted. Boil down till it is reduced to one-third ; then measure it, and for each pint of juice allow one pound of sugar. Heat the sugar and juice in separate pans, then put them together and boil slowly till the jelly sets—about twenty minutes.

Cherry jelly can also be made with equal parts

of cherries and red currants, or with equal parts
of cherries and raspberries.

43. CHERRY JELLY, No. 2

Take out the stones as carefully as possible, so as
not to lose the juice, and, having added a pound
of currant juice to every twenty pounds of cherries,
and half a pound of sugar to each pound of the
whole, cook over a sharp fire, stirring the fruit
gently. When done, proceed as with currant jelly.

44. CHERRY JELLY, No. 3

This should be made with cherries not quite ripe.
Put them in a covered earthen jar on the side of
the stove, or in a slow oven, till the juice is fully
extracted; strain, and boil till it is reduced to one-
third; then measure, and add one pound of sugar
for each pint of juice. Heat the sugar in a separate
pan, then add it to the juice, and boil till the jelly
sets—about twenty minutes or so.

45. CHERRY MARMALADE

Take out the stones, remove the stalks, and
reduce the cherries to one-half their bulk over a
slow fire; then make some syrup of double the
weight of sugar to the cherries, using very little
water, and, when the syrup has become quite thick,
put in the fruit, and let them cook together until
the marmalade is thoroughly done.

CRANBERRY

NOTE.—This has been already mentioned as marsh whortleberry; but (except in Cumberland, I believe) it is not very common in England. However, it is sold in most greengrocers' shops, which the other whortleberries hardly ever are. The shop cranberries come from the Scandinavian countries, from Russia, and from North America, where they are very extensively used. The cranberry is a valuable tonic and anti-scorbutic, containing a considerable amount of iron and of citric acid.

46. CRANBERRY JAM, No. 1

For every pound of the fruit use two pounds of sugar; pour a little water into the preserving-pan, then a layer of sugar, and then a layer of fruit; boil gently for twenty minutes, and skim.

47. CRANBERRY JAM, No. 2

Take two quarts of cranberries; pick them from the stalks, place in pan with four breakfastcupfuls of water. Let simmer for an hour; then remove to side of stove, and add one teaspoonful of carbonate of soda. Continue to stir and skim well until the fruit is soft enough to pass through a sieve. Measure the pulp, and allow an equal amount of sugar. Place all in pan, and simmer for half an hour. Pour off and cover.

48. CRANBERRY JELLY, No. 1

Place four pounds of cranberries in a preserving-pan with one quart of water. When tender, strain off the juice, measure, and place in pan. For each pint, allow twelve ounces to one pound of sugar. Stir and skim till the sugar has dissolved, but the jelly must simmer, not boil. As soon as it sets, pour it off.

49. CRANBERRY JELLY, No. 2

To each sixteen ounces of cranberries add half a pint of cold water. Let simmer gently for half an hour, then add sugar, allowing pound for pound. Let boil fairly fast for two hours; strain, boil up again, and pour off.

50. CRANBERRY JELLY, No. 3

Wash two quarts of ripe, but not over-ripe, cranberries, but do not dry them. Put them into a double-boiler, covered up, and boil them till they are fairly mashed. Strain them hard through a muslin or jelly-bag, and to each pint of juice allow one pound of crushed preserving sugar. Boil up again until the mixture jellies—about forty-five minutes.

51. CRANBERRY JELLY, No. 4

Pick the stalks from one quart of cranberries, add one breakfastcupful and a half of cold water; let simmer gently for an hour, or until tender; strain off the juice, and to each pint add one pound of warmed sugar; boil up again for three to five minutes after sugar is dissolved.

52. CRANBERRY JELLY, No. 5

Having washed the cranberries, allow half a pint of water to each pound of fruit; let them simmer gently for half an hour, then add sugar of equal weight to the fruit. Let boil fast for two hours, strain, give another boil-up, and pour off into glasses.

CURRANTS, BLACK

NOTE.—The black currant is a very distinct species, growing wild in woods in many parts of Britain. It is a common plant in the forests of Russia and Siberia. Of a tonic and astringent quality, it has always been in much request for colds, inflamed throats, etc., and this healing reputation is shared by all concoctions and decoctions of the berry. Its old country name was gazel or gozil. Black currant jam is dear to buy (I cannot think why), and cheap to make, if you grow your own currants; but it is a lengthy job, on account of the innumerable stalks to be picked off. Black currant preserve in some form or other should always be in the storeroom.

53. BLACK CURRANT JAM, No. 1

To every quart of fruit allow two pounds of sugar. Boil the fruit till tender, with just enough water to cover it when first put in; add the sugar, and boil for twenty to thirty minutes.

54. BLACK CURRANT JAM, No. 2

Take six pounds of black currants; pick off the stalks, and put them in an earthen vessel in alternate layers with sugar to the same weight. Let stand overnight. Take two pounds of rhubarb stalks (weighed after being peeled and sliced) ; add to these about one pound of stemmed black currants, and let cook till quite soft ; strain off as much juice as you can get, pressing the fruit with a wooden spoon. Pour this juice over the currants and sugar (if there is not enough to supply six breakfastcups of juice, you must boil down some more rhubarb). Let stand for twenty-four hours ; then drain off all the liquor, measure it, add an equal amount of sugar, and boil up in a preserving-pan ; then put in the fruit, and cook fast for a quarter of an hour, stirring and skimming well, but not allowing the fruit to get mashed or broken. Pour into glass jars, and cover.

55. BLACK CURRANT JAM, No. 3

Pick and weigh currants ; put them in preserving-pan ; when they have boiled a quarter of an hour, add the sugar. Let the sugar dissolve, and the jam boil for fifteen minutes ; it should then be ready to remove. It needs careful stirring all the while after the sugar is put in.

56. BLACK CURRANT JAM, No. 4

Gather black currants when just ripe ; stalk them, weigh, and place in a large bowl. Bruise them thoroughly with a wooden mallet ; do not leave a single berry whole. To every two pounds of fruit add one pound and a half of crushed sugar. Place in a preserving-pan, and boil not less than half an hour, stirring and skimming well. Pour off into heated pots.

57. BLACK CURRANT JELLY, No. 1

Take just-ripe currants; pick them from the stalks, place them in a large stew-jar. To every five quarts allow one pint of water. Tie a paper over the jar and set in a cool oven for two hours, or until the fruit is quite soft. Strain it through muslin. To every quart of juice allow one pound and a half of sugar broken small. Boil up the juice for twenty minutes, heating the sugar meanwhile; add the sugar, stirring till it is dissolved. When it boils, let boil for ten minutes over a clear fire, stirring well. Pour off into pots.

58. BLACK CURRANT JELLY (1815), No. 2

Put your black currants into a preserving-pan over the fire ; mash them with your spaddle, and just let them boil ; take them off and drain them through a very fine sieve ; boil them a quarter of an hour ; to every pound of currant juice put fourteen ounces of powdered sugar ; boil the jelly ten minutes ; put it in your pots ; let it stand two days before you cover it up, and put brandy papers over the jelly before you tie the papers.

59. BLACK CURRANT MARMALADE, No. 1

Pick the stalks from ripe black currants, crush them a little when placed in preserving-pan, and let simmer gently, stirring and moving them about, till all are quite soft. Strain off about two-thirds of the juice to make jelly with ; press the remaining juice and fruit through a sieve. The pulp must be weighed and boiled fast for fifteen minutes ; add twelve ounces of powdered sugar for every pound of pulp ; stir well till all is dissolved, then let boil fast for ten minutes or so, continuing to stir, and put into pots or jars.

60. BLACK CURRANT MARMALADE, No. 2

Pick the currants, crush them a little with a wooden spoon, so as to let the juice run, and let them simmer in a preserving-pan till they are sufficiently pulped to strain through a (not too fine) sieve. About three-fourths of the juice may be poured into another vessel, for jelly (see Black Currant Jelly), before the fruit is passed through the sieve. The pulp must then be weighed and given a fast boil for fifteen to twenty minutes.

CURRANTS, RED AND WHITE

NOTE.—These grow wild in Britain ; but so great is their antiquity as garden fruit, that nobody has ever been certain whether or no the wild ones were "escapes." The currant is of near kindred to the gooseberry, but much more acid. Red and white currants have not the specific medical value of the black currant ; but they are very good for intermixture with raspberries and other fruit in preserving, etc., or to make jams and jellies by themselves.

Dried currants, of course, are not in the least connected with these, being a kind of very small grape extensively grown in the Levant, and their name is derived from *Corinth*. They may, in fact, be considered as minute raisins.

61. RED CURRANT JAM

Pick and weigh the currants ; add an equal weight of sugar. Put the currants in a preserving-pan, and, when they have been boiling three minutes, add the sugar. Let the sugar melt and the whole boil up again ; if the jam sets then, remove and pour into pots.

62. RED CURRANT JELLY, No. 1

Pick the currants free of stalks, put them in a double-boiler, and let them stay an hour with the water boiling. Place them in a jelly-bag, but do not press or squeeze—leave the juice to drip all night. Next day, measure and put juice in pre-serving-pan, let boil for ten minutes, then add sugar, one pound and a quarter to each pint. The sugar should be heated. Boil up, and when the sugar has melted, the jelly should set.

63. RED CURRANT JELLY (1815), No. 2

Put your currants into a preserving-pan ; mash them and put them over the fire ; when they are all broken and just upon the boil, take your spaddle and put them in a hair sieve ; let all the juice drain through a flannel bag till it is quite clear ; if it is not clear enough first and second time, put it through again ; take as much sugar as you have got jelly, and let it boil almost to caramel ; then put your jelly in, and let it boil ten minutes; skim it all the time; then take it off—mind it is a clear jelly—and put it in your glasses.

64. RED CURRANT JELLY, No. 3

The currants must be picked free of leaves, etc., but need not be stalked. Wash and drain them, and place in a jar in a pan of hot water. Heat the fruit thoroughly, and mash it to a pulp with a heavy wooden spoon or pestle. Place it in a jelly-bag, and let drip all night. The following day, measure the juice; allow one pound of sugar to every pint. Heat the sugar in the oven, and put on the juice to boil. When it has boiled fast for twenty minutes, add the sugar; stir well, until it is dissolved; boil up for a minute, and pour off into heated glasses.

65. RED CURRANT JELLY, No. 4

Gather the currants dry and just ripe. Stalk them and place in a large stew-jar, with no water. Cover the jar or tie a paper over it, and let stand for one hour in a cool oven. Strain the fruit through muslin, and to every quart of juice add one pound and a half of loaf sugar. Stir gently till the sugar is melted, and boil fast for twenty minutes, skimming well. Pour off at once into jars.

66. QUIDDANY OF RED CURRANTS (1769)

Put your red currant berries into a jar, with a spoonful or two of water, and cover it close, and stand it in boiling water. When you think they are done enough, strain them, and put to every pint of juice a pound of loaf sugar. Boil up to jelly height, and put into glasses for use.

DATE

NOTE.—To my mind the most remarkable thing about the date is that it belongs to the same family as the coco-nut—the Palms or Phœnicaceæ. These two are without doubt the most useful fruit-bearing trees in existence, because their usefulness does not end with the fruit; for the sap, leaves, fibre, and wood are invaluable for various and widely differing purposes. The date, however, is so different from the coco-nut in its fruit, that it is almost impossible to realise their relationship. As a concentrated form of sugar, it is the portable food of millions; as a more-or-less luxury, it is familiar to every child. The name is remotely derived from the Greek *dactulos*, finger—in allusion to the oblong shape of the date.

67. DATE JAM, No. 1

To each pound of stoned dates allow one break-fastcupful of water and half a pound of sugar. Put the dates in the preserving-pan with the water, and let simmer eight or ten minutes; then add the sugar, and flavour according to choice—with lemon-rind and juice (half a lemon to each two pounds of fruit) or butter and spice. Boil till quite thick and smooth in texture.

68. DATE JAM, No. 2

Take five pounds of stoned dates (weighed after stoning); place in preserving-pan with three pints of

water ; cook gently until the dates are tender, then
stir in two pounds of sugar. Thoroughly mix, then
stir in one pound of chopped blanched walnuts.
Put into pots, and cover.

ELDER

NOTE.—This beautiful wild native tree, or bush,
is full of excellences and values. Every part of it,
root, bark, stem, shoot, leaf, flower, and berry, is
of use for medicinal or culinary purposes. I cannot
think why its berry is so little known, except to the
thrifty cottager, and why it is not still further
improved by selection and cultivation. Nowadays
it is chiefly employed for wine and syrup ; but as a
preserve it is not only acceptable, but beneficial,
and wholly unlike anything else.

69. ELDERBERRY JAM, No. 1

Pick and weigh ripe elderberries ; they must be
quite free from stalks. Allow pound for pound of
sugar, and to each pound of fruit the juice of one
large or two small lemons. Boil the berries in a
preserving-pan, slightly bruising them and stirring
them about. When the juice runs, put in one-third
of the sugar, and let simmer slowly up to boiling-
point. When the berries are thoroughly soft, press
them through a sieve. No seeds must go through.
Put the pulp, remaining sugar, and lemon - juice
back into the pan, also the lemon-rind, grated. Let
boil for half an hour, stirring and skimming continually. At the end of that time the jam ought

to set. Pour it into heated pots, but do not cover
it till cold.

70. ELDERBERRY JAM, No. 2

Take six pounds of ripe elderberries (weighed after
being picked from the stalks), and place in a preserving-pan with barely enough water to cover the
fruit. Boil for a quarter of an hour, then add four
pounds of sugar and one tablespoonful of orange-
flower water. Cook for forty-five minutes, stirring
and skimming well. Pour into pots, and cover.

71. ELDERBERRY JAM, No. 3

Pick and weigh ripe elderberries ; allow pound
for pound of sugar ; put the elderberries to heat in
the pan, then mash them with a potato-masher ;
add the sugar, and stir well till it is dissolved. Boil
till the jam thickens. Pour off and cover at once.

72. ELDERBERRY JELLY

Pick one quart of elderberries free of stalks ; add
one pint of water. Let simmer till quite soft, then
strain off the juice. Take one quart of crab-apples,
quarter but do not peel them ; add one pint of
water, and simmer till soft. Strain off juice, mix
it with elderberry juice, measure, and allow one
pound of sugar to every pint. Boil up the juice,
add the sugar, and boil about ten minutes or until
it sets.

FIG

NOTE.—The fig not only has the honour of being the first familiar tree mentioned in the Bible (Gen. iii. 7); but all over Europe and Asia it is associated with immemorial antiquity, and with the most curious, inexplicable beliefs. The peepul-tree of India (*Ficus religiosa*) is revered by the Hindus, because the deity Vishnu is reputed to have been born under it; by the Buddhists, because they believe that Gautama underwent his apotheosis beneath it. Under the name of Bo-tree there is a *Ficus religiosa* in Ceylon, which historical evidence proves to be a thousand years old. The invaluable indiarubber tree is a fig of sorts. But, most remarkable of all, the very name of Rome—anciently Ruma—is derived from her sacred fig-tree, the haunt of mystery and legend, whose roots are said to be still existent in the secret places of her most ancient site. There is something strange and occult—often something sinister—about the superstitions which encircle the fig-tree. I should like to see the whole subject thrashed out. . . . For the present, however, we must confine ourselves to its precious and invaluable fruit, which, whether green or dried, is of the greatest importance : wholesome, nourishing, laxative, and of very considerable food-value. Let me therefore emulate the Oriental fruit-seller, crying, " In the name of the Prophet, Figs ! "

73. FIG JAM, No. 1

Take small dried cooking figs, and scald them in a bowl with water which should be not quite boiling.

Drain them, slice each fig in half, remove the stems, and weigh. To each pound allow one pound of sugar, the juice of one lemon, and one teaspoonful of grated lemon-peel. Stew the figs, with the lemon-juice and rind, simmering slowly till quite clear and tender—a little water may be added, enough to cover the bottom of the pan and prevent burning; then add the sugar and cook slowly till the jam thickens and sets. Some people put the sugar in at once along with the figs; in this case a little water may be added at discretion during the cooking, if the preserve appears too thick. Stir carefully.

74. FIG JAM, No. 2

Either dried or ripe figs can be used for this. Dried ones should be steamed till soft. Fresh figs should be either steamed, or cooked in a double-boiler over boiling water. When they are tender, add about half their weight in sugar, place in a preserving-pan, and flavour either with lemon-juice and grated peel, or with chopped pineapple (fresh or tinned). Cook till the jam is thick, then rub it through a coarse sieve, and return it to the pan to reheat through before pouring it off into pots.

75. GREEN FIG JAM

Put the figs either in a double-boiler or a steamer, and let them get well heated through; then add half their weight in sugar, and (at pleasure) a little lemon-peel and juice. Boil till quite thick, stirring carefully; pass through a coarse sieve, reheat, and put into pots.

76. FIG JELLY

Slice the figs, adding one lemon, sliced through, to each pint and a half of fruit. Let it cook slowly in preserving-pan for an hour, in just enough water to cover bottom of pan; then strain, add sugar in the proportion of three-fourths of a pound to one pound of fruit-pulp, and boil for eighteen or twenty minutes.

GOOSEBERRY

NOTE.—The gooseberry, like its kinsfolk the white, red, and black currants, has grown wild in England so long that it may be considered indigenous; and it has been cultivated for at least seven centuries. It is an inhabitant of cool climates, and the further north you go in Britain, the better, as a rule, are the gooseberries. They were formerly known as feabes or feaberries. Whilst not of any very special dietetic or medicinal value, they are a pleasing, luscious, wholesome fruit, and make most excellent jam and jelly; while for bottling they are particularly in request. They have also this great advantage, that they can be cooked either ripe or unripe; and that all sorts, all sizes, all colours in which they can be found, are equally useful for the table. But they are at their best for preserving when half ripe. The small dark red hairy gooseberry is the most suitable for jelly making.

77. GOOSEBERRY JAM, No. 1

Take seven pounds of gooseberries; top-and-tail and wash them; add an equal weight of sugar, and put them in preserving-pan with enough water to cover the bottom of it—about a teacupful. Stir well until the sugar is all dissolved; then let boil about thirty minutes, stirring and skimming frequently. Let cool before covering.

78. GOOSEBERRY JAM, No. 2

Cook the gooseberries in preserving-pan till quite soft; pulp through a sieve; add an equal weight of sugar; replace in pan, and boil till the jam thickens and sets.

79. GOOSEBERRY JAM, No. 3

Take under-ripe gooseberries; top-and-tail and wash them; weigh, and place in preserving-pan with enough water to float them. Boil till soft; then add pound for pound of sugar, and boil fast for half an hour, or until the jam is a nice red colour. Currant juice may be used instead of water: the jam will set sooner and better.

80. GREEN GOOSEBERRY JAM (1805), No. 1

Take very large green gooseberries when they are full-grown, but not ripe; halve them, remove the seeds, wash, and drain on a sieve. Beat them in a mortar with their weight in sugar. Take a quart more gooseberries, boil them to a mash in a quart of water, then squeeze them, and to every pint of liquor put a pound of fine sugar. Boil and skim this, then put in your other green gooseberries. Boil them till they are thick, clear, and a pretty green; then put into glasses.

81. GREEN GOOSEBERRY JAM, No. 2

To each pound of fruit allow half a pint of water and twelve ounces of sugar. Make a syrup of this, and when it boils quite clear, put the fruit in, and simmer slowly till it will set and thicken.

82. GOOSEBERRY JELLY, No. 1

Take twelve pounds of gooseberries, top-and-tail and wash them, and place in preserving-pan with just enough water to cover them. Let boil forty-five minutes, stirring frequently. Strain off through jelly-bag, and to each pint of juice allow one pound of sugar. Return juice to boil up again; then add the sugar, and boil very fast for three minutes, stirring carefully. Pour off into jars. Let cool before covering.

83. GOOSEBERRY JELLY, No. 2

Put ripe gooseberries in the preserving-pan; let them heat and soften, pressing them with a wooden spoon to extract all juice. When ready, strain, and allow one pound of sugar for each pint of juice. Return to pan and boil till jelly sets, which should be in about ten minutes.

84. GOOSEBERRY JELLY, No. 3

Make gooseberry jelly the ordinary way, and when it is ready to take off the fire, have ready a bunch of elder flowers tied up in a piece of muslin, which you must turn round and round in the jelly until it has the desired flavour; it will be really like a most delicious grape.

85. GOOSEBERRY JELLY (1815), No. 4

Take two quarts of green gooseberries, and put to them two quarts of water ; boil, and mash them as they boil, until they are all to a pulp ; drain all the juice from them through a flannel bag ; when it is all drained, take as much more syrup as there is jelly from the gooseberries ; boil the syrup to "blow"; put the gooseberry jelly into it, and boil it about a quarter of an hour, and make it a fine jelly.

86. GOOSEBERRY JELLY, No. 5

Wash and top-and-tail two quarts of gooseberries ; put them in a lined stewpan, cover with water, and let simmer till they are soft. Put into a colander, over a basin, and strain the pulp through, leaving the skins. Strain the juice out of the basin through a fine gravy strainer, measure it, and to every pint allow one pound of sugar. Replace juice in pan and bring to boiling-point, when add a tablespoonful of lemon-juice, and the sugar, which should have been heated in oven. Boil up until the jelly sets.

87. GOOSEBERRY JELLY, No. 6

Place ripe gooseberries in a pan, with no water ; let them heat through, press out all the juice, then strain it. Measure, and to every pint of juice allow one pound of sugar. Heat juice and sugar separately, then mix and let boil for ten minutes.

88. GOOSEBERRY JELLY (EXTRA FINE), No. 7

Take small, dark red, hairy gooseberries ; top-and-tail, wash, drain, and rub through a sieve fine

enough to retain both seeds and skins. Measure
the pulp, and add double the amount of sugar; put
all into pan, and boil, stirring continuously, until it
sets and thickens. Pour it into heated jars at
once, and cover immediately with brandied paper.
The skins and seeds can be used for a cheap household jam, combined with tomatoes or carrots.

89. GREEN GOOSEBERRY JELLY

Six pounds of green gooseberries, four and a half
pints of cold water, sugar. Trim the gooseberries
" top and tail," wash and dry them, put them into
the water in a preserving-pan. Let them simmer
until broken and soft ; strain them through a jelly-
bag, and to every pound of juice weigh one pound
of preserving sugar. Boil the juice separately for
about a quarter of an hour, then take it off and
add the sugar, and boil all for twenty minutes or
so, skimming occasionally until it sets well.

GRAPE

NOTE.—Wholesome, nourishing, and delightful,
whether fresh or dried, the grape is, perhaps, the
oldest cultivated fruit in existence. It is no doubt
the most valuable, though the apple runs it close.
It contains an abnormal number of mineral salts,
and a large percentage of sugar ; but of course these
constituents vary with different kinds of grapes,
just as grapes themselves vary so amazingly with
different kinds of soils.

It is a matter for regret that the vine has been
let to fall into so much neglect throughout England.

In the Middle Ages, every monastery and abbey had its vineyard ; and the English outdoor grape, though not, of course, equal to the foreign or the hothouse one, is prolific and most useful for preserving (especially as jelly), or for wine. It is lovely and pleasant in itself—who that has ever had vine-blossom round the window can forget that unparalleled sweetness ?—its leaves and clusters are beautiful ; and it looks after its own growth surprisingly well.

The purple grape is the best for jelly, which is of a charming pink and a unique flavour.

90. GRAPE JAM, No. 1

Pick grapes from stem, put them in a double-boiler or a jar standing in a pan of boiling water, When they are heated through and soft, simmer them in preserving-pan for half an hour. When they are coolish, put them through a sieve, and weigh the pulp. To each pound allow one pound two ounces of sugar. Replace pulp and sugar in pan, and let simmer till it thickens and will set. Stir carefully and continually. Outdoor grapes, either ripe, unripe, or half-and-half, are available for this.

91. GRAPE JAM, No. 2

Take four quarts of green grapes ; stem, wash and drain them. Place in preserving-pan with one pint of cold water. Let simmer till soft ; pass through sieve, and measure ; add an equal amount of sugar, and return to pan. Boil fast for twenty-

five minutes, stirring well or the jam will burn.
Pour into glasses, and cover.

92. GRAPE JELLY, No. 1

This is made from outdoor grapes, and is extremely delicious, besides being a delicate, pretty
colour. Either ripe or green grapes, or equal quantities of each, may be used. Pick from the stalks
and simmer slowly till they are soft and the juice
runs freely. Strain through a bag of doubled
butter-cloth, but do not squeeze or press ; let drip.
Place the juice in a fresh pan, boil for twenty
minutes ; then add one pound two ounces for
each pint of juice (unless you wish to have a rather
tart jelly, when a pound to a pint will suffice), and
let it dissolve, stirring carefully. Boil for five
minutes, or until the jelly will set. Some people
add a flavouring of cinnamon and cloves, but this
is by no means necessary.

93. GRAPE JELLY, No. 2

Free the grapes from stems and leaves. Put in
preserving-pan; mash and heat slowly. After
reaching boiling-point, simmer for half an hour.
Put in a jelly-bag—it can drip all night; measure
juice, put in pan, boil for twenty minutes.
Measure equal quantity of sugar, add to juice, and
stir till dissolved. Put into jelly-glasses.

94. GRAPE JELLY, No. 3

Take some good ripe Muscat grapes ; remove their
stems, and place them in a pan over the fire, stirring

them gently till they burst and the juice runs freely.
Strain the juice through a cheese-cloth without
pressure, weigh it, and let boil fast for twenty
minutes. Remove from fire; add fourteen ounces
of fine sugar to every pound of juice. Stir it well
till dissolved, return to fire, and let boil for a quarter
of an hour longer, stirring and skimming well. It
should then set.

95. GRAPE JELLY, No. 4

Take a gallon of grapes; stalk, wash, and dry
them; place in a pan with a quarter of a pint of
water, and let simmer till quite soft. Strain the
juice, and measure it as quickly as possible, that it
may not get cool. Stir in one pound of heated
sugar for every pint of juice, and, directly the sugar
is dissolved, pour off the jelly into glasses. Another,
and probably a better-keeping method, is to proceed
on the usual jelly lines, and boil the juice quickly,
after straining it, for fifteen or twenty minutes;
then add the heated sugar, stir till it melts, bring
the jelly to boiling-point again, and pour it off.

96. UNRIPE GRAPE JELLY

Take whole bunches of unripe grapes, and simmer
them in an enamelled pan, with enough water to
cover them, until they are soft and broken—say,
about an hour. Strain off the juice through a
muslin bag or hair sieve, and to each pint of juice
allow one pound of preserving sugar. A very little
cinnamon may be added at discretion. Boil up
quickly, keeping it well skimmed, until it sets
firmly.

97. GRAPE MARMALADE, No. 1

Pulp the grapes; cook pulps till tender. Press through sieve and add skins, allowing three-quarters of a pound of sugar to half a pound of fruit. Cook slowly.

98. GRAPE MARMALADE, No. 2

Take one gallon of under-ripe green grapes; stalk, wash, and dry them. Place in a pan with one pint of cold water, and simmer until tender. Pass them through a sieve which will retain the seeds; weigh the pulp, add pound for pound of sugar, and return all to the pan. Let boil fast for twenty to twenty-five minutes, stirring and skimming; pour into pots, and cover.

GRAPEFRUIT OR POMELO

NOTE.—This large and handsome fruit is now to be seen at all greengrocers, and though not a cheap commodity (its usual price being 3d. and 4d. each), it makes a welcome variety from the other members of the Citrus family. Its name, which at first hearing seems singularly inappropriate, arises from the fact that it grows in groups or clusters, like the grape. Some consider it the best fruit going; others, again, are disappointed in it, because they eat it too soon in the year. It is not really mature till between March and June. The inner white tissue of grapefruit, like that of so many of its family, is particularly bitter, and must be removed with great care before using the fruit for preserve.

99. GRAPEFRUIT JELLY

Remove rind, slice it thinly, and leave it overnight in strongly salted water. Next morning, drain and place it in fresh water, changing the water till the bitterness is gone. Remove the white inner tissue and core or " rag " from the fruit, and place the pulp with the rind in preserving-pan. Allow one quart of cold water to each grapefruit; boil down till it is reduced to one-third of a pint of juice. Strain the juice, and add rather more than an equal amount of sugar. Return to pan and boil up until the jelly will set.

100. GRAPEFRUIT MARMALADE, No. 1

Remove the outer rind and cut it into thin strips. Put it into strong brine, let boil, then drain well and boil again in unsalted water. If the bitter taste still remains, repeat both boilings. Remove the white fibrous inner tissue from the fruit, slice in half, and take out the cores. Now slice the fruit lengthways, and let boil in preserving-pan; add the rind to it when ready, and let cook until the rind is tender and clear. Weigh, add pound for pound of sugar, and boil until the marmalade is thick and sets well—probably about half an hour.

101. GRAPEFRUIT MARMALADE, No. 2

This recipe is bitterer than the last, and more like Seville orange marmalade. Remove peel and slice thinly; remove white inner tissue; remove seeds. Cut fruit in slices with a silver knife. Weigh and place pulp and rind in preserving-pan, with enough water to cover it, and boil till tender. If very bitter, the water can be changed once. When rind is soft, add pound for pound of sugar, and let cook until it sets.

102. GRAPEFRUIT MARMALADE, No. 3

Take four grapefruit and cook them till tender, but not broken, in just enough water to cover them. Cook six oranges similarly in a separate pan. Turn out into bowls, water and all, and let stand overnight. Next day, halve the grapefruit, take out the pulp, and rub it through a coarse sieve which will retain the seeds and core. Cut the rinds into very fine shreds. Slice the oranges whole, and add them to the grapefruit. Save all the juice you can during these processes by cutting, etc., over a basin; add two quarts of water to the fruit, then measure the whole quantity in pints, and put all in a preserving-pan to heat through. Meanwhile heat sugar, allowing a pint and a half to each pint of fruit, and add it to the rest, along with the strained juice of six lemons. Simmer gently until thick, then pour off. Not to be covered for twenty-four hours.

103. GRAPEFRUIT PRESERVE

Remove the rind and as much of the white as possible. Cut the fruits in two; remove cores and seeds with a sharp knife. Slice and measure, place fruit in preserving-pan, with a very little water. Let it come slowly to boiling-point, then allow three-quarters of a pint of sugar to each pint of pulp; add it, and simmer gently for a quarter of an hour, or until it sets fairly firm.

GUAVA

NOTE.—The guava really belongs to the myrtle family, which accounts for its aromatic scent. It is very popular as an all-round culinary fruit in its native haunts; but here in Britain we are chiefly acquainted with it as jelly. Guavas are purchasable for the purpose of preserving; I therefore append some valuable recipes.

Mature guavas are not so suitable for jelly, etc., as quite under-ripe ones. Over-ripe ones should be entirely avoided. In any case, unripe ones should be used in the proportion of half-and-half along with the ripe. Guava jelly is better made in small quantities.

104. GUAVA JELLY, No. 1

Take some guavas which are well developed, but under-ripe and not coloured. Slice them and put in a preserving-pan with just enough cold water to cover the bottom of pan. Let simmer till the fruit is quite soft and falls to pieces; then strain it, without squeezing, through a jelly-bag. To each pint of *thick* juice allow half a pound of sugar and half a pint of water, which place in a separate pan and make into a syrup. When the syrup is fairly thick, add two pints of it to each pint of guava juice, and let it boil slowly till it will set.

105. GUAVA JELLY, No. 2

Take half the amount required in ripe guavas, and half in under-ripe ones, which are not quite coloured or mature. Slice the fruit and simmer as in No. 1. When the juice is strained, boil it quickly for twenty minutes (adding, if liked, the juice of half a lemon to each half pint) ; then measure granulated sugar (which has been previously warmed) cup for cup with the juice ; boil all together till it sets—about twenty-five minutes.

106. GUAVA MARMALADE

Proceed as for Guava Jelly (No. 1), but when the fruit is soft, pulp it through a sieve instead of straining ; then add an equal amount of sugar, and to each pint of fruit-pulp allow the strained juice of one lemon. Boil till thick.

107. GUAVA PRESERVE

Take ripe guavas ; peel, halve, and remove seeds. Measure, and to each pint allow one pound of sugar and three-quarters of a pint of water. Boil the sugar and water together till it will candy in cold water ; then add the fruit, and boil till it is clear and tender, but not broken.

LEMON

NOTE.—No traditions or old wives' fables are requisite to recommend the invaluable lemon. Its acid, as a germicide, as a liver tonic, as a remedy against fever and malaria, is one of the Creator's best gifts; not to mention the medicinal properties and delightful flavour of the rind. The pulp is not a common article of food, for obvious reasons; yet some folk eat it as they would an orange, with extremely beneficial results. Lemons are so largely employed to flavour other fruits or dishes, that they are not half sufficiently regarded "on their own." As preserves, they are cheap, they are delicious, and they are superlatively wholesome; I commend them on every ground to the British housewife.

108. LEMON JELLY, No. 1

Take twelve lemons; wash, dry, and cut them up into rough slices, removing the pips. Put them into an earthen jar, cover with five quarts of cold water, and let them stand twenty-four hours; then boil them for two hours, strain, allow one pound of sugar to every pint of juice, and boil fast for ten minutes. The pips can be soaked in a little of the water, strained, and the liquid added to the juice.

109. LEMON JELLY, No. 2

Twelve Seville oranges, four lemons; add two quarts of water to a pound of fruit. Let this stand twenty-four hours, boil until tender, then strain, and add fourteen ounces of sugar to one pint of juice. Boil up.

110. LEMON HONEY

Strain the juice of four lemons; add the grated rind of one; mix with one pint of water and two

pints of sugar; cook till thoroughly thickened.
Pour into jars, and cover.

111. LEMON MARMALADE, No. 1

Twelve lemons, water, preserving sugar. Slice
the lemons extremely thinly, removing the pips;
then weigh them, and to every pound of fruit add
three pints of water. Let it stand in the water
twenty-four hours, and let the pips also soak in a
little water. At the end of the time strain off the
pips and add the water they were in to the rest,
and boil the whole until the lemons are tender.
Pour off the whole into an earthen vessel and leave
it till next day; then weigh the pulp again, and
to every pound put one pound and a half of preserving sugar. Boil until the strips of lemon become transparent and the pulp jellies.

112. LEMON MARMALADE, No. 2

Take twelve lemons, and an equal weight in preserving sugar. Wash and wipe the lemons, then
halve them; strain out the juice, and put the pips
into a bowl by themselves with a tumblerful of
cold water. The peels must be put into cold water
in a lined pan, and boiled till thoroughly tender;
then take them out, and, having removed all the
white pith you can, cut the rinds into the thinnest
possible shreds or strips, about half an inch long.
Next put the lemon-juice, the water from the pips,
and the sugar into a preserving-pan, and let it
boil to a syrup; add the rinds, and boil till the
marmalade will " set."

113. LEMON MARMALADE, No. 3

Peel six pounds of lemons, put the peels into a pan of fresh water, and let boil till quite tender. Drain them, and, when cool, shred them into small, fine strips with a very sharp knife. Halve the lemon-pulp across middle, squeeze out the juice and pulp, and remove pips. Put the empty white lemon-pulps remaining into three pints of cold water, and let boil for thirty minutes ; then strain, and add the liquid to the rinds, juice, and soft pulp. Let boil together ten minutes, then add nine pounds of sugar (previously heated) ; boil till the marmalade thickens and sets. It must be potted and covered at once.

114. LEMON MARMALADE, No. 4

Take three pounds of lemons; wash, wipe, and peel them thinly. Shred the peel extremely fine with a sharp knife. Put the shreds into a small pan with one pint of water, and let boil for forty minutes. Remove the white outer tissue from the fruit, cut up the pulp, and place it in preserving-pan with two and a half pints of water ; bring to boiling-point, and then let boil an hour and a quarter, stirring well. Strain through a jelly-bag (but do not squeeze), and then add the shreds with the liquor they were boiled in. Measure the whole amount, and allow double the quantity of sugar. Replace all in the pan, with the sugar, and let boil half an hour. Pour off and cover.

115. LEMON AND ORANGE MARMALADE

Take an equal number of lemons, sweet oranges, and Seville oranges. Wipe them thoroughly clean, remove the peel, and soak it overnight in brine. Next day remove and drain, place in fresh water, and let boil. Take out, scoop out the white lining of rind, and finely shred the yellow rind. Place in preserving-pan with just enough water to boil it till quite tender. Have ready the sliced pulp and juice, cooked tender, in another pan; add this to the rind when it is ready, and continue to cook till the rind is clear; add pound for pound of sugar, and boil up till it is of the right consistency.

116. LEMON RIND PRESERVE, No. 1

This is a way of utilising lemons which have been emptied of their juice for lemonade or other purposes. Put them into a vessel of fresh water, and change the water every third day, for a fortnight; then scoop out the white inside, leaving the yellow rinds. These can be shredded, or left as they are. Add pound for pound of sugar, and let cook gently till the preserve is quite thick.

117. LEMON RIND PRESERVE, No. 2

Put the squeezed lemons, whole, into a pan of fresh water and boil until tender; then transfer to a syrup, which you must have ready boiling, composed of five pounds of sugar to one pint of water. Let boil until the preserve is clear and thick.

MEDLAR

NOTE.—This remarkable fruit, which, though wild in Britain, has been cultivated for many centuries, has apparently little justification for its existence. It is an apple of sorts; but it is not edible, in any form, till beyond maturity and on the high-road to over-ripeness. In fact, until the fruit has "bletted" or softened for from two to four weeks, no expert in medlars considers it worth his attention. The medlar is unknown to many people, though its fine bloom upon a gnarled and twisted growth renders it conspicuous in park or orchard. I give some recipes for preserving the medlar, with the proviso that not everybody will like its peculiar and quite original flavour.

118. MEDLAR JELLY, No. 1

Take medlars fully ripe, peel thinly and slice them, removing pips. Place in a preserving-pan with enough cold water to cover them, and to every twenty-four medlars allow the juice and thinly pared rind of half a lemon. Boil well until the fruit is thoroughly soft, then strain it through a jelly-bag, but *do not squeeze it*. Measure the juice, allow a pound of sugar to every pint, and replace in the pan. Allow about the same quantity of lemon-juice as before (one lemon to every fifty medlars), but no more rind. Keep boiling, skimming well until it sets—probably about one hour and a half. Be very careful that the jelly does not stick or burn. This recipe is reputed to equal the best guava jelly.

119. MEDLAR JELLY, No. 2

Put ripe medlars, peeled, pipped, and sliced, into a preserving - pan, with enough water to cover them ; or, better still, place them in a covered jar in the oven. In any case it will take some hours before the juice is all extracted. Strain the juice, letting it drip through the jelly-bag without any pressure. Measure it, and allow an equal amount of white sugar. Boil it till quite transparent, stirring and skimming well. Let cool a little before pouring into jars.

120. MEDLAR MARMALADE

Take the fruit pulp left from making medlar jelly ; rub it through a sieve, weigh, add an equal amount of sugar, and boil till it thickens and sets. Pour into pots, and cover.

MELON

NOTE.—The large water-melons, so cheap and so popular in latter summer, are hardly suitable for preserving. The smaller species—musk - melon, canteloupe, and citron melon—are those adapted for our purpose. These, of course, are more expensive—unless one has means of procuring them from a wholesale foreign fruit-seller or of growing them under glass. They are well worth using in any of the ways below stated. The melons, belonging as they do to the gourd family—related to the vegetable marrow, cucumber, pumpkin, etc.—are not an indigenous British fruit. But we have been acquainted with, and loved them, ever since their first introduction in the sixteenth century.

121. MELON MARMALADE

Take some large citron melons; quarter, but do not peel them. Take out the seeds, then weigh the fruit, and allow pound for pound in white sugar. Grate the melons on a coarse grater, omitting the rind. To every three pounds allow the grated rind of two lemons, and one teaspoonful of ground ginger; these are best mixed with the sugar. Put all into preserving-pan, and let boil till it thickens, becomes smooth, and will set. Steady stirring and skimming will be necessary. Pour into pots and cover up while hot. [The juice of the lemons, though not mentioned in original recipe, would, I think, be a great improvement.—*Ed.*]

122. MELON PRESERVE, No. 1

Take ten pounds' weight of citron melons; remove peel and seeds. Cut up into thin slices. Have ready a large pan containing enough water to cover the fruit, and two teaspoonfuls of powdered alum. Boil until the fruit is clear and tender; then drain it, and rinse in cold water. Prepare a syrup of six pounds of sugar, the juice of sixteen lemons, and the rinds of six, and four ounces of green ginger root. Let this syrup boil till it clears and thickens. Put the boiled fruit into it, with two sliced lemons, and let all boil up again; lift out the melon into hot jars, fill up with the syrup, and cover at once.

123. MELON PRESERVE, No. 2

Take some small citron melons; peel, slice, seed, and cut up small. Put in a large vessel overnight, with just enough slightly salted cold water to cover the fruit. Next day, drain the fruit and let it soak in fresh cold water for five or six hours. Place it in a preserving-pan, cover it with fresh cold water, add a small teaspoonful of powdered alum, and let boil till the fruit is clear and tender, but not mashy. Lift out and drain it; let it grow cold. Replace it in a pan on the fire, with one pint of sugar and about half an ounce of grated ginger root to every pint of melon, and enough water to moisten it. Simmer until the sugar candies, which will be in about two hours. Place the melon in jars, fill up with syrup, and cover.

124. MELON PRESERVE, No. 3

Take one musk melon; peel, seed, cut up small, and weigh it. Put it in a preserving-pan along with half a lemon thinly sliced; add just enough water to cover the fruit, and simmer till tender; then add the following: two tart cooking apples peeled, cored, and chopped small; one tablespoonful of preserved ginger finely chopped; one saltspoonful of ground cloves, and sugar to two-thirds the weight of the melon. Let boil fast until the melon becomes clear. Pour off, and cover.

MULBERRY

NOTE.—Nobody ever talks very much about the mulberry (except little boys who keep silkworms).

It is a handsome, beautifully coloured fruit;
exceedingly wholesome by reason of its potash and
" grape sugar " ; easy to grow, easy to gather ;
whose tree stands strong and full, outlasting generation after generation. It has been cultivated for I
don't know how many centuries in Europe, and
before that in the East. You may remember how
David was commanded to go forth to battle when
he should hear " a sound of going in the tops of
the mulberry trees." And yet how very, very
seldom one partakes of mulberry jam ! All recipes
appropriate to raspberries and blackberries are
suitable to mulberries also; which have been
termed superior to blackberries and raspberries,
" or indeed to almost any other fruit, in the matter
of jelly making."

125. MULBERRY JAM

Take ripe mulberries, weigh, and let simmer in
their own juice till they are tender but not broken ;
add pound for pound of sugar, and cook till the jam
thickens and sets. Mulberry jam may also be
made from the fruit used for jelly (which see) ; in
this case, pulp the strained mulberries through a
coarse sieve, add pound for pound of sugar, and
replace in pan to boil slowly till the jam is ready to
remove.

126. MULBERRY JELLY, No. 1

Ripe mulberries should not be used for this, but
those which, while red and full-sized, are still hard.
Allow one quart of cold water to three quarts of

mulberries, and let simmer slowly for the best part
of an hour. Add another quart of cold water, and
simmer for another hour, mashing the fruit with a
wooden spoon. Strain off the juice, and add a pint
of sugar (previously heated) for each pint. Place
fruit and juice in preserving-pan, boil up, skim well,
until the sugar has completely dissolved; then let
boil three to five minutes. The jelly should set well
after this; it should be a bright crimson colour
when cold.

127. MULBERRY JELLY, No. 2

Take equal parts of ripe mulberries and of hard
unripe ones, only just red. To three quarts of fruit
add one pint of water. Simmer very slowly in
preserving-pan, mashing the mulberries till the juice
is entirely extracted. Strain it off and return it
to the pan with an equal amount of heated sugar;
boil up as in No. 1.

128. MULBERRY MARMALADE, No. 1

Hard, red, unripe mulberries are suitable for this.
Stalk them, weigh, and chop with a sharp knife.
Put the fruit in an earthen jar, with about one teaspoonful of water to one quart of mulberries. Cover
and put the jar in the oven or at the side of the
stove till the fruit is soft and begins to simmer;
then for each quart of fruit add a pound and a
half of sugar (previously heated). Place the jar
over a hotter part of the stove, and stir until the
sugar is quite dissolved and the marmalade will set.
Pour into pots and cover.

129. MULBERRY MARMALADE, No. 2

Stalk and weigh the fruit ; allow pound for pound in crushed sugar. Place the mulberries in a preserving-pan (a large shallow one being best), and the sugar on top of them. Simmer and stir over a very slow fire until the juice and sugar have thickened into a syrup. Let boil up fast for five or six minutes, skimming well; pour off into jars, and cover.

ORANGE : SEVILLE ORANGE, ETC.

NOTE.—Familiarity breeds contempt. If we did not know the orange—if somebody were suddenly to spring upon us a blossom of exquisite ivory colour and wonderful perfume, which presently developed into a golden globe of surpassing sweetness, whose very rind was odorous, whose hue was a glory— with what rapture we should receive it ! The orange is really a most marvellous fruit ; and though you can buy it nearly four a penny—certainly forty for a shilling—its intrinsic marvel is not lessened. Yet a world without oranges is hardly to be conceived.

All oranges are supposedly descended from the sour or Seville orange, which grows wild still in many places, and was first imported by the Moors into Spain about A.D. 700. The sweet orange was not cultivated in Europe until the fifteenth century. The Spaniards apparently introduced both kinds into America and the West Indies. As for the mandarin and tangerine, small sweet oranges, they hailed originally from China and Japan—in all

probability from a sour species. The name orange
is derived from the Arabic *naranj*.

The bitterness of the Seville orange is presumed
to be tonic, and to counteract any undue sweetness,
in a preserved form. But as (for some inscrutable
reason) it is so much more expensive than the sweet
orange, and also requires so much more sugar,
there is no adequate reason why the latter should not
be extensively employed for cheap marmalades, etc.

NOTES ON ORANGE MARMALADE

The reader will probably be astonished to see this
very large variety of recipes for orange marmalade—
that indispensable article in the ordinary British
household. It may be said that no two recipes are
alike. The oranges may be all Seville, or all sweet
orange, or Seville intermingled with sweet oranges—
or, either way, with or without the addition of
lemons. They may be sliced right through, or the
peel removed and separately shredded. They may or
may not be soaked overnight in the water wherein
they are subsequently boiled, and this water may be
salted, or not. The proportion of water varies in
almost every obtainable recipe; but weight for weight
of fruit and water will make a solid marmalade, and,
for a thinner one, the water may be increased to
one pint and a half for every pound of pulp. The
treatment of the peel varies amazingly : it may be
grated, minced, finely shredded, sliced in thick
strips, or even cut in coarse squares, after the
manner of " Oxford " marmalade. The preserve
itself may be opaque or transparent ; the pulp may

be passed through a sieve, or not ; the peel may or may not be boiled separately from the pulp. The pips are too often thrown away ; but they should always be steeped, overnight if possible, in a little water. This liquor will jellify, and should be strained off and added to the first boiling of the marmalade—not that a second boiling is always indicated! Again, the proportion of sugar varies greatly, though " pound for pound " is usually advised in the case of all-Seville oranges ; and the length of boiling is never stated the same twice ; and the amount to be made at a given time ranges from the employment of six to forty oranges. When I was a country child, we made our marmalade fifty pounds at a time in the back-kitchen " copper," but for the life of me I cannot remember the exact recipe.

On the whole, that recipe may be considered the most fruitful of success which implies the most trouble : *i.e.*, the separate shredding and cooking of the yellow peel with white pith removed, the overnight steeping of the pulp—even to two nights running—and the addition of the sugar *when the pulp and peel are cooked tender* ; it is not the *sugar* which requires cooking, as has been suggested in Chapter I. The first recipe given, perhaps, approximates most nearly to this ideal, but the others have all been tested by time and family favour—it is just a question of which you personally prefer.

A slicing machine will save much time and trouble if it be desirable to make orange marmalade on a large scale. A silver knife should be used for dealing with the pulp.

Wipe or wash the oranges perfectly clean. It is possible, with good management, to make both jelly and marmalade by straining off a certain amount of juice first.

130. SEVILLE ORANGE MARMALADE, No. 1

Take twelve Seville oranges and three lemons; peel them, and cut up the peel into very thin strips. Cut up the pulp into rough pieces with a silver knife, removing as much as possible of the white tissue. Put the pips and any odds and ends to soak in a little water. Weigh, and place all in an earthen vessel. Pour an equal weight of water on, and leave for twenty-four hours. Next day, add the water from pips, boil the whole till tender ; put it back to stand another twenty-four hours. The third day boil it up fast, and add eight pounds of heated sugar. Stir well till the sugar dissolves, and boil for forty-five minutes, or until the marmalade is of the required colour and consistency.

131. SEVILLE ORANGE MARMALADE, No. 2

Take thirty Seville oranges ; peel them very thinly as you would lemons, using only the yellow outside rind. Weigh the peels, place in a preserving-pan, just covered with water, and boil for an hour and a half. Remove all the white pith from the fruit, and pull the pulp to pieces with your fingers over a basin. Remove all cores and pips, and put them to soak, just covered with water, in a separate bowl. When the peel is soft, drain it from the water, and mince it as finely as possible. Now weigh the juice, pulp, and peel all together, and place in the preserving-pan, along with one pint of water, which should include the water from the pips. Boil for half an hour, meanwhile heating sugar to an equal weight with the fruit, etc. ; add the sugar, and boil for an hour, stirring continually towards the end. Pour off into pots, and cover.

132. SEVILLE ORANGE MARMALADE, No. 3

Take twelve large Seville oranges ; slice them very thinly right through. Remove pips and put them to steep in a little water. Place the fruit in an earthen pan, cover it with twelve pints of water, and leave for twenty-four hours. Next day, boil up all for two hours, adding the liquor from the pips ; add twelve pounds of sugar, and boil for a further hour and a half, stirring continuously during the last half-hour ; add the juice of two lemons, pour off into pots, and cover.

133. SEVILLE ORANGE MARMALADE, No. 4

Take nine Seville and two sweet oranges and two lemons. Slice them right through as thinly as possible ; remove the pips and put them to soak in a little water. Place the fruit in a deep pan or bowl, add nine pints of cold water, and leave for twenty-four hours. Next day, boil until tender ; add nine pounds of heated sugar, and boil again until the marmalade thickens and sets.

134. SEVILLE ORANGE MARMALADE, No. 5

This can be made either with all Seville oranges or with four sweet oranges to every eight Seville. Wipe them well, slice them thinly. Remove the pips, pith, and cores, which should be left overnight in a bowl with a little water. Weigh the fruit, and for every pound add two pints of water. Let the oranges and water steep all night in an earthen pan. The following morning put all into a preserving-pan; strain in the liquor from the pips, boil up sharply for an hour ; return all to the earthen pan. Next day, weigh the contents of the pan ; allow fourteen ounces of sugar per pound of pulp. Boil all until tender (about one hour and a half), and as soon as it thickens pour off the marmalade into pots, and cover.

135. SEVILLE ORANGE MARMALADE, No. 6

Take Seville oranges, wash them well, and place in a large preserving-pan of slightly salted water. Boil them until a wooden skewer will easily pierce the peel. Take them out and plunge them into cold water ; leave them there till they are quite cold. Keep some of the water they were boiled in. When they are cold, cut them into quarters, scoop away the thick white pith from the peel, and shred the peel as finely as possible. Rub the pulp through a sieve and weigh it. Return it to the pan with an equal weight of sugar, the juice of sweet oranges and lemons to taste, and some of the original boiling-water—about one breakfastcupful to each pound of pulp. Boil for thirty minutes, or until the marmalade will set.

136. SEVILLE ORANGE MARMALADE, No. 7

Weigh the oranges first of all, and set aside for every pound twelve ounces of sugar. For every five oranges allow one lemon (grated rind and juice). Take off the peel in quarters, and boil it, well covered with water, until it is tender enough to be easily pierced with the head of a pin. Remove and drain, and set it aside to cool. Take out the pips from the pulp, and as much of the white pith as you can remove; boil the pulp, till tender, along with the sugar. When the peel is cold, scoop out the white from it, slice it very thinly, and add it to the pulp. Let cook till all is thick and dark.

137. SEVILLE ORANGE MARMALADE, No. 8

(Transparent)

Choose pale-coloured oranges; cut them in quarters, remove the pips and pith, and take out the pulp into a basin. Put the peel to steep all night in a little water, slightly salted. Next day, boil it till tender in plenty of water; shred it very fine, and add to the pulp. Weigh all together, and for every pound allow one pound and a half of preserving sugar. Boil gently together for twenty minutes, or until clear, which may be five or six minutes longer. Stir continuously, but very carefully so as not to break the peel. Do not cover till cold.

138. SEVILLE ORANGE MARMALADE, No. 9
(Transparent)

Slice the oranges thinly, take out the pips, and weigh. Allow three pints of water to every pound, and let it steep for twenty-four hours. Next day boil till the rinds are quite tender, and set aside for another twenty-four hours. The third day, weigh the pulp, allow one pound and a half of sugar to every pound, and boil until the rind is quite clear and the syrup jellies.

139. SEVILLE ORANGE MARMALADE, No. 10

Wash the oranges perfectly clean, and dry them; do not let them stay soaking in the water. Halve each orange; remove the pips, and drop them into a cup of warm water; slice the fruit as thinly as possible, and weigh it; add one pint and a half of cold water to every pound; let it all soak together for forty-eight hours; then gently boil it all together, until the peel is tender enough to cut with a spoon handle; add the strained water from the pips; measure, and allow one pound of sugar to each pint of pulp. Heat the sugar while the pulp is being boiled up again, then add it, and boil for about twenty minutes.

140. SEVILLE ORANGE MARMALADE, No. 11

Take four pints of oranges chopped very small—including pulp, rind, and juice; add four pounds of run honey, and boil gently till the marmalade is of the proper colour and consistency.

141. SEVILLE ORANGE MARMALADE, No. 12

To each dozen of Seville oranges add two lemons, and allow one pint of water for each fruit. Cut each fruit in four. Take off peel and slice in machine cutter (these can be hired from most large fruit shops for sixpence a day). Have the required amount of water in a large earthenware pan, into which throw the cut peel. Squeeze each piece of pulp into this as well. Keep out the pips. Chop up the inner skins and throw in (the very tough inner skins can be thrown with the pips into another vessel with all the waste bits). Let all stand till next day—twenty-four hours, if possible. The waste bits can be boiled separately and their juice added to the rest; then boil at least one hour (or till the skins are tender). Empty back into earthenware pan. Now measure out for cooking. To each pint of the pulp allow one pound and a quarter of best lump sugar, and boil till it jellies when tested by cooling a little on a plate. Usually it requires at least one hour and a quarter to do this.

142. SEVILLE ORANGE JELLY, No. 1

To every four pounds of Seville oranges allow the juice and rind of two sweet oranges and two lemons. Peel the Seville oranges, quarter the pulp, take out pips, and place the pulp in the preserving-pan with just enough water to cover it, and press it with a wooden spoon. Boil until it thickens slightly, then remove the rinds of lemon and sweet orange, strain the liquid through a fine sieve, and measure. Allow one pound of sugar to each pint of juice, return to pan, and boil up till the jelly will set.

143. SEVILLE ORANGE JELLY, No. 2.

Take ten Seville oranges, two sweet oranges, and one lemon. Grate the peel (removing the white inner rind); cut up the pulp into rough pieces, and place all in preserving-pan with enough water to cover it. Let simmer for two hours and a half. Rub through a fine sieve. Measure the juice thus obtained, return to pan, and boil for a few minutes, while sugar to the same amount as the fruit is being heated in oven; add sugar to juice, boil up for five or six minutes, pour into pots, and cover.

144. SEVILLE ORANGE JELLY MARMALADE, No. 1

Twelve Seville oranges, three sweet oranges, two lemons, water, sugar. Having peeled the Sevilles very thinly, divide the peel into the thinnest possible strips, and tie these up in a muslin bag large enough to give them plenty of room to swell. Remove as much as possible of the white inner rind from the rest of the fruit, and cut it up, making about three slices of each orange. Slice the sweet oranges and lemons the same way. Put the strips in the bag in a large preserving-pan, or, better, a deep earthen pan, such as a bread-pan. Put the fruit in also, and cover all with twelve pints of cold water, and leave it overnight for twelve hours or so. Next day, boil all together fairly fast for three hours, then remove the muslin bag and empty out the strips. When the pulp has been strained twice, return the strips to it, weigh it, and add an equal amount of sugar. Clean out the preserving-pan, and boil the jelly till it sets, which will take at least twenty-five minutes. Let it stand nearly three-quarters of an hour before pouring off into jars.

145. SEVILLE ORANGE JELLY MARMALADE, No. 2

Take five pounds of oranges ; wash, and peel them very thinly. Put half the peels into a pan of cold water, slightly salted ; let this come to the boil, and then simmer till the peels are tender. Remove the pips and pith from the pulp, cut it up with a silver knife, and place in a preserving-pan with about seven pints of water. Let boil fast for an hour, then strain through a muslin jelly-bag, and measure ; add one pound and a half of sugar for every pint of juice, and return both to the pan ; boil for forty-five minutes. Meanwhile, take the peels, if sufficiently tender, and drain and shred them as finely as possible. Put them to the jelly when it has boiled half an hour. Stir and skim well, and, when it sets, pour off into glasses.

SWEET ORANGES

146. SWEET ORANGE HONEY

Take twelve good oranges ; grate the rind off them, and add it to two pounds of honey strained clear from the comb ; add the strained juice of all the oranges, and mix thoroughly. Let boil gently in a preserving-pan ; when it has boiled for half an hour, put into jars, and cover.

147. SWEET ORANGE JELLY, No. 1

To the pulp of five sweet oranges add one Tangerine orange, and the rind and pulp of a seventh orange. Cut up the fruit in slices, take out pips, and put in preserving-pan with half a pint of cold water. Let simmer till the whole is reduced to half a pint. Strain and boil up again, then add a good half a pound of sugar to each half a pint of juice, and cook until the jelly sets.

148. SWEET ORANGE JELLY, No. 2

One ounce of isinglass, one pint of hot water. Rub some loaf sugar on the rinds of six oranges and four lemons until they appear white. Put the sugar into the water, and let it remain until the isinglass is dissolved; then add the juice of the fruit and let it just boil; then strain into jars. (This will not keep so long as No. 1.)

149. SWEET ORANGE MARMALADE, No. 1

Wipe the oranges with a clean, damp cloth, and with a sharp knife cut the rind downwards and round the middle. Remove it and place in a pan of cold water; let boil until it is quite tender, when cut it into thin strips. Meanwhile have ready the pulp—halve it, remove pips, take out the " rag " at the core, and slice it. Place in a separate pan and cook till quite tender. When the rind is ready, add it to the pulp, and measure; add pound for pound of sugar (which should be warmed), and boil up until the marmalade is cooked enough to set— *i.e.* about twenty minutes.

150. SWEET ORANGE MARMALADE, No. 2

Take twenty ripe oranges, remove the peel and white " rag," and squeeze the pulp with a lemon-squeezer. Boil the juice till it is quite clear, then add five pounds of sugar and the rind grated. Let boil till clear and thick. You can add, while it is still thick and hot, an equal amount of apples, and boil the fruit together ; but it is better left as it is.

151. SWEET ORANGE MARMALADE, No. 3

Take two dozen sweet oranges ; wipe them well with a dampish cloth, and grate the rinds off into a large bowl containing about a breakfastcupful of cold water. Only use the yellow part of the rind. Remove the white inner tissue. Place the pulps of the fruit in a second bowl, and the pips and cores (just covered with boiling water) in a third. Leave all for forty-eight hours; then add the pulps to the peels, also the strained water from the pips. Weigh the whole, and add eighteen ounces of sugar for every pound of fruit, etc. Place sugar and all in a preserving-pan, and boil till it thickens and sets—which should be in about an hour and a half.

152. SWEET ORANGE PRESERVE, No. 1

Take sound sweet oranges, wipe well, slice in halves, core, and remove as much of the " rag " or stringy part as you can, also the pips. Place in preserving-pan, just covered with water, and boil the fruit till tender and clear but not broken.

Change the water once; add an equal quantity of warmed sugar, and let simmer till the preserve is thick and will set.

153. SWEET ORANGE PRESERVE, No. 2

Take the rind from some sweet oranges, remove the inner white lining, slice the fruit in quarters, removing the pips. Let simmer until tender, and add an equal quantity of sugar, and cook till the preserve will set.

154. TANGERINE ORANGE MARMALADE, No. 1

NOTE.—This can be made by any Seville orange marmalade recipe, if you allow one sweet and one Seville orange to every six tangerines. The following methods are, however, especially adapted for this fragrant and attractive little fruit.

155. TANGERINE ORANGE MARMALADE, No. 2

Take thirty-six tangerine oranges; weigh, wash, and dry them well; place them in a preserving-pan with as much water as will float them, and let boil till they are soft. Pour off the water, slice every orange into four, remove the pulp, and take out the pips. Take away as much white pith from inside the peel as you can, and shred the peel into thin uniform strips. Put the pips into a pint of cold water, and let stand overnight. Mash the pulp and leave it in a separate dish. Next day put into a preserving-pan twice the (original) weight of the oranges in white sugar, the strained water from

the pips, and the juice of six large lemons. When the
sugar has dissolved, boil it to a syrup; then add
the peel and pulp. Continue to boil until the
juice will set—about thirty-five to forty-five minutes.
Do not cover until cold.

156. TANGERINE ORANGE MARMALADE, No. 3

Take sufficient tangerine orange-rinds to make
two pounds' weight; add four lemon rinds—all
should have the white pith removed so far as possible. Strain the juice of the fruit into a basin,
and put the pips into a separate basin, covered with
half a pint of boiling water. Chop the rinds, and
put them, with the rest of the squeezed pulp, into
a preserving-pan with four pints of cold water.
Let stand for two hours, or until all is well softened.
Strain the liquid into another pan; strain in also
the fruit-juice and the water from the pips. For
every half-pint of liquid add one pound of sugar,
and boil up for half an hour at least; it may require a little longer, but you must stand by it and
skim, and remove from the fire the moment that
it sets.

157. TANGERINE ORANGE MARMALADE, No. 4

Take twenty-four tangerines and two lemons;
wipe and dry them; place in a preserving-pan with
enough water to float them, and let cook till the
rinds are tender enough to pierce with the head of
a pin. Drain and quarter them; put the pips to
soak overnight in a pint of water; remove the pulp

and mash it; slice the peel as thinly as possible. Weigh the pulp, allow double its weight in sugar, and put the sugar, with the strained liquor from the pips and the strained lemon-juice, to boil up into a thick syrup; add the rinds and pulp; boil until the marmalade will set, which should be in about half an hour, more or less.

VARIOUS

158. AMBER MARMALADE

Take two oranges, two lemons, and two grape-fruits (or a larger sweet quantity in proportion if preferred); slice them very thinly; take out the pips and as much of the white " rag " as possible, especially the cores; measure and allow three times the amount in water; place all in an earthen pan overnight. Next day put it in a preserving-pan; let boil for a quarter of an hour; remove and pour off into the pan. Leave overnight again. The next morning replace in pan, with heated sugar in the proportion of pint for pint, and let boil until it will set—probably about two hours.

159. ORANGE MARMALADE CONSERVE

Take three Seville oranges, one sweet, one lemon, five pounds of sugar, five pints of water. Cut fruit in half, squeeze all the juice out, put straight in preserving-pan. Cut up the peel as finely as possible with a very sharp knife, put it into the pan and also five pints of water. Leave to soak for twenty-four hours. Put the pips to soak in a little water separately, boil them for some time, and strain off into the other pan. Boil all for one hour without sugar, and then, without letting it cool, for two hours with sugar. When the juice begins to jellify on a cold saucer, it is done.

PEACH AND APRICOT

NOTE.—I class these together, because they have very many points of resemblance, and, for practical preserving purposes, they may be regarded as the same. The peach is so ancient a fruit (supposed to have originated in China), that its early history is "wropt in mistry." Darwin believed it to be an evolution of the wild almond, to which it is undoubtedly akin. Its botanical name is Prunus (or Amygdalus) Persica, under the idea that it hails from Persia; the apricot is Prunus Armeniaca, which credits it with an Armenian origin. The nectarine is a smooth-skinned variation of the peach.

Peaches and apricots, as grown in England, are of extraordinary beauty, lusciousness, and fragrance. They are also extraordinarily expensive, and although our eighteenth-century ancestors seem to have made jam of them with a light heart, such a procedure would seem to us to savour of "wasteful and ridiculous excess." I can only suppose that they were then much more commonly grown, in walled gardens, and that their quantity justified the use of them in jam, because they could not all be eaten. This, however, is only a private theory.

Meanwhile, we see any amount of "shop" apricot jam, dried peaches, etc. These fruits come,

pulped or desiccated, from Spain and from America,
and they are very different from the English speci-
mens. But a mid-seasonal variety of English
apricot, the Moor Park, is grown for preserving purposes chiefly.

The reader is referred to the Note on Plums, etc.,
p. 106, as to the danger of using too many kernels of
stoned fruit; a few, however, make an admirable
and natural flavouring for preserve.

All recipes given for peaches apply equally to
apricots.

160. PEACH JAM (1815), No. 1

Get the ripest peaches, stone and bruise them ;
put them in a preserving-pan and let them boil ;
mash them very much, stirring them with your
spaddle ; when they are soft, pass them through a
large sieve ; pound some bitter almonds with powdered sugar, to keep them from oiling; put half an
ounce of them to a pound of jam ; put the jam
and almonds over the fire, and boil them a quarter
of an hour ; add ten ounces of powdered sugar to
every pound of jam ; mix the sugar and the jam
together, boil it half an hour, stirring it all the
time from the bottom ; when it is boiled enough,
put it into your pots, and when cold put brandy
paper over that. [Some peach kernels would be a
substitute for almonds.—*Ed.*]

161. PEACH JAM, No. 2

Take good ripe peaches ; peel, stone, weigh, and
simmer gently for an hour ; add sugar, pound for
pound, and let cook till quite stiff. Cover at once.

162. PEACH JELLY, No. 1

For this it is best to use a mixture of ripe and unripe fruit, which should be washed, stoned, and sliced, but not peeled. It must be placed in a covered earthen jar in the oven, or in a double-boiler at side of stove, for very many hours, until the juice is all extracted. The juice can be put to drip all night in a butter-muslin or cheese cloth jelly-bag. Next day, heat sugar separately, one pound per pint of juice, and reduce the juice a little before adding the sugar. Put in the sugar gradually and let boil up.

163. PEACH JELLY, No. 2

Take half ripe and half unripe fruit. Wash, stone, and quarter, but do not peel it. Put it in a covered earthen jar in a moderate oven, or at the side of the stove, or in a double-boiler; no sugar or water is required with it. It may take a long time, up to twenty-four hours, before the juice is all extracted. Strain it through butter-cloth, measure, and allow a pound of sugar to every pint of juice. Next day, heat the sugar and juice separately, and let the juice boil down a little before you begin to add the sugar. This should be done a little at a time, stirring and skimming carefully. When all the sugar is in, boil up for a few minutes until the jelly sets.

164. PEACH MARMALADE, No. 1

Peel, stone, and weigh some peaches; slice the pulp finely. Crack a few stones and add the kernels to the fruit, which must be cooked fast till soft; add an equal weight of sugar, boil gently for a quarter of an hour, and pour into jars.

165. PEACH MARMALADE, No. 2

Peel, stone, weigh, and slice peaches; to every pound allow twelve ounces of sugar. Mash sugar and pulp thoroughly, put in a covered earthen jar in oven, and leave to cook for several hours. When it will set, pour off into jars.

166. PEACH MARMALADE, No. 3

Peel and cut ripe peaches, and put them into a preserving-pan, with three-quarters of a pound of sugar for every pound of fruit, taking care that they do not burn; boil them until they are soft, take them out, and dip them in cold water; put them on again to boil, with some clarified sugar, until no more scum rises; then take them off, and pour into jars.

167. PEACH MARMALADE, No. 4

Pare, slice, and weigh the peaches, and allow twelve ounces of sugar to every pound of fruit. Mash and mix all well together, place in a covered earthen jar in a good oven, and let cook for several hours, until the whole is like an opaque jelly. To be covered at once.

168. APRICOT JAM, No. 1

NOTE.—The " shop " apricot jam is largely manufactured from foreign fruit-pulp—not unmixed with pumpkin. A very good imitation of real apricot jam can be made from Victoria plums, gathered fully ripe and *skinned* before using. The next best fruit for the above purpose, perhaps, is the Magnum Bonum plum.

169. APRICOT JAM (1815), No. 2

Get the ripest apricots you can, cut them to pieces, and take the stones from them ; put them in a large preserving-pan, and mash them as much as you can ; put them over the fire to warm, mashing them all the time ; pass them through a colander and keep pressing them with a small pestle ; when they are all broken, put them over the fire and just let them boil for ten minutes, stirring them all the time ; then put fifteen ounces of powdered sugar to every pound of apricots ; let them boil together half an hour, stirring them all the time with your spaddle, that it may not burn at bottom ; when it is boiled enough, put it into pots; when cold, put brandy papers over the jam before you cover the pots, and let them stand two days before you put them by.

170. DRIED APRICOT JAM, No. 1

To every pound of dried apricots allow two and a half pounds of sugar and the juice of one lemon. Soak the fruit for forty-eight hours in sufficient water to cover it. Strain off the water, add the sugar to it, and boil; then add the fruit, and let it continue to boil until the jam will set.

171. DRIED APRICOT JAM, No. 2

Two pounds of dried apricots, six pints of water, six pounds of preserving sugar, two ounces of bitter almonds (blanched and chopped or grated very small). Wash the apricots lightly ; let them steep in the water for twenty-four hours ; then boil them slowly till they are quite tender. Mix the sugar and almonds well in, and boil half an hour longer. This is a cheap jam, and is said to taste like one made of fresh fruit. Larger quantities to be made in above proportions.

172. DRIED APRICOT JAM, No. 3

Take two pounds of dried apricots ; wash them well, drain, slice each apricot in half, and put the fruit to soak in three quarts of water for three days and three nights. On the fourth day, empty all into a preserving-pan. Have ready two ounces of Valencia almonds, shelled, blanched, and finely chopped ; add these to the apricots, and bring all slowly to boiling-point ; add six pounds of loaf preserving sugar, and let boil till the jam thickens and sets—say about thirty minutes.

173. APRICOT MARMALADE, No. 1

Take any apricots for this which are unsuitable for preserving in syrup owing to being slightly bruised, etc. Boil them quite soft in as little water as possible (having removed the stones). Beat them to a pulp, or rub them through a sieve. Weigh the pulp ; take half its weight in sugar. Make a

syrup with this sugar and just sufficient water to
dissolve it; boil and skim well, and, when it is clear,
add the apricot pulp, and boil up until the marmalade thickens and sets, which should be in a few
minutes.

174. APRICOT MARMALADE, No. 2

Take ripe apricots; stone them and put them at
once into a pan of boiling water, deep enough to
cover them well. Cook till soft, but not broken;
remove and gently wipe them. Weigh, and allow
pound for pound in sugar. Dissolve the sugar in
sufficient water and boil until it candies or "blows";
put in the apricots and boil fifteen minutes, and
"then glass them up," says the old-world recipe
from which the above is adapted.

PEAR

NOTE.—The pear, which is closely related to the
apple, in no way equals it for general value and
utility. It is regarded somewhat as a luxury if
for eating *au naturel*, and the cooking pear does
not rank high as a comestible. As a matter of fact,
it is a fruit quite wealthy in sugar, valuable acids,
and mineral salts; its rich juiciness and strongly
individual flavour render it most attractive. But it
should be used, whether for eating or preserving, at
the exactly right moment: a "sleepy" pear is
decidedly to be avoided, and an obviously unripe one
is devoid of half its worth. Taken all round, the
pear is best for preserving whole; but it can be

utilised very successfully for other methods of preservation, and no pear need ever go to waste.

175. PEAR HONEY

Take one peck of just-ripe pears; peel, core, and
put them through a mincer. Weigh them, and put
into preserving-pan, with eight ounces of sugar and
one breakfastcupful of water to every pound of
fruit. Bring to boiling-point, and add grated pineapple (one small tin of chunks), and the juice and
grated rind of two lemons. Let simmer for two
hours, or until quite thick, then put into jars and
cover at once.

176. PEAR JAM

Take sound, hard pears; remove the stems, wipe
but do not peel, and weigh them. To every four
pounds allow three pounds of sugar and two ounces
of grated green ginger root. Slice the fruit very
thinly, place in an earthen vessel, and leave for
twelve hours. Place in a preserving-pan, with the
grated rind and juice of two lemons to every four
pounds of fruit. Bring gradually to boiling-point,
and let simmer for three hours, or until quite thick
and clear.

177. PEAR JELLY

Peel and cut ripe pears into quarters, and boil
them with a very little water till quite soft; then
pass the pulp through a sieve so as to have only
the juice, and boil it with sugar in equal portions;

when it is become sufficiently thick by boiling, put
it into glasses and cover over.

178. PEAR MARMALADE, No. 1

Take rather juicy pears; peel, core, and halve
them. To each pound of fruit allow one pound
and a half of sugar, with the juice and grated rind
of one lemon. Simmer the fruit till tender, add
the sugar and lemon, and boil till the marmalade
sets.

179. PEAR MARMALADE, No. 2

Take large pears, not over-ripe; peel, halve, and
core them; let boil gently in just enough water to
cover them. When they are tender, remove carefully from pan, and put in the parings and cores,
which boil till they are reduced by half. Strain off
the liquor and add sufficient water to it to make
a syrup of twelve ounces of sugar and one pint of
water to every pound of fruit. Boil the syrup till
it sets well upon the spoon, then put the pears into
it, and let them boil for five or six minutes.

180. PEAR MARMALADE, No. 3

Take six pounds of small pears, and four pounds
of sugar. Put the pears into a saucepan with cold
water; cover it and set it over the fire till the fruit
is soft, then put the pears into cold water; pare,
quarter, and core them; put to them three teacupfuls of water, and set them over the fire. Roll
the sugar fine, mash the fruit fine and smooth, and
put the sugar to it; stir it well together till it is
thick and sets like jelly.

181. PEAR MARMALADE, No. 4

Take ripe pears of good quality, and, having peeled them, boil them until they are quite soft; press them through a sieve, and put the marmalade over the fire; when it is become thick, moisten with syrup, and add powdered sugar in such proportion that the whole quantity of sugar employed (including syrup) may be equal to one pound for a pound of fruit. The sugar and fruit are to be made well hot, and stirred frequently, taking care, however, never to pass the state of simmering; when the preserve is thoroughly heated, and of a proper thickness, put it into pots in the usual way.

182. PEAR PRESERVE, No. 1

Take eight pounds of good sound pears; peel, core, and quarter them. Place in preserving-pan with barely enough water to cover them; add six pounds of sugar, four ounces of ground ginger, juice and thin rind of two large lemons, and about a saltspoonful of cayenne. Boil all together until the fruit is thoroughly tender and will set.

183. PEAR PRESERVE, No. 2

Take the largest stewing pears when they are on the turn. Pare them nicely, cut them in halves, leaving the stem in. To every pound of pears add three-quarters of a pound of loaf sugar, and to about fifty pears put a pint of water, the juice and peel of four lemons (the peel to be pared thin and cut in long strips), a small cup of cloves, and a little

cochineal to colour them. Let them stew very
gently over a slow fire, turning them constantly
until you can pass a straw through them; then add
a teacupful of brandy and let them boil two or
three minutes longer. Put them in jars and tie
down like other preserves; they will keep good for
twelve months.

PINEAPPLE

NOTE.—This delightful fruit, which does not
grow on a pine and is not an apple, but derives
its name from its outward resemblance to a pine-
cone, is to some extent a luxury in England, unless
you live near a big seaport. I have known magni-
ficent pineapples sold for sixpence each in Southamp-
ton. The juice, uncooked, is extremely valuable for
its digestive properties, no less than for its unique
and delicious flavour. Cooking of any kind, to a
certain extent, somewhat reduces both the above
qualities; but as a pineapple soon deteriorates, it
is better to cook than to waste it. Do not attempt
to pare it whole; cut it up in thick slices, peel them
with a sharp knife, and subsequently remove the
" eyes." This operation should be performed over
a bowl or dish, so as not to lose any of the juice.

184 PINEAPPLE HONEY

Take some ripe pineapples; remove the peel and
eyes; pass the fruit through a mincer. Weigh, allowing pound for pound of fruit and sugar. Mix the
sugar well in, and, when it has stood till dissolved,

place in preserving-pan and let simmer gently till the honey is clear and soft. It will need skimming. Put into glasses and cover at once.

185. PINEAPPLE JAM

Peel and prepare one or more pineapples as above directed; grate the fruit, allow an equal amount of sugar, pound for pound, and put all into preserving-pan. No water will be required. It must heat through slowly, for twenty minutes, then simmer for about an hour.

186. PINEAPPLE JELLY

Take one good-sized pineapple, wipe it well, cut off the crown, slice it thickly, but do not peel it; cut the slices in half; add two lemons, thinly sliced right through, and one pint of water. Place in preserving-pan and let simmer for several hours. Strain off, squeeze through jelly-bag, return to pan, and boil up again; then strain it into another pan, let boil again, and add equal amount of sugar to juice. Let cook till it sets—about ten minutes longer.

187. PINEAPPLE MARMALADE

Take some sound, ripe pineapples; slice, pare, and cut into little cubes; add three-quarters of a pound of sugar to each pound of fruit; mix well, and leave overnight in a bowl in a cool place. Next day, put fruit into preserving-pan, simmer quietly for an hour; then pulp it through a coarse sieve. Return it to pan; let cook until it is transparent and gold-coloured—about half an hour longer—and will set well.

188. PINEAPPLE PRESERVE

Cut the pineapples in slices before peeling them and removing " eyes "; then weigh an equal quantity of sugar, and lay it in alternate layers with the fruit in a preserving-pan. Allow half a breakfastcupful of water to every pound of fruit, and pour this in on top of the fruit and sugar. Let the whole come to a boil, then remove the fruit and place it on dishes to dry in the sun. Let the syrup continue to boil slowly for nearly three-quarters of an hour; then replace the fruit in it, and let cook for twenty minutes. Take out the fruit into jars, pour the boiling syrup over it, and cover at once.

PLUM, DAMSON, GREENGAGE, SLOE

NOTE.—Not the most wholesome of fruit when uncooked (most stone fruits have a tendency to disagree if raw), the plum is admirably adapted for preserving in almost any way, and is not only palatable, but delicious when properly dealt with. A great variety of opinion prevails about what should be the very simple operation of making plum jam, as will be seen from the following recipes. Personally I prefer the method indicated in No. 1, the results of which are admirable, and keep particularly well.

There is also a difference of opinion as to the best

plums for the purpose of jam, but the *Victoria* can hardly be beaten. *Magnum Bonum* and the black plums, formerly termed Mogul, are best preserved whole.

The best damson plums are, I think, those to be found in Cheshire—large, sweet, and juicy. Those which are saleable in Southern markets are much more like bullaces (from which the damson was originally evolved), and, consequently, are not half so good for culinary purposes.

In all stone fruits the kernels should be used with care and sparsely ; they contain a distinct amount of prussic acid.

189. PLUM JAM, No. 1

Take twelve pounds of good, sound **Victoria** plums, not over-ripe, and wipe them with a clean cloth. Split and stone them with a silver knife ; allow equal weight of crushed preserving sugar. Place the fruit and half the sugar in layers in a deep earthen bowl, or on large dishes ; let stand overnight. Next day, boil it up in preserving-pan, stirring carefully ; when it begins to be soft, add the rest of the sugar, and let boil until it thickens and sets.

190. PLUM JAM, No. 2

Take under-ripe plums of suitable kind, such as Pershore Egg or Victoria ; cook them, in enough water to cover and float them, until tender. Lift them out, remove the stones, and weigh fruit. Allow sugar of equal weight, and boil it up along

with the water in which the plums were cooked;
then replace plums in pan, and boil until the jam
thickens and sets—about thirty minutes.

191. PLUM JAM, No. 3

Take sound plums, just ripe; cook them down
to a pulp, with just enough water to float them.
Rub the pulp through a sieve which will retain the
stones and skins; weigh it, add equal weight of
crushed sugar, replace in pan, and boil for half an
hour, stirring well.

192. BLACK PLUM JAM (1815)

Get the ripest black Mussel plums; cut them to
pieces, stone them, and put them into a large copper
pan; bruise them as much as you can with your
spaddle; warm them over the fire till they are soft;
pass them through a colander with a pestle, and get
as much pulp through as you can; boil it one hour,
stirring it from the bottom all the time, or else it
will burn; put twelve ounces of powdered sugar to
every pound of jam; take it off the fire to mix it;
put it over the fire ten minutes; then take it off
and put it in brown pots, and sift some powdered
sugar over it.

193. PLUM JELLY

Wipe, skin, stone, and weigh juicy plums. Put
them in a preserving-pan with just enough water
to cover them; when this boils, pour it off and add
fresh (boiling) water. Cook till the plums are soft.
Strain through a jelly-bag, without pressure; let

drip all night if need be. Return juice to pan, boil it down by one-fourth; add sugar of equal weight to the fruit; skim well. The jelly should set in about twenty minutes after the sugar has dissolved.

194. PLUM MARMALADE, No. 1

Take twenty-five pounds of good, sound plums; halve, remove stones, place in pan with one quart of cold water, a handful of granulated sugar, and one teaspoonful of cinnamon. Boil till soft, stirring frequently. Press fruit through a sieve; weigh, and allow twelve ounces of sugar to every pound of pulp. Boil sugar, with two gills of cold water, for ten minutes; add plum pulp; boil twelve minutes, stirring constantly, and pour into pots. Do not cover till cold.

195. PLUM MARMALADE, No. 2

Take large, ripe, sweet, soft plums; remove the skins and stones, and place in covered earthen jar in slow heat to extract juice. When the juice is all out, strain it through a sieve, and weigh the remaining pulp. To each pound of pulp allow one pound and a half of sugar. Let simmer very gently (having added the juice at discretion), and remove as soon as it sets—about twenty minutes.

196. DAMSON JAM, No. 1

Take sound, large, ripe damsons; wash, halve, and remove stones. Weigh, put in preserving-pan with just enough water to cover them, and cook till the skins break; add sugar, pound for pound, and boil till the jam thickens and sets.

197. DAMSON JAM, No. 2

Take just-ripe damsons; cook them to a pulp in barely enough water to cover them. Rub them through a coarse sieve which will retain the stones and skins; weigh the pulp, return it to the pan with an equal weight of sugar, and boil for twenty minutes, stirring well.

198. DAMSON JELLY

Take just-ripe damsons; wipe them well, and put them in a pan with barely enough cold water to cover them; cook until tender (probably about thirty minutes). Strain through a jelly-bag, and measure; allow an equal amount of sugar. Boil up sugar and juice for about a quarter of an hour, and pour into glass jars.

199. GREENGAGE PLUM JAM

Take firm greengages; wipe them with a cloth, stalk them, remove the stones, and weigh fruit. Set aside an equal weight of sugar, and put it in the oven to heat. Crack some of the stones, and blanch the kernels, which add to the fruit, and place in a pan, with not more than an inch deep of water. Let it come gradually to boiling, then boil fast for ten or twelve minutes. Put in the sugar, stirring well till it dissolves, and continue to boil fast for twenty minutes, when place it in jars, and cover.

200. SLOE JAM

Take just-ripe sloes; wash, and place in preserving-pan with just enough water to float them. Let boil gently till quite tender, then pass through a coarse sieve. Weigh the pulp, and return it to pan with an equal weight of sugar. Stir well till the sugar has dissolved, and boil up until the jam thickens and sets. Pour into pots, and cover at once.

POMEGRANATE

NOTE.—The name of this ancient and remarkable fruit is a corruption of *Punica granatum*—*i.e.*, a fruit hailing from Carthage and possessing grains, kernels, or seeds. Particularly beautiful as regards both flower and fruit, and of distinct astringent, medicinal value, the pomegranate belongs, strange to say, to the Loosestrife family or *Lythraceæ*; it is a relation of those tall purple or golden spires which fringe our English rivers. It has always been accounted a valuable and recherché fruit; yet its nutrient qualities are not extremely great. For preserving it, care must be taken to withhold the seeds, and not to crush them in doing so, or they will injure the flavour of the fruit.

201. POMEGRANATE JELLY

Place under-ripe pomegranates in a covered earthen vessel in the oven or at the back of the range until they become quite pulpy and the juice flows freely. Strain without any pressure through a jelly-bag, which can drip all night. Measure the juice, boil it up, and add pint for pint of heated sugar. When the sugar has dissolved, boil up for a few minutes until the jelly will set. It is a lovely colour. Pour off into glass jars, and cover when cold.

202. POMEGRANATE MARMALADE

Take rather under-ripe pomegranates ; halve and place in a preserving-pan with a very little water and cook till tender. Pass through a sieve fine enough to retain the seeds ; weigh the pulp, return it to pan, and give it a boil-up while you heat an equal amount of sugar ; add the sugar, stir well till it dissolves, and boil a little longer till the marmalade thickens. Pour off and cover.

QUINCE

NOTE.—The oddest thing about the quince, which belongs to the Malaceæ or apple family, is that it is practically never eaten uncooked. It has beautiful blossom, exquisite perfume, and pleasing appearance ; yet it is only considered as an adjunct to the apple, to which, when cooked, it imparts a peculiar and most attractive taste. I have heard a man at a seaside boarding-house grumble for a whole afternoon because there was *no quince* in the apple-pie at lunch ! However, in the province of preserves, the quince at last comes into its own, for quince jelly and quince marmalade are truly delectable concoctions, nor are they so common as to be disdained. A distinct food-value is attached to the preserved quince, and nobody need be afraid of its disagreeing with the most delicate.

The Japanese quince (*Cydonia maulei*) also yields an excellent preserve.

It is interesting to note that, as before mentioned, the word *marmalade* is supposed to have been derived from *marmelo*, the Portuguese word for quince. This looks as if quinces had always been chiefly used for preserves and confitures, which indeed one must suppose to be the case.

203. QUINCE HONEY

Take two large quinces; wipe well, and grate them let cook till tender. Have ready a syrup made with one pound of sugar to one pint of water, which must cook for about five minutes, or till it arrives at the " soft ball " stage (see p. 14) ; then add the grated quince and let simmer for another twenty minutes. Stir continually.

204. QUINCE JAM, No. 1

Take fourteen to sixteen good-sized ripe quinces, and about four quarts of ripe sweet apples. Wash and dry; peel, core, and quarter them. Put the quince cores to steep in a little cold water. Slice all the fruit thinly, and place it in an earthen vessel overnight, in alternate layers with sugar (five to six pounds), and pour one pint of water over all. Let stand overnight. Next day boil all slowly, adding the strained liquor from the cores, until the fruit is tender and the syrup becomes transparent and sets.

205. QUINCE JAM, No. 2

Half a pound of sugar to one pound of fruit; about a large teacupful of water to five or six pounds of fruit. Cover the stew-pan close during the last ten minutes to improve the colour. The hard, dry quinces are better if peeled and put into a jar with a small quantity of sugar, the peelings put on the top, and covered with paper and put into the oven after the bread is out, and then preserved in the usual way.

206. QUINCE JELLY, No. 1

Take ripe quinces; peel, core, and slice them; place in a preserving-pan with sufficient water to float them; boil for two and a half hours; strain through a jelly-bag, and allow one pound of white sugar to every pint of juice; boil up again until the jelly will set. This makes a bright red jelly, of extremely attractive flavour.

207. QUINCE JELLY, No. 2

Take the liquor in which quinces have been boiled (see No. 211), and place the parings, cores, etc., in it; boil till the contents of the pan are quite soft, then press through a fine sieve; add one pound of sugar to every pint of fluid, and boil for half an hour. This will not be a very clear jelly.

208. QUINCE JELLY, No. 3

Wash, peel, core, and quarter the quinces; put the peels and cores in a little cold water. Place the

fruit in a pan, cover with water, and cook slowly
for several hours. If the water boils away, strain
the liquor from the cores and add it. Boil the fruit
to a pulp, and let it drip all night from a jelly-bag.
Next day measure, boil up the juice for twenty
minutes; add an equal amount of heated sugar,
and, when this is dissolved by stirring, boil for
twenty minutes and pour off.

209. QUINCE JELLY, No. 4

Take quinces and cut them up small, without
peeling or coring. Put them in a preserving-pan,
cover with cold water, and cook slowly for many
hours until they become a soft pulp; add more
water if need be. Let drip all night through a
muslin jelly-bag; proceed as for No. 3.

210. QUINCE MARMALADE

Peel the quinces and cut them into quarters, and
to every pound of fruit allow three-quarters of a
pound of loaf sugar with a little water. Boil them
gently for three hours and put into jars; simmer
the seeds in water to a jelly and add to the above
while boiling.

211. QUINCE PRESERVE

Peel and quarter the quinces, and boil in just
sufficient water to keep the pieces from becoming
pulped and broken. When they are quite tender
but still whole, remove them, and add one pound of
white sugar to each pound of quinces; cover the
fruit with the sugar, and let stand overnight; then

replace in preserving-pan and let boil for twenty minutes.

RASPBERRY, LOGANBERRY, WINEBERRY

NOTE.—The raspberry is, like the blackberry, a variety of the *Rubus* genus; and both belong to the great Rosaceæ family which furnishes nearly all the fruit for temperate climes. Raspberries are easy and cheap to grow; their fruit, for some occult reason, is very dear to buy; and hence it is not worth while preserving unless you can provide it from your own garden, or procure it, at wholesale price, very fresh. The seeds of the raspberry are the bother: they always remain more or less hard and harsh, after any amount of cooking. Therefore, although raspberry jam is a very popular preserve, especially for culinary purposes, raspberry jelly is a far superior article. Red currants are so frequently admixed with raspberries that many people regard them as essential. Yellow raspberries should be intermixed with white currants.

The loganberry, gradually becoming well-known, is a large recent hybrid between blackberry and raspberry. It is very suitable for preserving whole; next to that, for jelly.

The wineberry is a beautiful scarlet fruit, *Rubus phœnicolasius*; it is allied to raspberries and blackberries, and can be preserved by any method appropriate to them, but may require rather more sugar, being somewhat more acid. It has a distinct and pleasant flavour, and is very juicy. Its origin, I believe, is Japanese.

212. RASPBERRY JAM, No. 1

To every four pounds of raspberries add one pint of red-currant juice. Let boil for half an hour, stirring well, and mashing the fruit with a wooden spoon. Press through a fine sieve, so that no seeds can pass ; weigh, and for each pound of fruit allow twelve ounces of sugar. Boil up the fruit again, then add the sugar, and boil till the jam will set, which should be in twenty minutes.

213. RASPBERRY JAM, No. 2 (1815)

Put the raspberries into a large copper pan, stir them well at the bottom of the pan with a large spaddle about three feet long ; mash the raspberries as much as you can ; put them over the fire and keep stirring them all the time ; when you find they are almost ready to boil, take them off. Have a large hair sieve over another pan, and pass the raspberries through the sieve ; the hair of the sieve must be large enough to let all the seeds of the raspberries through ; mind there are no pieces of raspberries left. Put them over the fire and stir them with your spaddle ; let the raspberries boil half an hour, stirring them well from the bottom as they boil to prevent them from burning ; put in fourteen ounces of powdered sugar to every pound of raspberries ; take them off the fire, mix them well together, and boil the sugar and the raspberries together half an hour ; sift some powdered sugar over the top of the pots before they are covered.

214. RASPBERRY JAM (UNBOILED), No. 3

One and a quarter pounds of best lump sugar
to each pound of raspberries. Put on the fruit,
bring it to boiling-point, but do not let it boil more
than two or three minutes; add the sugar; stir
till quite dissolved; again bring to boiling-point.
Pour it at once into warm jam-pots and cover while
hot. Keeps well. Is of splendid colour and re-
tains the flavour of fresh fruit.

215. RASPBERRY JAM, No. 4

Gather ripe, dry raspberries; pick them very carefully from the stalks; weigh, then crush them in a
bowl with a silver or wooden spoon; add half their
weight of red currant juice (currants previously
cooked and strained as for jelly), and set them over
a clear, slow fire. Boil for thirty minutes, or until
quite soft; add pound for pound in heated sugar,
stir well till it dissolves, and boil up for a few minutes
until the jam thickens and sets.

216. RASPBERRY JAM, No. 5

Pick and weigh the raspberries; allow pound for
pound of sugar, and a quarter of the weight of the
fruit in red currants. Wash, pick, and mash the
currants, strain the juice through a fine sieve, and
cook it with the sugar for about twenty minutes.
Put in the raspberries; let simmer, stirring well, for
about twenty-five minutes.

217. RASPBERRY JAM, No. 6

Weigh the raspberries, and set aside pound for pound of sugar. Let the fruit simmer by itself till reduced by a third, then gradually sprinkle in the sugar (heated), and stir well till it is thoroughly melted. Give the jam a boil-up, pour into pots, and cover immediately.

218. RASPBERRY JAM, No. 7

Pick the raspberries thoroughly, and set the finest on one side, till about half are selected. Take the rest, weigh, and add half a pound of picked red or white currants for every pound of raspberries. Mash and strain them through a cheesecloth, and when all the juice is extracted, put it in a preserving-pan with twelve ounces of sugar for every pint of juice, and twelve ounces for every pound of the raspberries set aside. Boil the juice and sugar for twenty minutes, stirring and skimming well; then add the raspberries and boil for ten minutes, or until the syrup sets. Pour off and cover at once.

219. RASPBERRY JELLY, No. 1

Put into a jar two pounds of raspberries and two pounds of white currants; set the jar in a saucepan containing some water, and in this way heat the fruit thoroughly; then press the fruit, and pass the juice through a jelly-bag; now boil the juice with a pound of castor sugar to every pint; when it has boiled once, take it off and skim it, and repeat the same operation three or four times, until it is quite clear.

220. RASPBERRY JELLY (1815), No. 2

Put your raspberries in the preserving-pan over the fire, stirring them all the time they are on; when they are ready to boil, take them off and pass them through a hair sieve into a pan; let no seed go through. Put your jelly into another pan and set it on the fire, and let it boil twenty minutes before you put the sugar in it; stir it all the time, or else it will burn at bottom; put fourteen ounces of sugar to every pound of jelly; let it boil twenty minutes; stir it all the time; when cold, put it in brown pots, and sift a little powdered sugar over it; let it stand one day and then cover it up.

221. RASPBERRY JELLY, No. 3

Pick the raspberries on a dry day. Stem them and put them in a jar in boiling water (or in a double-boiler) till quite pulped—about an hour. Place in a jelly-bag, but do not squeeze; let the juice drip all night. Next day measure, then boil it up for ten minutes; add one pound and a quarter of heated sugar for every pint of juice, and stir well till the sugar is dissolved, keeping the jam boiling. Pour off at once, but do not cover till cold. This jelly, like most others, is better for standing in the sun.

222. RASPBERRY JELLY, No. 4

Proceed as above until the fruit is soft, then strain off the juice, applying pressure, and measure it. Allow twelve ounces of sugar to every pint; let the juice boil for twenty minutes; meanwhile heat the sugar, and add it, stirring thoroughly till it dissolves. Boil up for five minutes, but not longer.

223. LOGANBERRY JAM

Take sound, ripe loganberries; weigh, crush, and heat them through in a covered pan. Let simmer slowly for half an hour; then add an equal weight of sugar, and let boil for half an hour; at the end of that time the jam should set.

224. LOGANBERRY JELLY

Put the loganberries in preserving-pan with a very little water, enough to keep them from sticking; let the water boil, then move the pan and let the berries simmer till they are quite pulped. Pass through jelly-bag, measure, allow one pound of sugar to each pint of juice. Boil up the juice, add the sugar, and boil for twenty minutes or until the jelly sets.

225. WINEBERRY JELLY

Place the wineberries, well stalked, in a double-boiler, without water. The outer part must be filled with cold water; gradually bring this to the boil, and let the fruit be cooked till soft. Mash it with a wooden spaddle, and strain through muslin or a fine sieve; measure, and boil the juice for twenty minutes. Stir in an equal amount of sugar previously heated in oven; when this is thoroughly dissolved, give the jelly a fast boil-up, and pour it into glass jars.

RHUBARB

NOTE.—Rhubarb, among the cheapest and commonest of comestibles, is not a fruit; neither is it, in the ordinary sense, a vegetable. It is the stalk of a plant whose root is strongly medicinal. It originated in Central Asia, and was introduced to this country more than 300 years ago. I should say that it was the nearest approach to fruit, and the best substitute for it, that has ever been discovered. Stewed, it is singularly wholesome and refreshing; it proves invaluable for tarts; it results in an excellent wine; and in preserved form it is delicious. It can be combined with other fruits, fresh or dry; but to my thinking, the simpler you have it, the better. It has been said that rhubarb "takes all flavours but gives none," yet this would seem a libel on its peculiar and delectable taste.

Some people eke out their rhubarb jam with sago, which seems an unnecessary economy; still, there is no reason against it, provided you counterbalance the insipidity of the sago with sufficient lemon, candied peel, or other flavouring. Rhubarb is one of those articles which are best prepared one day and left till the next before cooking, covered with sugar.

Rhubarb juice is admirable as a substitute for water in syrup for other fruit.

226. RHUBARB JAM, No. 1

Weight for weight of fruit and sugar. Pare the rhubarb and cut in three-inch pieces; pound one-third of sugar and put over rhubarb; let it stand all night. Pour off the juice in the morning, and boil it with the remainder of sugar; pour this over the fruit, and let it stand till cold. Then put it through a hair sieve, and boil the juice again for fifteen minutes; add the fruit and let it boil till tender. Essence of ginger to taste should be put in a little before it is taken off the fire.

227. RHUBARB JAM, No. 2

Eight pounds of rhubarb, eight pounds of sugar, four level teaspoonfuls of ginger, one pound of candied peel. Wipe the rhubarb and cut into pieces about one inch long; put in a pan, slightly crush the sugar and spread this over it. Leave it till next day; then cut the lemon peel up thinly, add the ginger, and boil the whole till it turns a nice red colour, probably one hour and a half. Pour into dry scalded jars and cover down at once.

228. RHUBARB JAM, No. 3

Take red fresh stalks, cut them into four-inch pieces, and weigh four pounds. Mix this with one pound of stoned raisins, the juice and grated rind of one orange and two lemons, and four pounds of sugar. Let all stand, well mixed, in a bowl for thirty minutes; then place in preserving-pan and boil forty-five minutes, stirring and skimming well.

229. RHUBARB JAM, No. 4

Wipe the rhubarb, cut it into small pieces; allow three-quarters of a pound of preserving sugar to

each pound of rhubarb, and two or three lemon
rinds grated finely. Let all simmer gently; skim
and stir occasionally. When the jam is tender and
will set, turn it into a heated bowl, and stir in the
juice of the lemons. Pour into pots and cover
while hot.

230. RHUBARB JAM, No. 5

Take red-stalked rhubarb, and string it carefully
so as to leave plenty of red. Cut it into half-inch
slices, and leave it overnight covered with an equal
weight of sugar. Next day, place it in preserving-
pan with the juice and grated rind of one lemon to
every three pounds of rhubarb, and one ounce of
finely chopped blanched sweet almonds to the whole.
Let boil thirty minutes after reaching boiling-point;
then simmer quietly for thirty minutes longer.

231. RHUBARB JAM, No. 6

Take four pounds of rhubarb; wash, peel, and cut
into one-inch lengths; add one pound of stoned
raisins, five pounds of sugar, and the juice and
grated rind of one lemon and two oranges. Mix all
thoroughly, and let stand for thirty minutes; then
put on to cook, and when the jam reaches boiling-
point, let it boil for three-quarters of an hour. Stir
and skim well.

232. RHUBARB JELLY

Take young, fresh, red rhubarb. Wash and dry
it; no peeling is required. Slice it in half-inch
pieces, and place in preserving-pan with just enough

water to cover the bottom of pan; let simmer till the juice is all out, then strain and measure. Allow one pound of sugar to each half-pint of juice. Boil up sugar and juice, stirring well; and let boil till it sets, say about twelve minutes; then pour off.

The above is for plain rhubarb jelly; but it may pleasantly be varied at discretion by using a little grated lemon-peel and cinnamon, or essence of lemon and essence of almond.

233. RHUBARB MARMALADE, No. 1

Take four pounds of rhubarb; wash, wipe, and cut in small bits; add the grated rinds of five lemons and half a breakfastcup of water; place in a preserving-pan and boil for twenty minutes; add twelve ounces of blanched almonds, grated in a nut-mill or chopped very fine, one tablespoonful of essence of ginger, and six pounds of heated sugar. Let boil fast until the marmalade clears and sets— about twenty minutes.

234. RHUBARB MARMALADE, No. 2

(This is for making in autumn when the rhubarb is fairly dry.) Take six pounds of rhubarb, cut it in inch lengths, then in narrow strips like orange-peel for marmalade. Take three lemons, and cut the rinds in similar strips. Allow one pound of sugar to every pound of rhubarb, and half a pound of sugar to every lemon. Let all the sugar and fruit be put together, and remain for twenty-four hours; then boil, and add the juice of the lemons last thing, just when the marmalade is nearly done.

235. RHUBARB PRESERVE

Take some sound, fresh, red stalks, wash and wipe dry, slice into six-inch lengths, and let dry for forty-eight hours. Place in a preserving-pan four pounds of sugar, half a pound of grated lemon-peel, half a pound of preserved ginger chopped small, and one gill of water. Stir well until the mixture has boiled five minutes; then put in four pounds of the dry rhubarb and let it boil thirty minutes, taking care how you stir, lest the sticks should break. Pour into pots and cover at once.

ROWAN OR MOUNTAIN ASH

NOTE.—This brilliant and glowing berry-cluster is much utilised in Scotland, in Switzerland, and, I believe, in Scandinavian countries. Known in Ireland as quicken, and in Scotland as rowan, it has from time immemorial been credited with all manner of mystical and romantic qualities. Certainly it contains a large amount of malic acid; though I doubt whether that is enough to corroborate the ancient Irish tradition that quickenberries will restore the oldest man to the age of about thirty and the possession of his full strength. Mountain ash is allied to the hawthorns, the apples, and the inevitable Rosaceæ. As a preserved fruit, not everybody likes it; but unquestionably it is best as a jelly.

236. ROWAN OR MOUNTAIN-ASH JELLY, No. 1

The berries should be not quite ripe. Wipe them well, pick off the stalks, place in preserving-pan with just enough water to cover them; boil till quite soft, mashing with a wooden spoon occasionally; strain off the juice, and measure; add one pound of sugar to every pint, and boil up together for thirty minutes; stir and skim well. Some people add apple juice, pint for pint; if this be done, an extra pound of sugar must be added for every pint of apple juice.

237. ROWAN JELLY, No. 2

Pick the mountain-ash berries clean from the stalks, and stew them down to as near a pulp as you can, with enough water to cover them and a very little " race " ginger. Crush and strain the pulp, and boil it up again for half an hour with two-thirds of its weight in sugar.

238. ROWAN JELLY, No. 3

Pare, core, and slice two pounds of good preserving apples of the juiciest kind, and boil them for twenty minutes or more in one quart of water, till they are well to pieces; strain off the water, and add to the apples in the preserving-pan three pounds of mountain-ash berries. Let all simmer gently until quite pulped; then strain off the juice, and to every pint measure one pound of sugar. Let the juice boil fast for twenty minutes; then put in the sugar, which should be warmed and crushed; boil for fifteen minutes more, skimming well, and then pour off the jelly into heated pots. Some people put a leaf of scented geranium, such as oak-leaf, into every pot.

239. ROWAN JELLY, No. 4

Put ripe rowan berries in preserving-pan, with just enough water to cover them. Let the water boil, then move it from fire and let simmer gently till the berries are quite soft; strain and measure the juice; allow one pound of sugar to every pint. Boil the juice; then add the sugar, and boil for twenty to thirty minutes; skim well. If mixed with an equal quantity of strained apple juice, with one pound of sugar to every pint of the latter, this jelly is much improved.

240. ROWAN JELLY, No. 5

Take ripe mountain-ash berries; pick them from their stalks, weigh, and place in a preserving-pan with enough water to float them (about half a pint to every two pounds of fruit). Let simmer till quite soft, crushing the berries with a wooden spoon. Strain the juice, without pressure, through a jelly-bag, and measure it. Return it to the pan and boil it up; add one pound of heated sugar for every pint of juice (some people put double this quantity), and boil fast for half an hour, stirring and skimming well. It is advisable to stir in a little boiled and strained blackberry juice just at the last—about one cupful to four pints of the jelly.

STRAWBERRY

Note.—This is, perhaps, of all fruits the most widely distributed in its wild state; although the blackberry runs it close. But the wild strawberry

is so *easy*, so handy, so unprotected with barbed
wire of thorns or defensive attitude of branches;
I have seen it growing, in the Isle of Wight, literally at the wave's edge, along the skirts of a crum-
bling cliff, where the salt spray rained upon it twice
a day. The wild strawberry is said to be more easily
digestible than any other berry. This happy state
of things, unluckily, does not apply to the garden
strawberry. For various reasons, it disagrees
most heartily with certain people. Undoubtedly
the "shop" strawberry, with its moist, luscious
surface, is a trap for innumerable germs during its
journeying from garden to market; by the time it
finally rests upon your table, it must be a crowded
mass of bacilli. Fresh-gathered fruit, as a rule,
should cause no dyspeptic disturbances.

The strawberry very quickly matures, and should
be preserved at the right moment—*i.e.*, just under-
ripe. Squashy, pulpy berries are often sold for jam,
but are by no means likely to keep as will the sound
and perfect ones.

241. STRAWBERRY JAM, No. 1

Weigh pound for pound of sugar and strawberries;
boil the sugar until it candies when dropped into
cold water. Then add the fruit and let boil about
ten minutes. Put into jars and cover while hot.

242. STRAWBERRY JAM, No. 2

To every pound of ripe strawberries allow twelve
ounces of sugar. Put the fruit in preserving-pan
over fire; strew a little sugar on it; as the juice

begins to run, add more sugar ; and so on till it all is dissolved. Bring to boiling point and boil for twenty minutes, or until the jam sets ; stirring very carefully lest you break the strawberries. This is not too sweet a preserve, which strawberry jam usually is.

243. STRAWBERRY JAM (1815), No. 3

Pick the stalks from the strawberries, and put them into a large copper preserving-pan ; mash them with your spaddle to break them as much as you can ; put them over the fire, make them quite hot, almost to boil ; pass them through a very fine colander ; boil the strawberries again for twenty minutes, stirring them all the time with your spaddle ; weigh them, and allow fifteen ounces of powdered sugar to every pound of strawberries ; put in the sugar and boil all together, stirring well from the bottom, for half an hour over the fire ; fill your pots, and sift some powdered sugar on the tops of them before you put them by, and the next day put papers over them.

244. STRAWBERRY JAM, No. 4

Choose good, sound strawberries, not over-ripe nor green ones. Allow pound for pound of sugar and fruit, and make a strong syrup with the sugar, which must be boiled until it will set hard. The strawberries should then be carefully put into the pan and boiled fast for ten to fifteen minutes. Do not stir much, lest the fruit should break, but skim well.

245. STRAWBERRY JAM, No. 5

Measure and let boil the required quantity of strawberries, mashing them a little to extract the juice, till they are quite tender, and add for each pint of fruit three-quarters of a pound of sugar; boil slowly till the jam is of proper consistency.

246. STRAWBERRY JAM, No. 6

Take strawberries gathered just under-ripe and perfectly dry; weigh and stalk them; allow an equal weight of crushed sugar, half of which has been passed through a coarse sieve. Put the strawberries and sieved sugar in alternate layers in a large bowl or dish, and let stand overnight. Next day place in a preserving-pan the rest of the sugar with one pint of red currant juice and half a pint of cold water to every four pounds of strawberries (as first weighed). Let the sugar dissolve, stirring and skimming carefully; let it come slowly to the boil, and then simmer till it threads (about half an hour). Put in the strawberries and let them come gently to boiling-point, stirring them very carefully that they shall not break, and boil until the syrup sets firm. Pour off and cover.

247. STRAWBERRY JELLY, No. 1

Put ripe strawberries in a double boiler, and mash them to extract the juice; let the water boil till all the juice is out. Strain it, and to each pint add either half a cupful of strained red-currant juice or the juice of a smallish lemon. To each pint of mixed juice add one pound of sugar. Return to pan and boil up till the jelly will set.

248. STRAWBERRY JELLY, No. 2

Choose sound fruit, rather under-ripe ; place in a jar or pan at the side of the range until it is a soft pulp. Strain the juice through a jelly-bag, measure, and place in the oven to heat, one pound of sugar for every pint of juice. Put the juice in a preserving-pan, boil for twenty minutes, stir in the sugar, and, when it is well dissolved, boil for another quarter of an hour and pour off into glasses. Do not cover till cold.

249. STRAWBERRY JELLY, No. 3

Take freshly gathered fruit, only barely ripe ; stalk it, and place in the preserving-pan over a clear but not fierce fire, till the juice is flowing freely ; the berries may be crushed a little with a wooden spoon. Let simmer for about twenty-five minutes, then strain off and measure the juice. Return it to the pan and boil fast for ten minutes or so, while you heat (in the oven) sugar to the amount of twelve ounces per pint. Stir the sugar in very gradually, a little at a time : this is best done with the pan off the fire. Boil up fast for a few minutes—until the jelly sets.

250. STRAWBERRY MARMALADE

Crush two pounds of fine strawberries, and pass them through a sieve ; then mix them with a strong syrup made with two pounds of sugar, and cook till the marmalade is done.

251. STRAWBERRY PRESERVE

Choose sound clean berries, just under-ripe. Stalk and measure them : for every five breakfast-cupfuls, set aside in a preserving-pan four cupfuls of sugar and one of cold water. Bring this syrup to the boil, then put in the strawberries and let cook fast for about ten minutes. Do not stir, for fear of breaking them, but shake the pan to and fro. Lift them out very carefully one by one into glass jars, and when these are three-quarters full, give the syrup another boil-up for five minutes, and pour it into the jars. Let the strawberries settle down before you cover them up, and, if need be, fill up more with the rest of the syrup.

TOMATO

NOTE.—The tomato presents this paradox, that, whilst really a fruit, it always ranks as a vegetable, to be eaten, cooked or uncooked, with salt. The idea of making jam of it is, to many people, at first blush, most unappetising. In itself it is somewhat insipid ; but, properly flavoured, it forms the basis of cheap, wholesome, and attractive preserves.

252. TOMATO JAM, No. 1

Take ripe but firm tomatoes ; peel, slice, and weigh them ; do not lose any juice if you can help. Add pound for pound of sugar, and to every seven

pounds of fruit allow the juice of three lemons.
Place the fruit, etc., in a bowl or large dish overnight; next day, drain the liquid into the preserving-pan. Let boil five minutes, then add the
rest; let boil twenty minutes; stir in a little
essence of ginger, about a small teaspoonful if the
preserving-pan is full. Ladle out the pulp into your
jars a little at a time, and then pour in the syrup,
up to the top.

253. TOMATO JAM, No. 2

Four pounds of sound tomatoes (ripe but not
over-ripe), four pounds of preserving sugar, four
lemons, water. Pour boiling water over the tomatoes, thus you can easily remove their thin outer
skins; then cut them up. Boil the lemons soft
in two pints of water, then chop them finely and
remove pips. Put tomatoes and lemons, well mixed,
into a preserving-pan, with the water in which
the lemons were boiled; simmer for about an hour
and a quarter.

254. TOMATO JELLY

Take firm red tomatoes, wipe and quarter them.
Simmer in preserving-pan till all the juice is extracted; strain and measure juice, boil it up again;
add sugar, one pound to every pint, and boil until
it sets. Some people allow the juice and grated
rind of a lemon to every pound of tomatoes; the
rind should be put in with the whole tomatoes and
the juice when the sugar is added.

255. TOMATO MARMALADE

Four pounds of tomatoes; four pounds of preserving sugar; three lemons; water. Dip the tomatoes (which must be sound, hard, just-ripe ones) in boiling water, to loosen and remove the skins, and cut them in slices about half an inch thick. Take three lemons (the pips being removed), and cut them in slices about a quarter of an inch thick. Make a syrup of four pounds of preserving sugar and about half a pint of water, and when it has boiled for five or six minutes, put in the fruit. The marmalade must boil fast, and be well skimmed, until it is thick enough to set.

256. GREEN TOMATO MARMALADE

Take six pounds of green tomatoes; stalk, wash, quarter, and place in a large basin; add four and a half pounds of sugar, the juice and grated rinds of two lemons, and leave for twenty-four hours. Next day place all in a preserving-pan; add one ounce and a half of root ginger, one-eighth ounce of chillies, tied up in muslin. Boil until quite tender—probably about an hour and a half. Take out the ginger, etc., and put in two ounces of candied peel, shredded very fine. Boil up, pour off, and cover.

VEGETABLE MARROW, CUCUMBER, ETC.

NOTE.—The large and simple vegetable-marrow, while not very specially interesting or nourishing in itself, forms a good basis for preserves. It must be highly flavoured and seasoned to render it worth while; and lemons, ginger, candied peel, etc., are almost indispensable. It becomes a fairly colourable imitation of preserved ginger, when properly prepared, and is a popular, not to say economical, form of jam.

Cucumbers, which are of the same race, can be preserved very much in the same way.

257. VEGETABLE MARROW PRESERVE, No. 1

Procure a good, sound, well-ripened marrow, twelve pounds in weight. Peel it and cut it into cubes two inches square; add the juice and very thinly cut rind of four lemons; mix in one pound of sugar to every pound of marrow, and place in an enamelled preserving-pan, or in a deep earthenware jar, for twenty-four hours; then add three ounces of bruised "race" ginger and a quarter of an ounce of chillies (this is optional) in a muslin bag. Let the mixture boil for one hour and a half in the preserving-pan (counting from the time that it comes to the boil); and just before it is done add half a pound of candied peel cut into very thin strips.

258. VEGETABLE MARROW PRESERVE, No. 2

Take young, firm marrows, not too small. Peel, take out seeds, and slice up into cubes; weigh and put into a bowl. To every eight pounds of marrow allow a large tin of pineapple chunks with the syrup, and the grated rind and juice of three lemons. For every pound of marrow allow twelve ounces of sugar ; spread it over the fruit, and let stand overnight. Next day, let all simmer gently in preserving-pan for two hours, adding a little root ginger in a muslin bag. Pour into pots and cover while hot.

259. VEGETABLE MARROW PRESERVE, No. 3

Take four pounds of marrow, peeled, seeded, and cut into cubes ; add four pounds of sugar, the juice and shredded rind of four lemons, one ounce of root ginger, four ounces of green ginger, and a few grains of cayenne. Place all in an earthen vessel overnight, till the liquid covers the marrow ; then boil until the fruit is clear and tender, and the preserve will set.

260. VEGETABLE MARROW PRESERVE, No. 4

Cut the marrow in long, narrow strips ; peel and weigh equal quantities of loaf sugar ; sprinkle a little sugar on the fruit, and leave it for a night. Next day, boil it with its own syrup, and the rest of the sugar, and one lemon to every pound of fruit ; put about thirty pepper pods to every four pounds ; two glasses of spirits to be added before taking it off the fire. Before adding the spirits, it is well to take out the fruit and boil the syrup with some more sugar, then pour over the fruit. It should be quite clear. The lemons should be cut in circles ; only half the rinds. Tie the pepper in muslin.

261. VEGETABLE MARROW PRESERVE, No. 5

Take a good, well-ripened marrow; peel and cut it in two-inch pieces; weigh it, and to every pound allow one pound of sugar, three-quarters of a lemon, and two ounces of race ginger. Cover it with sugar and leave it to stand twenty-four hours : then add the lemon peel finely shredded, the lemon pulp (with the pips removed) thinly sliced, and the ginger cut very small. Boil all together for one hour and a half.

262. VEGETABLE MARROW PRESERVE, No. 6

Take a good-sized marrow, not less than six pounds; peel, remove seeds, cut up into cubes, and weigh. Place in an earthen jar with sufficient water to cover it, and leave it for three days ; the water must be changed daily. The third day, make a syrup with sugar (one pound to each pound of fruit), three chillies, half an ounce of root ginger (in a muslin bag), and half a teaspoonful of saffron. When this boils, put in the marrow and cook till quite tender—about thirty minutes.

263. VEGETABLE MARROW PRESERVE, No. 7

Take four pounds of marrow, peeled, seeded, and cut into inch cubes. Add one pound of apples, peeled, cored, and chopped, the grated rind of four lemons and juice of two; four teaspoonfuls each of cinnamon and of ground ginger, and three pounds of sugar; boil all together till it thickens and sets. The above is rather highly spiced, and half the quantity of cinnamon, ginger, and lemon-rind would suffice for most people.

264. CUCUMBER JAM

Take some large ripe cucumbers; slice, but do not peel them. Put them in a large bowl over-night, covered with an equal weight of sugar. After twenty-four hours, drain off the juice into a pre-serving-pan; add half an ounce of root ginger to every pound of sugar, and boil for ten minutes or so; put in the cucumber, and let boil fifteen minutes; carefully lift out the cucumber, and let the juice stand till cold, then add it to the cucum-ber. Leave overnight again; next day boil up all again for ten minutes, or until the jam will set.

CHAPTER III

PRESERVES OF MIXED FRUITS

NOTE.—These are to a certain extent a matter of individual taste. They are cheap, easy, and popular, especially in the form of jellies. That they should possess the exquisite individual flavour of the single fruit is, of course, impossible (here I must except the récherché Bar-le-Duc preserves); on the other hand, the intricate combination of various flavours is often very pleasing. The most elaborate and delicious mixed fruit preserve is that which you will find in Chapter VII, No. 470, which, being brandied, does not come within the range of this section.

It should be observed that in making mixed preserves, the fruit should be selected, so far as may be, of the same quality and of the same degree of ripeness, and it should be most carefully prepared for the preserving-pan. It need not be of such superfine quality as that required for bottling, nor even so good as that for individual jams ; but it must not be sour in one case and squashy in another.

265. APPLE AND BLACK CURRANT MARMALADE
Take four pounds of black currants, pick them well, and cook till soft, in preserving-pan. Enough

water to cover the bottom of the pan may be added, but is not essential. Wipe four pounds of apples, examine carefully to see that they are sound ; quarter and core, but do not peel them ; cook in separate pan till soft, and mix thoroughly with currants. Press through a colander; measure, and put into preserving-pan, and let boil till thick ; add an equal weight of sugar, and cook till the marmalade will set.

266. APPLE AND DAMSON JELLY

Take six pounds of sound apples ; wipe, slice, and core, but do not peel them ; add six pounds of damsons, and place in a preserving-pan, just covered with cold water. Boil till tender ; strain through a jelly-bag. Measure juice, and return it to pan with an equal amount of sugar. Boil up for a quarter of an hour, and pour off into glasses.

267. APPLE AND DATE PRESERVE

Take two pounds of dried apples ; leave them to steep overnight in sufficient water to cover them. The following morning drain off the water, cut the apples small, and add them to six pounds of stoned dates (which can be cut small at discretion). Place the fruit in a preserving-pan with two pounds of sugar and three pints of water ; boil for half an hour, and pour into pots.

268. APPLE AND GINGER PRESERVE

Take two ounces of root ginger and put it through a mincer ; place it in a preserving-pan, with one saltspoonful of cayenne, six pounds of sugar, and one pint of water. Let this mixture be heating while you prepare six pounds of tart cooking apples, by coring, paring, and chopping fairly small; add these to the rest, and let cook gently till they are clear and tender, but not broken. Pour into jars and cover.

269. APPLE AND GRAPE JELLY

Take four pounds of sound grapes; remove them from the stems, and wash them by letting water run upon them in a colander. Take fourteen pounds of good apples, and slice without peeling them; remove the cores. Put the grapes and apples into a preserving-pan, let boil till quite soft, then strain the juice through a large muslin bag; it can be left to drip all night. Next day measure, and allow one breakfastcupful of sugar for each breakfastcupful of juice. Heat the sugar separately, and add it to the juice when the latter has boiled for twenty minutes. Boil up together for a quarter of an hour, then put into glass jars and cover.

270. APPLE, PEAR, AND PLUM PRESERVE

Take an equal amount of apples, pears, and plums. The plums must be plunged in hot water and skinned, then halved and the stones taken out. The apples and pears must be peeled, cored, and sliced. Weigh, and allow an equal weight of sugar. Place the three fruits in a preserving-pan, in alternate layers, with sugar between each layer, and let cook very slowly at the side of the fire until all is perfectly blended, and quite thick and smooth. Place in pots, and cover.

271. BANANA AND ORANGE JAM

Take twelve good-sized bananas, slightly under-ripe; peel and slice thinly and evenly. Weigh, and allow twelve ounces of sugar to every pound of fruit; add the pulp and juice of six medium-sized sweet oranges and four lemons. Let all cook slowly together for forty-five minutes; pour off and cover.

272. BARBERRY AND APPLE JAM

Take two gallons of ripe barberries; pick off the stalks, measure the fruit, wash it, and place in a preserving-pan with just sufficient water to float it; add one quart of treacle, and simmer all till the barberries are soft. Meanwhile, peel, quarter, and core four gallons of ripe sweet apples, and when the barberries are tender, take them out with a skimmer; put the apples into the syrup, and cook till soft; then lift them out and put them with the barberries; boil the syrup till it thickens, pour it over the apples and barberries, and let stand overnight. Next day put all into the preserving-pan, boil up for a few minutes, and place in jars. Cover at once.

273. BARBERRY AND PEAR JAM

Take ripe barberries; stem, wash, dry, and weigh them. Allow an equal weight of sugar, and make a syrup with it, using one pint of water to two pounds of sugar. When it boils quite clear, add the barberries, and let boil till they are cooked quite tender, but not broken ; this will take very nearly an hour. Remove the barberries very carefully and put them aside. Take peeled, cored, and quartered pears of an equal weight with the barberries, boil them in the syrup till tender, then lift them out and put them with the barberries. Mix them carefully and place in heated pots. Let the syrup boil for half an hour longer, and then pour it into the pots, and cover.

BAR-LE-DUC PRESERVES

NOTE.—These are very choice and special preserves, prepared chiefly at Bar-le-Duc, near Verdun. They are so treated as to retain the shape of the fruit, which is contained in a clear jelly. Red and white currants, raspberries, and strawberries are the fruits chiefly employed, and so minutely careful are the methods, that in some cases (large white currants, for instance), every seed is pushed out with a needle before the preserving process begins. Naturally these preparations are, as a rule, too expensive, and " too bright and good for human nature's daily food." I have only included those which are practicable for the average British housewife. It will be seen that the essential of success is the reversal of ordinary jam-making methods—i.e., the fruit must not boil and must not be stirred.

274. BAR-LE-DUC CURRANT, No. 1

Take ripe red and white currants ; pick off the stalks, weigh, and place in a covered preserving-pan.

They must heat very gradually and then simmer for half an hour; add heated sugar—two breakfast-cupfuls to each pound of fruit—and blend it with the fruit by gently shaking the pan; it must not be stirred in, or the fruit will be broken. Let the fruit be kept as hot as possible without boiling, until the sugar is thoroughly melted; then pour into glass jars and cover immediately.

275. BAR-LE-DUC CURRANT, No. 2

Take the very finest grape currants, either red or white. Pick off the stalks extremely carefully, weigh the fruit, and to every pound allow one pound and a half of fine sugar (granulated cane). Make the sugar into a clear syrup, using as little water as possible; skim and boil till it is absolutely transparent, then put the fruit in, very carefully, not to break it. Let the syrup just return to boiling-point, and take it off the fire at once. Pour off into small glasses, putting so far as possible the same amount of fruit in each, and cover at once. Do not stir the fruit at all.

276. BAR-LE-DUC GRAPE

Take green grapes; wipe them clean with a damp cloth, halve them with a sharp knife, take out the seeds. Now weigh the fruit, and allow pound for pound of sugar. Place the grapes in the preserving-pan, with enough water to float but not to cover them. Let them heat through very gradually, until they almost boil, and then dust in the sugar, in small quantities, letting it dissolve before adding more. If you stir at all, do it as carefully as possible, not to break the grapes. It is best to stand the pan on an asbestos mat, to prevent any scorching. Continue to simmer very slowly after all but the sugar is in, skimming occasionally, until the syrup will set; then gently remove the grapes into glasses, and fill up with the syrup. Cover at once.

277. BAR-LE-DUC RASPBERRY AND RED CURRANT

Take four pounds of raspberries and one pound of red currants. Crush the currants, strain the juice, and weigh again. For each pound of fruit together, add three-quarters of a pound of sugar. Let the currants and sugar simmer, then boil for twenty-five minutes; then put in the raspberries (unmashed) and boil until the jam sets—about a quarter of an hour; then pour into jars and close while still hot.

278. CHERRY AND CURRANT JAM

Take one quart and a half of red currants; pick and wash them, place in a preserving-pan, and, when the juice runs, mash the fruit with a wooden spoon and strain it through a fine sieve, obtaining as much juice as possible. Stone six quarts of cherries, place in pan along with four pounds of sugar and the currant juice, and let heat very gradually. When the jam boils, skim it well and let simmer for a quarter of an hour, then pour into pots and cover.

279. CHERRY AND LEMON PRESERVE

Take six pounds of tart cooking cherries, and to every pound allow the rind of half a lemon. Simmer the lemon-rinds separately in a pint of water, then strain off the water and make a syrup with it, three pounds to the pint. Remove the pips and strings from the lemon pulp, and cut it up small. When the syrup boils, skim it and put in the cherries; when they have boiled five minutes, put in the lemon pulp and let boil another three minutes. Lift out the fruit into heated jars, fill up with the hot syrup, and cover at once.

280. CRAB-APPLE AND PLUM MARMALADE

Take three-fourths of whole crab-apples to one-fourth of sweet plums. Cook separately till quite soft and pulpy; rub through sieve, and measure. Allow one quart of plums to every three quarts of crab-apples; mix them, add one pound of sugar for each pound of fruit, and let simmer gently until thick and smooth.

281. CRANBERRY AND CRAB-APPLE JELLY

Take a peck of crab-apples; cut them up small, but do not peel or core them; place them in a preserving-pan with barely enough water to cover them, and let them simmer till about half done; add one quart of cranberries, well picked and washed; let cook till all the fruit is quite tender. Place it in a jelly-bag and leave it to drip all night. Next day measure the juice and bring it to the boil;

place an equal amount of sugar to heat in the oven. When the juice has boiled for twenty minutes, add the sugar, stir well till it is melted, boil fast for three minutes, and pour off into hot glasses.

282. CURRANT AND RAISIN JAM

Take two pounds of muscatel raisins ; wash, wipe, stone, and chop them small ; put them in preserving-pan, and let them be slowly heating. Have ready prepared three quarts of white-currant juice, the fruit of which should be boiled in a separate pan, mashed, and strained ; mix three pounds of sugar with this juice, and add it to the raisins ; stir and mix thoroughly ; let boil, skimming well and stirring continually. When the jam is thick and smooth and sets easily, remove it from stove and let it cool before placing in pots.

283. DAMSON AND APPLE JELLY

Take an equal weight of damsons and of apples, and to every pound of fruit allow half a pint of cold water. Boil all together until quite soft and pulped ; strain through a muslin bag ; measure the juice, and let it boil fast for a quarter of an hour ; add one pound of sugar for every pint of juice, and boil for thirty minutes, skimming well.

284. DATE AND BANANA PRESERVE

Take one pound of dates, stone them, and slice in strips lengthways. Take four bananas peeled and very thinly sliced. Put into a preserving-pan with one pound of sugar, and let simmer for twenty minutes, stirring and skimming well. Then boil until the preserve is thoroughly thickened and will set.

285. DATE AND CARROT PRESERVE

Take three pounds of dates, stone and chop them fairly small; peel two pounds of carrots and put them through mincer. Place both in preserving-pan with three-quarters of a pint of water and two pounds of sugar; let boil twenty minutes; add one-third of a teaspoonful of essence of almonds (or not more than twenty drops), and simmer for another quarter of an hour. Pour off into pots, but do not cover till next day.

286. DATE AND PINEAPPLE PRESERVE

Stone and chop three pounds of dates; add two pounds of preserving sugar, and a small tin of pineapple chunks, thinly sliced. Put all in preserving-pan, along with the pineapple syrup and three-quarters of a pint of water. Let boil half an hour ; then simmer till the fruit is tender and sets well.

287. FIG AND APPLE JAM

Take two pounds of figs ; wash and quarter them, and place in preserving-pan with four breakfastcupfuls of cold water. Let simmer for two hours, and turn out into a bowl. Take eight pounds of cooking apples, wipe them with a damp cloth, and quarter but do not peel them. Place them in a pan, with

five pints of water, and bring to boiling-point ; then
simmer for an hour and a half. Strain the juice,
without squeezing, through a muslin or cheesecloth
jelly-bag. Put the apple liquor, with the figs, into
a preserving-pan ; when it boils, let boil for a
quarter of an hour, then put in eight pounds of
warmed sugar, and about four ounces (or to taste)
of root ginger. Stir all well together till the sugar
dissolves, and boil until the jam thickens and sets.

288. FIG AND APPLE MARMALADE

Take five pounds of apples ; peel and core them,
and chop them very small, or put them through a
mincer. Put two pounds of figs through a mincer
(having removed the stalks), and place them in a
preserving-pan, along with the apples, two quarts
of cold water, the juice and grated rind of two
lemons, twelve cloves, a quarter of a teaspoonful each
of grated nutmeg and powdered cinnamon. Cook
slowly until about half tender, then add one pound
of warmed sugar ; stir it in well, and cook faster
until the mixture thickens and sets, when pour into
jars and cover.

289. FIG AND LEMON MARMALADE

Take six lemons ; soften them by beating with a
rolling-pin or potato-masher ; place them in lined
pan with a quart of water, and boil. Change the
water once, and replace it with boiling. Keep a pint
of the first water. When the lemons are tender
enough to pierce with a wooden skewer, remove
them and cut them up when cool ; retain the

pulp, slice the peel in thin shreds, and remove the white pith and pips. Put one pound of figs through a mincer (having picked off stalks), and put them to the lemons, with the pint of lemon-water and two pounds of white sugar. Place all in a preserving-pan, and boil until the mixture sets. Not to be covered until cold.

290. GREEN FIG AND GINGER MARMALADE

Take six pounds of figs; remove the stalks and slice thinly ; add to these one pound of crystallised ginger, cut up into small even strips. Boil four pounds of brown sugar in three pints and a half of water, and when it is clear, dissolve in it one ounce of isinglass. Put in the fruit to the syrup, and let boil thirty minutes ; then simmer gently for an hour, when it ought to set. Pour it off into pots, but do not cover till next day.

291. FOUR-FRUITS JAM

Take one quart of gooseberries; " top-and-tail " them ; add one pint of stalked raspberries, one quart of picked red currants, and two quarts of stoned cherries. Weigh the whole, and add twelve ounces of sugar for every pound of mixed fruit. Boil all together until the jam thickens and sets. Pour off and cover.

292. FOUR-FRUITS JELLY

Take an equal amount of cherries, currants, strawberries, and raspberries. The cherries must be

stoned, but do not lose any of their juice. Mix the
four fruits, place in a double boiler ; they will require plenty of mashing and crushing. When all
are quite soft, strain off the juice, and to each fruit
allow one pound two ounces of sugar. Place in
preserving-pan and boil for at least twenty minutes,
skimming carefully.

293. GOOSEBERRY AND APRICOT JAM

Top-and-tail three quarts of gooseberries. Have
ready one pound of dried apricots, which have stood
twenty-four hours with one quart of boiling water
poured on them. Strain the liquor from the
apricots into preserving-pan ; add the gooseberries ;
when they are at boiling-point, gradually add five
pounds of sugar, and the apricots. Let simmer
gently, stirring and skimming, till the jam thickens
and sets.

294. GOOSEBERRY AND RED CURRANT JAM

To every four pounds of gooseberries allow three
pounds of sugar and two cupfuls of red-currant
juice. Make a syrup of the sugar and juice, and
let the berries simmer in it till they are quite clear
—about forty minutes ; remove and pot at once.

295. GOOSEBERRY AND WHITE CURRANT JAM

Take four pounds of gooseberries, four pounds of
currants, and eight pounds of sugar. Put all together in preserving-pan, and let simmer slowly,
crushing the gooseberries now and then with a

wooden spoon. When the jam is quite thick and
tender, it is ready to pot. This jam will keep better
if boiled longer, say an hour, but it will not be
such a good colour.

296. GOOSEBERRY AND PINEAPPLE JAM

Top-and-tail five quarts of half-ripe gooseberries.
Peel and slice a large pineapple, remove the " eyes,"
chop it up ; add the gooseberries and weigh all
together. Allow twelve ounces of sugar for each
pound of fruit, and make a syrup of it with one
breakfastcupful of water. When it has boiled till
clear, put the fruit in, and cook gently until the
whole thickens and sets.

297. GRAPES AND PEARS (RAISINÉ), No. 1

Take an equal weight of grapes and of ripe
pears. Wash and seed the grapes, and stem them ;
simmer them until quite soft in just enough water
to cover bottom of preserving-pan ; pass them
through a sieve or fine colander, and add the pears,
which must be peeled, cored, and sliced, but not
cooked. Let simmer till quite thick, stirring well ;
then sweeten to taste and place in pots.

298. GRAPES AND PEARS (RAISINÉ), No. 2

Take ripe grapes ; stalk them, and squeeze the
juice through a damp cheesecloth. Measure, and
place the juice in a preserving-pan ; boil it down to
little more than half, stirring well ; then add an

equal quantity of pears (ripe sweet ones), peeled, cored, and sliced. Continue to boil till the pears are tender and clear, then lift them out into glasses and fill up with the grape-juice. Sugar may be added before the juice is boiled, according to the sweetness of the grapes, but not more than five ounces to the pint of juice.

299. GRAPE AND RAISIN CONSERVE

Two pounds of grapes, one pint and a half of sugar, one pound and a half of seeded raisins, half a pound of shelled and blanched walnuts. Remove pulp from grapes; boil five minutes; put through a colander to remove seeds; add raisins, sugar, and walnuts chopped fine, and boil thirty minutes till thick.

300. ORANGE AND APPLE MARMALADE

Quarter and core, but do not peel, some apples. Place in sufficient water to cover them, and cook till tender. Strain through a jelly-bag, pressing well. Weigh the juice, add an equal amount of sugar, and boil until the syrup drops in beads. Have ready an equal amount (less will suffice) of orange pulp and shredded or grated orange peel, cooked till tender, and simmer till the mixture is thick and sets.

301. ORANGE AND DRIED APRICOT JAM

Take twelve oranges; peel, remove the white pith, shred the peel finely, and slice the pulp. Place in an earthen vessel, pour over sufficient boiling water to cover fruit, and leave overnight. Place two pounds of dried apricots in another vessel, cover with cold water, and leave overnight. Next day empty both vessels into a preserving-pan and simmer for thirty minutes. Remove from fire, measure, add an equal amount of heated sugar, and let boil till thick, stirring and skimming well.

302. ORANGE, GRAPE, AND RAISIN JAM

Take six oranges; peel the rinds thinly as though they were lemons, and chop them up (or put them through a mincer), along with two pounds of stoned raisins. Take six pounds of ripe grapes; skin, remove the seeds, and simmer the pulp till tender; then put in the skins and let cook a quarter of an hour; add the orange-peel, orange-juice, raisins, and four pints of sugar. Mix thoroughly till all is blended and the sugar is dissolved: then simmer until the jam thickens and sets.

303. ORANGE AND PINEAPPLE PRESERVE

Take six oranges wipe them thoroughly clean, and leave them overnight in an earthen vessel, with three pints of cold water. Next day put oranges and water into a preserving-pan; boil till the fruit is quite cooked; take it out, chop it up small, and replace it in the pan with the contents of a large tin of pineapple, chopped small, and four pounds of sugar. Let boil fast, skimming and stirring continually until the preserve thickens and sets. Fresh pineapple is the best, if obtainable; two large ones will be required.

304. ORANGE AND PRUNE JAM

Take four pounds of prunes; scald them well in hot water, rinse them in cold water, cut open and remove stones. Put the prunes through a mincer; measure, and add an equal amount of orange pulp cut small, with the grated rind of half the number of oranges used; add eight ounces of sugar and two breakfastcupfuls of cold water. Mix all thoroughly, place in a preserving-pan at side of fire, and let cook very slowly until smooth and thick; put into pots and cover.

305. PEAR AND GINGER PRESERVE, No. 1

Take eight pounds of pears; pare, quarter, and core them. Take four ounces of root ginger and cut it into small pieces; add the grated rind of three lemons, and place in alternate layers with the pears, and with eight pounds of sugar, in a preserving pan. From one to two breakfastcupfuls of water should be put in, according to the juiciness of the pears. Let this cook very slowly (two hours will probably be needed), and, when it is rather more than half done, add the strained juice of six lemons. Continue to simmer gently until the pears are clear and tender, and the syrup sets.

306. PEAR AND GINGER PRESERVE, No. 2

Take four lemons; wash and place them in a small pan with just enough water to cover them. Let boil for one hour. Meanwhile take eight pounds of pears; pare, core, and slice them evenly; add six

pounds of sugar and one pound of (dry) preserved
ginger chopped small. Place in a preserving-pan and
let cool for an hour ; then take out the lemons ;
drain them well, slice them, and remove the pips.
Put them to the pears, and let simmer for an hour
longer. Pour into pots, and cover at once.

307. PEAR AND GRAPE PRESERVE

Take an equal weight of cooking pears and of
ripe grapes. Stem the grapes and wash them ;
place them in a pan with just enough water to float
them. Boil till soft, then put them through a sieve
fine enough to retain the seeds. Weigh the pulp
and return it to the pan, along with the pears, which
must be pared, cored, chopped, and then weighed ;
cook slowly till the preserve thickens, and add
twelve ounces of sugar for each pound of fruit.
Boil up for five minutes after the sugar has dissolved.
Pour into pots, and cover.

308. PEAR AND LEMON PRESERVE

To every pound of pears, peeled, quartered, and
cored, allow four ounces of thinly pared lemon-peel.
Make a syrup with one pound and a half of sugar
and half a pint of water for every pound of fruit ;
when it is clear, lay the fruit in it, and cook gently
till it is quite tender and sets.

309. PEAR AND PINEAPPLE PRESERVE

Take eight pounds of cooking pears; peel, quarter,
and core them. Peel, slice, and remove the eyes

from two large pineapples. Be careful to save as much juice as you can in the process. Pass all through a mincer, place in a preserving-pan, add four pounds of sugar, and boil until the whole is clear and thick—probably about thirty minutes. Pour into glasses, and cover.

310. PRUNE AND APPLE JAM

Take four pounds of large prunes; wash well and leave steeping in water overnight. Next day simmer them till tender, using the water they were steeped in, sufficient just to cover them. Remove from fire and let cool; take out the stones. Replace in preserving-pan. Have ready nine large apples, peeled, cored, and sliced, one pound of sugar, and the juice of two oranges and two lemons; add these to the prunes, mix thoroughly and stir well, and let cook until the jam is smooth and thick. Place in pots, and cover.

311. RHUBARB AND FIG PRESERVE

Cut up small six pounds of rhubarb and one pound of figs. Thinly shred one pound of candied peel; add the grated rind and juice of three lemons; mix well, and let stand overnight, placed in layers with five pounds of sugar. Next day let cook very slowly, for not less than an hour.

312. RHUBARB AND GOOSEBERRY JAM

Take equal quantities of rhubarb (washed, peeled, and cut into one-inch pieces) and of just-ripe

gooseberries (topped and tailed). Measure, and set
aside one pound of sugar for each pound of fruit.
Allow one gill of water to each pound of fruit ; boil
it together in a preserving-pan till all is tender,
then add the sugar. Cool gently till the sugar dissolves, then boil till the jam will set.

313. RHUBARB AND ORANGE JAM

Take two good-sized oranges ; peel them ; remove
the pips, and as much of the white inner pith as
you can. Slice the fruit and place in preserving-
pan, with the finely sliced rind of six oranges and
three pounds of sugar crushed small. Have ready
two quarts of young rhubarb, peeled and thinly
sliced ; mix it with the oranges, and let simmer
slowly for an hour, stirring and skimming well. At
the end of this time it should be ready to pour off.

314. RHUBARB AND ORANGE MARMALADE

Take one quart of red rhubarb stalks ; string
lightly and cut up small. Peel six sweet oranges ;
boil peel till tender, then slice it very thin. Put
the pulp of the oranges (having carefully removed
the pips and white pith) to the rest ; add one pound
and a half of sugar; boil all together very slowly
till they are well reduced and thickened, and will
set.

315. RHUBARB AND PRUNE PRESERVE

Take eight pounds of rhubarb, cut it up small, put
it in a dish or bowl, and cover it with two pounds

of sugar, leaving it overnight. Wash four pounds
of prunes, and leave them soaking overnight in
just sufficient water to cover them. Next day, place
the rhubarb in the preserving-pan, also the prunes,
water and all, and six lemons cut into quarters;
let simmer quietly for an hour; then add eight to
nine pounds of sugar, according to taste, and boil
fast for thirty minutes. Take out the lemon and
pour the jam into pots.

316. RHUBARB AND RASPBERRY JAM

To every three pounds of rhubarb allow four
pounds of raspberries and six pounds of sugar. Slice
the rhubarb small, let it cook till tender (adding
six tablespoonfuls of water), then put in the raspberries and mix them well. Bring to boiling-point,
add the sugar, and boil till the jam sets.

317. STRAWBERRY AND PINEAPPLE JAM

Take ripe pineapples; peel, slice, and remove
the eyes. Chop them fairly small; weigh, and
add an equal weight of just-ripe stalked strawberries;
add pound for pound of granulated sugar; place all
in preserving-pan, and cook slowly till the jam is
extremely thick. Stir well. Put into jars, and cover.

318. TOMATO AND PINEAPPLE JAM

Take seven pounds of unripe tomatoes; slice them
thinly, allow twelve ounces of sugar to every pound,
and boil all together till soft; then open small tin
of pineapple, and add the juice to tomatoes; mince

fruit to a mash, put it with the rest, and boil for a
quarter of an hour, stirring and skimming; add a
quarter of an ounce of isinglass, let boil up, and
pour into pots, but do not cover till next day.

319. VEGETABLE MARROW AND PINEAPPLE PRESERVE

Take a fair-sized but not too old marrow ; peel,
remove seeds, cut into narrow strips, and weigh ;
add twelve ounces of sugar for every pound of
marrow, and leave both overnight in a large basin
(not a tin one).   Next day, open a tin of pineapple
chunks, and put one chunk, cut into four cubes, to
every three pounds of marrow.   Let boil two hours,
till the marrow is tender but not broken, and the
syrup will set.

320. MIXED FRUIT PRESERVE, No. 1

Take two pounds each of plums, of pears, and
of apples.   Stone the plums, peel and core the
apples.   Place the plum-stones and apple-peelings
in a preserving-pan; add two breakfastcupfuls of
water; let simmer for half an hour, and strain.
Have ready the pears, peeled and cored ; slice them
and the apples.   Put the strained liquor from the
parings to boil with five pounds and a half of sugar,
and when it boils, add the fruit, and boil for half
an hour.

321. MIXED FRUIT PRESERVE, No. 2

Take one quart each of red currants, red raspberries, and red cherries ; pick, stem, and stone

them respectively. Take two large oranges, and slice them into small pieces, peel and all; peel and shred one ripe pineapple; pick, wash, and dry one pound of sultana raisins. Weigh the whole fruit together, and let simmer for an hour over a slow fire; it will need frequent stirring. Have ready heated an equal weight of sugar; let the fruit just boil up, and add the sugar; continue to cook until the whole thickens and sets.

CHAPTER IV

FRUITS PRESERVED WHOLE IN SYRUP OR SUGAR

NOTE.—This is a delicious and delicate method of preserving fruit, as a rule whole, or only halved. It is also known as bottling, and (by the Americans) as canning. A good deal of sugar is required ; but not so much as you might think, because in many cases the same syrup can be utilised for different batches of fruit, till all have been cooked in it. The fruit in question may be of almost any kind ; but probably stone fruit is the best for the purpose. In any case it must be exactly ripe, perfectly sound, and of a good quality : this is not a method suitable to odds and ends and windfalls.

The selected fruit should be as uniform in size as possible. It may be peeled, cored, stalked, or stoned, according to its species, and placed uncooked in bottles, the syrup being poured over it, the bottles corked, and the cooking finished by standing them up to their necks in a large vessel of boiling water until the fruit reaches boiling-point inside the bottles. (If this method be adopted, the bottles must be left in the water till both are cool.)

The second, and perhaps the better, way is to

cook the fruit in cold water—stoning large fruit very carefully so as not to break it in two or spoil its shape, and pricking smaller (stone) fruit right through with a darning-needle. In this case the water should be brought to boiling-point, and the fruit immediately removed, rinsed in cold water, and drained on a sieve. It is subsequently boiled up in syrup (to "thread") (*see* Chap. I), and the syrup is boiled up again day after day and re-added to the fruit. This somewhat tedious process may be continued from three to six days; on the last day the fruit is once more boiled up in the syrup, and bottled and corked at once.

The third method is simply to pour boiling syrup of the "thread" degree over uncooked fruit arranged in bottles, without further procedure. This is really only available for quite soft fruit, such as strawberries and raspberries. Many authorities, however, believe in using *cold* syrup for all *red* fruit : it preserves the colour better. Cold syrup is made by letting the sugar dissolve in *cold* water instead of by boiling (using one pint of water to two pounds of sugar), and takes very much longer to prepare than by the heating process. It is heavier and thicker than boiled syrup.

The fourth method consists in filling up rubber-ringed bottles, on top of the fruit, with thin syrup—made according to the kind of fruit : three-quarters of a pound of sugar to a quart of water for sweeter fruits, a pound for a quart to the more acid such as black currants and damsons. First stand the fruit in jars in pans containing two inches of boiling water. The jars must have the glass tops on without the rubbers. Put into a moderately hot oven for fifteen minutes ; then remove, one jar at a time, and fill up with boiling syrup. Put the rubber on and cover tightly.

The fifth method of preserving whole is to pack small soft fruits in the jars in layers, with powdered sugar—allowing about four ounces to each pound of fruit—and fill up all spaces firmly until the pots are filled. One-pound pots are the best for this.

Remember to select fruits of uniform size, and to arrange them in concentric circles or layers in the bottles, as evenly and compactly as possible.

Other slightly different methods will be found in this chapter. The reader is referred to Chapter I as regards further particulars regarding syrup and bottling.

VARIOUS NOTES RE SYRUP

There is nothing in which experts differ more remarkably than in the proper proportions of sugar and water for preserving fruit.

The Board of Agriculture says that pure water is " equally as suitable and a little more transparent than syrup," and that a thin syrup "spoils the natural flavour of the fruit," while not making it sweet enough to use (eventually) without sugar. Half to one pound of cane sugar to a quart of water is therefore recommended, if syrup is to be used.

American writers vary the amount of sugar with the kind of fruit to be preserved : from three table-spoonfuls of sugar to one pint of water for raspberries, to a pound per pint for grapes, etc., etc.

Certain English authorities define a good average syrup as twelve ounces of sugar to one quart of water, and say that syrup preserves the flavour of the fruit better than water. Soft fruits, such as strawberries and raspberries, are undoubtedly better if treated by the dry sugar method—*i.e.*, packing them in alternate layers with the sugar till the jar is full. Four ounces of sugar per pound of fruit is supposed to suffice in this case; but I should not care, myself, to risk the fruit with so little sugar.

However, the reader will find plenty of variety among the recipes to follow.

322. TO BOTTLE FRUIT IN SYRUP

Perfectly sound fruit, just ripe, must be used, as uniform in size as possible. It must be wiped with a dry cloth, and placed carefully, so as not to bruise it, in wide-mouthed jars; these must be well filled. Tap them on the table now and then to make the fruit settle down firmly. Place the bottles, which must not touch each other, in a warm oven, and leave them until the fruits begin to crack; take the bottles out of the oven, and fill them with a boiling syrup, made with eight ounces of sugar to one quart of water. On top of this pour a thin layer of hot mutton fat, or of fine salad oil. Tie down at once with bladder.

323. DUTCH RECIPE FOR BOTTLING FRUIT

Make a syrup to the proportion of two cups of sugar to four of water. Let it boil for a few minutes in a preserving-pan; if it is not clear, strain through butter-muslin. Then put two or three pounds of fruit in it at a time while the syrup is boiling, and simmer from ten to twenty minutes, according to the kind of fruit; the latter should be soft and clear when done, and unbroken. Take the bottles, previously warmed, fill to the top with fruit and a little syrup; screw them down tightly. Then add more fruit to the boiling syrup until it is used. Do not forget to screw the covers more tightly the following day. If you have no screw bottles, pour boiling mutton suet on the top of each bottle when cold, about a quarter of an inch thick. Any syrup left over can be bottled and used as a fruit drink; add vinegar and water to it at the table. Must be stored in a dry place. Will keep for months.

324. APPLES OR PEARS PRESERVED WHOLE, No. 1

Take twelve good apples or pears, well-flavoured, peel and core them neatly (but do not remove the pear-stalks), and put them into salted water for twenty-four hours; then remove and wash them, and leave them for some hours in fresh cold water; wipe them very dry. Make a syrup with one pound of sugar, one breakfastcupful of water, and the juice of a lemon. When it is thick, put in the fruit, only one layer at a time, and let simmer very slowly until quite clear. If preferred, they may be done thus in slices. They can be either bottled in the syrup, or taken out and dried on sieves.

325. APPLES PRESERVED WHOLE, No. 2

Take eight pounds of tart cooking apples; pare and core them. Make a syrup with eight pounds of sugar, two pints of water, and one teaspoonful of dissolved citric acid; boil with care, and when the syrup is clear and thick, lay the apples in it, and turn them often that they may become thoroughly covered and coated with it. When the fruit is quite clear, bring the syrup to boiling-point; carefully lift out the fruit, taking care not to break it. Place it in the jars, fill up with the boiling syrup, and cover at once with brandied paper and bladder.

326. APPLES PRESERVED WHOLE, No. 3

Take ten pounds of sound, unblemished apples, just ripe; wash and dry them thoroughly. Have ready three quarts of syrup (one pound of sugar to one pint of water: increase in proportion), and let boil eight or ten minutes. Put in the apples, and boil till the skin begins to crack; then lift out very carefully, put into large seven-pound jars, and fill up with boiling syrup. But as you need not add the syrup till just before covering the jars, you can use it until all the apples have been boiled.

327. GREEN APRICOTS PRESERVED WHOLE (1815)

Take green apricots when they are the size of a small walnut, put them in a bag with a great deal of salt, and shake them in it for the salt to take off the silkiness of the skin; then take them out put them into a large pan with water; place them

over a slow fire just to scald them, and when you
find they grow soft, have a flat preserving-pan
with a very thin syrup boiling in it; but before
you put them in, drain the apricots well from the
water through a sieve. When the syrup boils, put
them in, but do not put too many in the pan at a
time, only let the syrup cover the apricots; but
mind you do not crowd them in the pan; boil your
syrup about a quarter of an hour, then take them
out, put them in a flat earthen pan, and cover them
with a sheet of paper, that no dust can get in. The
next day boil them half an hour, and if you find
they look well, drain the syrup from them twenty
minutes, then put the apricots in again, and just
give them two or three boils; then put them in
the flat pan, and cover them close with paper,
minding to keep them covered with syrup as it
boils. When your syrup is of a fine thickness and
the apricots look well, put them into your pots,
and when cold cover the tops.

328. RIPE APRICOTS PRESERVED WHOLE (1815)

First take a large knife, split the apricots in half,
and with a small knife peel them fine. Have a preserving-pan on the fire with water boiling; put
some of the apricots in; when you find they grow
soft, have two basins of cold water on each hand,
and put the softest by themselves, as those that
are broken will spoil the rest. Have a preserving-
pan on the fire with thin syrup boiling, drain all
the water from them, and put the hardest ones in
and let them boil ten minutes; then put them in

a flat earthen pan, and cover them with paper;
then have another preserving-pan on the fire with
syrup boiling ; put the soft ones in and just give
them a boil or two ; then put them in the same pan
as the others, and cover them. The next day boil
the hard ones five minutes, and put them in the
same pan again, but drain the syrup from the soft
ones ; boil it and pour it on them when hot ; do
the same four or five days successively, then put
them in pots, and be careful the pots are not in the
least damp, for that will make them ferment and
grow sour.

329. BARBERRIES IN BUNCHES OR SPRIGS, PRESERVED IN SYRUP (1815)

Cut the sides of the barberries open, take the
stones out of them, tie six bunches to a piece of
wood about an inch long and about the sixth part
of an inch wide, wind them on with red thread ;
put your barberries in bunches on a sieve, and have
a preserving-pan with syrup, and boil the syrup
half an hour ; put the barberries in the syrup, boil
them, and skim them with paper ; give six or seven
boils, always get the scum clean off ; put them in
pots, and cover them with paper ; those tied on a
stick are called bunches, but what you would wish
in sprigs must not be tied to a stick ; you may
put them in pots, as other sweetmeats.

330. BLACKBERRIES PRESERVED WHOLE, No. 1

Take equal weight of fruit and sugar, put it into
jars in layers, and leave it all night. The fruit

should be at least three inches below top. Close
the tops securely, and set the jars in boiling water
till they come to boiling-point. After five minutes,
fasten up with bladder, etc., and let cool off.

331. BLACKBERRIES PRESERVED WHOLE, No. 2

Take perfectly sound just-ripe blackberries; stalk
them, and place in large glass bottles. Have ready
a syrup which has been made in the proportion of
eight ounces of sugar to one quart of water, and
boiled half an hour, then allowed to grow cold.
Fill up the bottles with this, cork tightly, and place
in steriliser or boiler as indicated.

332. BLACK CURRANTS PRESERVED WHOLE

Pick the black currants carefully from the stems,
see that all are quite sound, and proceed as for
blackberries.

333. CHERRIES PRESERVED WHOLE, No. 1

Take four pounds of ripe but perfectly sound
cherries; stalk them, and take out the stones very
carefully with a sharp knife, so as to preserve the
shape of the fruit. Have ready a syrup made with
one pint of white-currant juice and three pounds
of sugar, and when it is boiling fast, place the
cherries in it and let boil about a quarter of an hour.
It will need skimming. Empty all slowly and
gently into a large bowl, and let stand overnight.
Drain the fruit on a sieve, and boil up the syrup
alone until it is reduced and thickened. Put in

the cherries, to boil about five minutes; then lift
the pan from the fire, carefully transfer the cherries
into wide, heated jars, and fill up with syrup. Cover
when cold.

334. CHERRIES PRESERVED WHOLE, No. 2

Cooking cherries or morellas must be used.
Wash, wipe, and stem the fruit. For every six
pounds allow three lemons; thinly peel these, and
let the rind simmer for half an hour; then strain
off the water, and make a syrup with a pint of it
to three pounds of sugar. Slice the lemon pulp,
removing any strings, pips, and white pith. Boil
up the syrup; add the cherries; and when they
have boiled five minutes, put in the lemon pulp;
boil three minutes more, then lift out the fruit into
pots, and fill up with the hot syrup.

335. CHERRIES PRESERVED WHOLE, No. 3

Take perfectly sound and unblemished cherries,
just ripe, and remove stalks. Have ready a syrup,
allowing twenty ounces of sugar and one gill of
water to every pound of cherries. Let boil five
minutes, then put in the cherries; boil ten minutes,
skimming well; pour off all into a heated pan,
and let stand overnight. Next day give another
boil-up for ten minutes and return to pan. The
third day, bring to boiling-point and remove from
fire. Put the cherries into jars, fill up with syrup,
and cover when cold.

336. CHERRIES PRESERVED WHOLE (1815), No. 4

Let your cherries be the best Kentish you can get; stone them, put them into a tub with boiling hot syrup over them, and cover them till the next day ; then boil and put them into the tub again. The third day boil them softly twenty minutes, and put them into the tub again; continue this for eight days ; then make a thick syrup for them, put them into it, then into an earthen jar ; put some apple jelly over the tops, and brandy papers over them. If you want to dry sweet cherries, put them into your preserving-pan, warm them, and drain them well from the syrup through a sieve ; put them into the hot stove, and shift the sieve every day till they are dry ; then put them into your boxes. Whole cherries are preserved the same way as those, only you leave the stones in and the stalks on them.

337. CHESTNUTS PRESERVED WHOLE

Slit the chestnuts on one side with a sharp knife ; let cook a minute in boiling water, drain thoroughly, and when dry, place in a pan over the fire with one teaspoonful of butter to each pint of nuts. Stir and shake well for four or five minutes ; then remove the shell and skin together. Keep the nuts hot by covering them with a thick cloth, and they will shell better. Put them into cold water, acidulated with citric acid and lemon-juice. The water must just cover them—about one dessertspoonful of acid to each pint of shelled chestnuts. Let stand eight hours; then put into boiling water, which must quite cover them. Let boil; then only just simmer for two hours, or until tender. Drain off the water, and cover the chestnuts with syrup made of sugar and water each equal in weight to the weight of the nuts, and a piece of vanilla bean; keep hot for two hours, but do not let boil. Pour off half the syrup; boil it down by one-half; pour over the chestnuts; keep hot one hour. Then drain off all the syrup, reduce it a little; let grow cold, and pour over the nuts. Place in jars, which must be tightly corked.

338. CITRONS PRESERVED

Put them into water overnight; boil them till quite tender; cut them in halves, and to every pound of citron add a pound of sugar. Put about a tablespoonful of water to every pound of sugar; when all is dissolved, pour it on the citrons, then put all on the fire and let them boil about half an hour. Soak a few races of ginger in water three or four days; boil them first with a thin syrup, and afterwards with the citrons.

339. CRAB-APPLES PRESERVED WHOLE, No. 1

Take eight pounds of crab-apples. Core the larger ones, and leave the lesser ones as they are. Peel neither, and leave the stems on. Parboil them, and then place them in a syrup made with one quart of water, in which a teaspoonful of citric acid crystals is dissolved, and eight pounds of sugar.

Let simmer carefully a few minutes, but mind that the fruit does not break. It ought to become translucent, and to arrive at boiling-point; then remove and place it in jars, and fill up with syrup. Cover it at once.

340. SIBERIAN CRABS PRESERVED WHOLE, No. 2

Make a syrup with a pound of loaf sugar to half a pint of water. Simmer till clear; then boil the crabs in this, very gently, till done, having first pricked them all over to keep them from bursting. A little ginger, lemon, and cochineal to be added before boiling. The stalks are to be left on.

341. CUCUMBERS PRESERVED WHOLE, No. 1

Take large and small cucumbers free from seeds ; put them into salt and water, with cabbage leaves on the top to keep them down. Tie a paper over, and put them in a warm place till they are yellow ; then wash them out and put them into fresh salt water. Continue to change the water till they are a good green ; then take them out, and cut out all the pulp, and put them into cold water to take out the salt. Let them so remain two or three days, changing the water twice a day. Take one pound of fine sugar and half a pint of water ; put on the fire and skim it clear ; add the rind of a lemon cut very thin, one ounce of ginger. When cold, wipe the cucumbers and put them in. When the syrup comes to " thread," remove the cucumbers into an earthen jar, and pour the syrup over them. Boil up the syrup three times a week for three weeks.

342. CUCUMBERS PRESERVED WHOLE, No. 2

Gather the cucumbers when fresh and green ; rub them smooth with a coarse cloth ; put them in strong salt and water ; tie them down close and set them by the fire ; change them from top to bottom till quite yellow, then put them in a skellet with layers of vine leaves and strong salt and water, and a small piece of soda and alum. Put it over the fire at some distance till quite scalding hot, but not boiling. If not green in a few hours, change the water and leaves, and put them on again ; when green, drain them on a sieve, and throw them in fresh water for three days, changing it every day. Make a thin syrup with one pound of sugar and a gallon of water boiled an hour and cleared with the white of an egg. When nearly cold, pour it over them, repeating the same for a week, each day a little warmer ; the last day let them boil five minutes.

343. CUCUMBERS PRESERVED (1815), No. 3

Let your cucumbers be clear and free from all spots ; put them in salt and water ; let them stand two or three days, then take them out and drain them well ; put them in another pan of water, scald them in a tub, and let them stand all night ; then drain the water from them, put them into a pan of water, and to every two quarts of water put half a pint of syrup ; put them in, and let them boil over a slow fire five minutes ; put them into the tub again, and let them stand till the next day ;

then boil them again, drain that syrup from them, and have a clean pan with the syrup of a proper thickness; let it boil, put the cucumbers into it, and let them boil gently for a quarter of an hour; then put them into a flat brown pan, and cover them; let them stand two days, then drain the syrup from them; boil the syrup one minute, and pour it over them; the next day boil them and the syrup together three or four minutes, and repeat the same for five days; then put them in pots, and cover them up.

N.B.—Always observe to let your preserved fruits stand two or three days before you put them up.

344. CURRANTS IN BUNCHES PRESERVED WHOLE (1815)

Take some of the best currants you can get; take a small piece of stick, tie about six bunches to this stick with thread, and lay them on a sieve; have your preserving-pan on the fire with your syrup in it; boil the syrup about twenty minutes on a brisk fire; put your currants in bunches into the syrup; only cover the bottom of the pan with them, do not put too many in; let them have five or six boils, and take the scum off with paper; put them in your pots.

345. RED CURRANTS PRESERVED WHOLE

Weigh and stalk the currants, and lay them in a shallow dish, sprinkled with crushed preserving-

sugar in the proportion of one pound to a quart of
currants; let stand overnight. Next day, place
in preserving-pan, and when at boiling-point, let
boil one minute. Place in jars, and cover while
hot.

346. DAMSONS PRESERVED WHOLE

To every pound of fruit allow half a pound of
preserving sugar; fruit to be sound and not too
ripe. Put the fruit into large jars; sprinkle the
sugar over the fruit. Place saucers over the jars,
and place them in moderately cool oven for an hour
or two, until the fruit is tender. When cold, cover
the top of the jars with white paper cut to the size
of the jar. Pour over this melted mutton fat,
about two inches thick; cover over with brown
paper, and keep in dry place. As a rule they
keep till February, but the fruit must not be
too ripe.

347. FIGS PRESERVED WHOLE

Let the figs be thoroughly heated through, as
in Fig Jam (No. 74). Have ready a thick syrup,
boiling; put the figs into this, take it off the stove
and leave it overnight. Next morning boil it up
again, and let it get cold again. Boil again, drain
off the syrup, place figs in close layers in wide jars;
re-heat the syrup and pour it into the jars. Lemon-
peel and ginger, or lemon-peel and juice, may
be added: I think they are a great improvement.

348. GREEN FIGS PRESERVED WHOLE

Take green figs, weigh, cut a small slit across the top of each, and place them in strong brine for eight days. Drain and put in preserving-pan with enough water to cover them ; boil till tender ; drain again, and put in a pan, covered with cold water, for three days. The water must be changed every day. The third day, prepare a syrup, allowing for each pound of figs, one pound of sugar and half a pint of water. Let boil, place the figs in, and boil for ten minutes. Pour off all into a pan or bowl, and repeat three days running, or until the figs are quite green and tender, then put them into jars, fill up with syrup, cover, and keep in a dry place.

349. GOOSEBERRIES PRESERVED WHOLE, No. 1

Make a syrup with one pint of water and two pounds of sugar. Place the gooseberries in the syrup, having pricked them well with a large needle. Bring to boiling-point ; then remove from fire, and let stand all night. Repeat the boiling and removing next day ; the third day, do not let the syrup quite boil, but again let stand overnight. The following morning, place the gooseberries in bottles ; pour syrup over them, and stand them in a large boiler or fish-kettle with cold water till the water boils ; remove at once and close the bottles. If the berries begin to crack before the water boils, remove the bottles immediately.

350. GOOSEBERRIES PRESERVED WHOLE, No. 2

Take equal quantities of fine red gooseberries and loaf sugar. Allow rather less than half a pint of cold water to each pound of sugar. Top-and-tail the gooseberries and see that none are broken. Put the sugar in the preserving-pan, and add the water gradually ; when the sugar is all dissolved, place the pan on the fire and allow it to come to boiling-point without stirring ; skim well, and when the syrup threads, put the fruit into the syrup and allow it to boil until it is tender, but not broken. Strain the syrup through a sieve very carefully without crushing gooseberries. Return it to the saucepan and boil it alone until it threads ; put in the fruit again, and stir gently to prevent it sticking ; let boil, and when the jam begins to coat the slice, it is done, and may be turned into pots. The fruit should be quite whole and of a bright red colour.

351. GOOSEBERRIES PRESERVED WHOLE, No. 3

Top-and-tail some sound gooseberries. Have ready a syrup made with two pounds of sugar to one pint of water. Prick the gooseberries with a needle, and put them in the boiling syrup ; let the temperature reach 160°, and remove pan from fire ; leave it as it is overnight. Repeat boiling up to 160° two days running. The third day, re-heat but not to boiling-point ; let cool overnight ; bottle, and finish up in a bain-marie or large pan of boiling water, till the syrup boils inside the bottles.

352. GREEN GOOSEBERRIES PRESERVED WHOLE

The small hairy kind are suitable for this. Top-and-tail the gooseberries; place them in wide-mouthed glass jars or bottles. Make a syrup in the proportion of three pounds of sugar to one quart of water; let boil five minutes and then cool off; pour it over the fruit in the bottles, cork them, cover with bladder; stand them, with straw beneath and between them, in a pan of cold water up to their shoulders; bring the water to the boil, let boil twenty minutes; take off fire, let cool; leave the bottles in the water till it is quite cold.

353. GRAPES PRESERVED WHOLE, No. 1

Take just-ripe grapes; wash them, and cut them off the bunch, leaving a little stem to each. Have ready a syrup made with one pound of sugar to every quart of water. Put the grapes in jars (previously heated) in a large pan of cold water; let them heat gradually. When the water boils, pour boiling syrup into the jars till nearly full. Let the water boil ten minutes longer, then fill up jars with syrup; remove, and cover at once.

354. GRAPES PRESERVED WHOLE, No. 2

Take some good, sound grapes; remove them from the stems, wipe them with a clean damp cloth,

and place them in a perfectly clean, dry jar. Pour
boiling water over them (a silver spoon in the jar
will avert cracking), and drain it off : this should be
done three times. Have ready a syrup made with
a pint of sugar to a pint of water ; pour it, boiling,
over the grapes while they are hot, and cover at
once.

355. GREENGAGES PRESERVED WHOLE

Take firm, sound greengages ; wipe them well,
prick them here and there with a darning-needle.
Place in a pan, barely covered with cold water,
and let heat very gradually till the fruit just
simmers ; then take it out and drain it in a sieve.
Make a syrup with three pounds of sugar and the
liquid remaining in the preserving-pan, and boil
fast until it becomes thick and sticky. Replace
the fruit, and boil up again until it bubbles ; then
pour off the whole into an earthen vessel, and
leave overnight. Next day drain off the syrup,
give it a quick boil-up again, and pour over the
fruit, to stand another night. The third day, put
all into the pan, and let boil for five or six minutes ;
then pour off, and cover.

356. LEMON CHIPS IN SYRUP (1815)

Take some fine lemon peels ; pare off all the rind
with a knife, cut it all into pieces, if you can, about
a quarter of an inch wide ; put them into a cab-
bage-net, and into a preserving-pan with water ;
boil them quite tender ; then have another pan with

syrup boiling, and when the chips are boiled enough in the water, take them out of the net and put them into the boiling syrup.

N.B.—Let them be well drained before you put them into the syrup, and let them boil a quarter of an hour ; then put them into a large earthen pan, and let them stand till next day ; then drain the syrup from them and boil it ten minutes, and pour it over them ; cover them till the next day ; then boil the chips and syrup together twenty minutes, and put them into the tub again ; keep them covered with the syrup, and when you think it is well soaked into them, boil all together, and bottle them.

357. LEMON PEELS IN SYRUP (1815)

Take the largest and clearest lemon peels you can get, and throw them into a large preserving-pan with water ; let them boil till you find them quite soft and tender ; then take them one at a time out of the water, and with a tablespoon take all the pith out of the inside clean from them ; throw them into a tub of cold water as you do them ; let them stand in the water four or five days ; then put your lemon peels one within the other, and place them in a large deep tub ; have a large preserving-pan of syrup boiling over the fire, pour some of the syrup over them, and cover the tub ; let them stand two days, and boil the syrup three or four minutes ; pour it over the peels again, and keep them always well covered with syrup ; repeat boiling the syrup in this manner for eight or ten days ; then bottle them.

LIME

NOTE.—This very useful member of the *Citrus* family is chiefly known to us in the form of lime-juice, that excellent mild tonic and anti-scorbutic. It is not used, as a rule, for jam, marmalade, or jelly, but is preserved whole in syrup.

358. LIMES PRESERVED WHOLE

Take just-ripe limes; wipe well, and place in boiling water. Boil fast until they are tender enough to pierce with a wooden point; then drain off the water, pour on more hot water, and let it reach boiling-point again; then remove the limes, throw cold water over them, and drain them in a folded cloth. Have a syrup ready boiling, made with one pound of sugar to rather under one quart of water, and a pinch of salt. Put the limes into this for about twenty minutes; then remove from the fire and let stand till next day. Boil them up in the syrup four or five times, letting them cool off (in the pan) for quite an hour between each boiling; finally place them in jars. Reduce the syrup till it thickens, fill up the jars with it, and cover.

359. MELONS PRESERVED

Gather the melons when fresh and green; rub them smooth with a coarse cloth; put them in strong salt and water; tie them down close and set them by the fire; change them from top to bottom

till quite yellow, then put them in a skellet with
layers of vine leaves and strong salt and water,
and a small piece of soda and alum. Put it over the
fire at some distance till quite scalding hot, but not
boiling. If not green in a few hours, change the
water and leaves, and put them on again ; when
green, drain them on a sieve, and throw them in
fresh water for three days, changing it every day.
Make a thin syrup with one pound of sugar and a
gallon of water boiled an hour and cleared with the
white of an egg. When nearly cold, pour it over
them, repeating the same for a week, each day a
little warmer ; the last day let them boil five
minutes.

360. MELON-RIND PRESERVE

Thinly pare the green outer rind of the melon
(water-melon can be used), and cut up the rest of
the rind into small uniform pieces or strips. Weigh,
and put to soak in water which will cover the rind,
adding one tablespoonful of salt to every quart of
water. Leave this overnight ; next day give it a
good draining and rinsing, and put it into boiling
water. When it becomes transparent, carefully
drain it. Have ready a syrup made with twelve
ounces of sugar and half a breakfastcupful of
water for every pound of rind. When it boils,
put in the rind, and add, for each pound of melon,
half an ounce of ginger root and a lemon sliced
thinly. Let cook about twenty minutes, and
remove the rind into heated jars ; let the syrup
boil till it thickens, and fill up the jars with it.

361. MULBERRIES PRESERVED WHOLE

Choose large and very ripe mulberries; put them gently into some strong syrup, and let them boil, covering over the pan, and shaking it gently from time to time; then take them off the fire, skim the syrup, and let them stand for two hours; they are then to be put on again, and boiled until the syrup has become exceedingly thick; pour into glasses and pots, and cover.

362. PLUMS PRESERVED WHOLE, No. 1

Take six pounds of large ripe (but not over-ripe) plums, and place them in a large bowl. Cover them with boiling water, cover them up, and let stand till cold. Have ready a syrup of six pounds of sugar and six teacupfuls of water; let boil five minutes. Drain off the water thoroughly from the plums, and pour the boiling syrup over them, so as to cover them completely; then leave them for twenty-four hours. Drain the syrup from the plums; boil it for five minutes after reaching boiling-point, and again pour it over plums and let stand twenty-four hours. The third time, boil up the syrup, place the plums very carefully in it; let boil till they are tender and translucent (twenty-five to thirty minutes). Remove them very carefully, and place in bottles. Give the syrup an extra boil-up until it thickens (about ten minutes more), then fill up the bottles and cover them.

363. PLUMS PRESERVED WHOLE, No. 2

Wipe and weigh the plums; prick them in several places with a needle; put them in preserving-pan, with an equal weight of sugar, placed in alternate layers with the fruit; bring slowly to a boil. Remove the plums; drain them well, and put them on large plates to dry in the sun. Let the syrup simmer slowly for thirty minutes; then put the plums in, and let boil ten minutes; drain and dry again. When the fruit is quite cold, put it into jars or bottles; have the syrup boiling, and cover the plums with it.

364. PLUMS PRESERVED WHOLE, No. 3

Six pounds of plums, six pounds of preserving sugar, three pints of cold water. Boil the sugar and water in a preserving-pan to a thin syrup. Wipe the plums quite clean, stalk them, prick them with a silver fork, and leave them in an earthenware jar for forty-eight hours, with the syrup (when cool) poured over them. Then boil all gently, until the plums are tender, when they must be lifted out into jars, and the syrup must boil until it is quite thick before being poured over the plums.

365. GREENGAGE PLUMS PRESERVED WHOLE
(1815)

Let your greengages be very sound; prick them with a fork six or seven times or more about the stalks; put them into cold water, or else they will turn black; scald them, and have another preserv-

ing-pan with boiling syrup ; drain the water from
the gages, and put them into a deep, earthen pan ;
place them regularly, and pour the boiling syrup
over them ; let them stand till next day, then
drain all the syrup from them ; boil it again, and
put it over them ; repeat so for seven or eight
days ; then take another flat earthen pan, drain
the syrup from them, place your gages in this pan ;
boil some fresh syrup for half an hour and pour it
over them ; place in pots and cover.

366. MOGUL PLUMS PRESERVED WHOLE (1815)

Take the largest Mogul plums you can get with
clear skins ; prick them with a fork about ten or a
dozen times, mostly about the stalk ; throw them
into cold water, otherwise they will turn black
where you have pricked them ; put them over the
fire just to scald them ; have a pan half full of
boiling syrup ; drain all the plums from the water
through a sieve, and put them into the syrup ; do
not put too many in, only just to cover the bottom
of the pan ; boil the plums and the syrup ten
minutes, then put them into a flat earthen pan
and cover it with paper. The next day drain the
syrup from them through a sieve, let the syrup
boil, put the plums in it and let them boil together ;
put them into the same pan, and repeat the same
five or six days ; bottle and cover them.

367. YELLOW PLUMS PRESERVED WHOLE (1815)

Let your plums be the soundest and best you can
get ; prick them with a fork, and put them into

cold water ; have a very thin syrup, so thin as to be hardly sweet, scald them in it, and let them have but one gentle boil ; put them in an earthen pan, let them stand till the next day ; then drain all the syrup from them, boil and pour it over them ; repeat the same eight or nine days successively, then let them have a gentle boil, and put them in your pots ; take care that your pots are not the least damp ; let it be three days before you cover them up, and keep them and all other sweetmeats in a dry place.

368. SMALL YELLOW PLUMS PRESERVED WHOLE (1815)

Let your plums be clear from spots ; run a fork in once at each end and no more ; you must not have the plums too ripe ; boil a pan of syrup ten minutes ; drain all the water from the plums and put them in the syrup ; boil and skim them. Repeat the same four or five days, then put them carefully into pots ; mind you do not break them, for they are very tender, and take care your pots are very dry ; let them stand two days before you put them by ; cut small pieces of writing-paper, dip them in brandy, and put them over your fruit in every pot ; this should be done to all fruits ; it must be put close, that no air can get in, then another paper over that ; tie them up.

369. QUINCES PRESERVED WHOLE

Pare and core the quinces ; cook them in water enough to cover them, which has a little citric acid

in, and when they are quite tender, have ready a
syrup made with one pint of water to three of
sugar ; place the fruit in this, and when it boils,
let boil five or six minutes. Lift out the quinces
into jars, pour the boiling syrup over them, and
cover at once.

370. QUINCES AND APPLES PRESERVED WHOLE

To every two pounds of pared and cored quinces,
allow one pound of pared and cored sweet apples.
Cook the quinces till tender, then remove them and
cook in syrup, as in No. 369 ; take them out and
keep hot whilst the apples are simmered in the syrup ;
cook the apples for an hour, or until they are quite
red and clear. Place the apples and quinces
alternately in the jars, fill up with boiling syrup,
and cover at once.

371. SLICED PRESERVED QUINCES

Pare, core, quarter, and weigh the quinces ; allow
six ounces of sugar and about one pint of water to
every pound, which make into a syrup. Steam the
quinces till tender, but not broken ; then place in
jars and pour some syrup in. When it has boiled
five minutes, let the jars stand in boiling water for
half an hour ; then completely fill up with syrup
and cover.

372. RASPBERRIES PRESERVED WHOLE, No. 1

Make some very strong syrup, and when it is
quite thick, put the raspberries into it and boil them

for five minutes, taking off any scum that may arise ; take them off the fire, and add a little sifted sugar ; then boil again, skimming as before : this process, and the powdering with sugar, is to be repeated three or four times.

373. RASPBERRIES PRESERVED WHOLE, No. 2

Take some of the finest raspberries you can get ; then with a large pin prick those that are large and dry ; just cover the bottom of a sieve with them. Put a preserving-pan on the fire with syrup in it ; boil the syrup ten minutes ; then put the raspberries in, let them boil, and skim them as they boil, with whited brown paper ; ten or twelve minutes are sufficient, and mind that the pots are quite dry before you put your raspberries in, for if they are the least damp it will spoil your fruit ; let them stand in the pots two days before you tie them up.

374. RASPBERRIES BOTTLED WITH SUGAR

Take sound, large red raspberries ; stem them, and place them in clean dry jars in alternate layers of fruit and sugar ; this will take about three table-spoonfuls of sugar to one pint of raspberries. Do not fill the jars more than two-thirds. Stand them in a large boiler, or fish-kettle, *with a lid*, and fill the boiler with cold water up to the height of the fruit in the jars. Cover the boiler, and put it over a moderate heat. When the water boils fast, take out the jars, one at a time, and cover immediately.

375. STRAWBERRIES PRESERVED WHOLE, No. 1

Take sound, just-ripe strawberries; stem them, wash them lightly in a colander without rubbing them; drain, place in a bowl in a steamer over boiling water, and steam them fast for ten minutes. Have ready a syrup, made pint for pint of sugar and water. Place the fruit in sterilised jars and fill up with the syrup. Cover at once.

376. STRAWBERRIES PRESERVED WHOLE (1815), No. 2

Mind to get the strawberries for this purpose in very dry weather—that is, if it has not rained for three or four days; pick the largest and finest you can get. Put some syrup into a preserving-pan; boil it over a brisk fire for half an hour, and put your strawberries in while it boils; do not put many into the pan, only one strawberry deep; let them boil twenty minutes, and take off all the scum with paper carefully; if you find they are likely to break, take them off immediately, and put them into your pots; when cold, put apple jelly over, and be very careful that your pots are not the least damp.

377. STRAWBERRIES PRESERVED WHOLE, No. 3

Mash some strawberries, let simmer for twenty minutes, and strain juice. For each pint allow one pint of sugar; re-heat juice, and heat sugar separately; and when the juice boils, mix both. Have sound, whole strawberries ready in heated bottles

or glass jars about three inches short of the tops,
and when the syrup is thick, fill up the bottles with
it. Do not cover till cold.

378. PEACHES PRESERVED WHOLE

Take equal weight of fruit and sugar ; lay the
fruit in a large dish, and sprinkle half the sugar
over in fine powder ; give them a gentle shaking ;
the next day make a thin syrup with the remainder
of the sugar, and instead of water, if you have it,
allow one pint of red-currant juice to every pound
of peaches ; simmer them in this till sufficiently
clear.

N.B.—Pick them when not dead ripe.

379. PRESERVED PEARS, No. 1

Take the largest stewing pears when they are on
the turn; pare them nicely, cut them in halves,
leaving the stem on.

To every pound of pears add three-quarters of a
pound of loaf sugar, and to about fifty pears put
a pint of water, the juice and peel of four lemons
(the peel to be pared thin and cut in long strips), a
small cup of cloves, and a little cochineal to colour
them.

Let them stew very gently over a slow fire, turning them constantly until you can pass a straw
through them ; then add a teacupful of brandy and
let them boil two or three minutes longer. Put
them in jars and tie down like other preserves ; they
will keep good twelve months.

380. PRESERVED PEARS, No. 2

Weigh an equal amount of pears and preserving-sugar ; then divide the sugar, reserving half, and making a thin syrup with the rest—one quart of water to one pound of sugar. Having peeled, halved, and cored the pears, place each half, as you finish it, into a bowl of water in which lemon juice has been dropped ; this will make them keep their colour. When the syrup is cool, lift out each piece of pear, wipe it with a soft cloth, and let the fruit simmer in the syrup over a slow fire until half-cooked ; then put it (very carefully so as not to break the fruit) into a large bowl or pan, and leave it, covered with a cloth. Leave it for forty-eight hours ; then drain off the syrup and add the rest of the sugar ; to each quart of liquid allow the juice of one lemon and its rind peeled very thin, and half an ounce of root or " race " ginger. Boil this syrup for ten minutes or so, skimming well ; then replace the pears, and let them simmer till they become transparent. Lift the fruit with care into wide-necked jars or bottles, cover with the syrup ; cover firmly and securely.

381. PRESERVED PEARS, No. 3

Blanch ripe pears, then peel and cut them into quarters, taking out the cores ; boil them in strong syrup for a short time, and leave them for twelve hours after boiling in the syrup ; then take out the pears and drain them, and give the syrup another boil ; put the fruit in again, and let it boil for a short time. The quantity of sugar used should be equal to the weight of the fruit.

382. PRESERVED PEARS, No. 4

Peel some small, sound pears, but do not remove stems. Allow pound for pound of sugar, and make a syrup, with one pint of water and one teaspoonful of citric acid (dissolved) to every four pounds of sugar. Melt the sugar with the acid in the double boiler ; let boil one minute, then set aside at back of stove. Boil the pears with sufficient water to cover them, and a little citric acid. When they are tender but not broken, boil up the syrup again ; let the pears be in it for thirty minutes ; place in jars and cover at once.

383. PRESERVED PEARS (1815), No. 5

Get some baking pears that are of a very hard nature ; put the pears in a large preserving-pan with water ; let them simmer over the fire till you find them rather soft ; take them out of the boiling water with a skimmer, and put them into a basin with cold water. Pare them in this manner : first cut off the end of the pear, then hold the stalk end in your hand, and bring your knife down the skin straight, so as to make the skin come off in five pieces all round the pear ; throw them into another basin with cold water. Have the preserving-pan with syrup in it ; let the syrup boil for ten minutes, then put the pears in ; but first drain the water well from them ; let them boil in the syrup

again about ten minutes ; skim it with paper ; boil
them in the same manner six days, draining the
syrup off the paper every time, till the syrup is of a
fine thickness ; let them remain in this syrup till
you want to candy them ; or bottle them.

384. PRESERVED PEARS, BAKED

This is a good method for using small, hard
pears. Peel, core, and place them in an earthen
jar, putting thinly pared lemon peel in layers with
them. Mix equal quantities of water and treacle,
sufficient to cover the fruit. Leave overnight, and
next day bake as long as possible in a slow oven.
When the pears are darkened and tender, place them
in jars ; boil down and reduce the syrup and pour
it over them ; cover at once. The pears should be
boiled very long and very slowly.

385. PRESERVED JARGONELLE PEARS

Pare very thin and simmer for ten minutes in a
syrup of one pint of water and one pound of sugar.
Let them lie a day or two. Make the syrup richer
and simmer again. Repeat this till they are clear
and the syrup the thickness of honey.

386. PINEAPPLES PRESERVED WHOLE (1815)

Take the pineapple, chip off all the small pieces
of leaves from the bottom of the pine ; take the
top and stalk, and have a preserving-pan on the
fire with water, and to every two quarts of water
put half a pint of syrup, so as to make it very clear,

thin syrup, and only just sweet; be sure that it
boils before you put the pines in, and let it simmer an
hour over the fire. The next day let the fruits boil
gently another hour; take them off and cover them
carefully; the next day let them boil gently about
half an hour; put some syrup as thick as you use
to other fruits; the next day drain this syrup off
and boil it, repeating the same seven or eight days;
then put the pines into pots, and be very careful
that your pots are very dry.

CHAPTER V

FRUIT CHEESES AND PASTES

NOTE.—These were popular in England for centuries ; recently they seem to be almost ignored. On the Continent they are always to be had. They are an excellent method of using up windfalls, and small or unripe fruit. The only one still in vogue with us is damson cheese ; but apples, apricots, black currants, cherries, elderberries, and quinces make particularly good pastes. This method of preservation is particularly to be recommended, because so little sugar is, or need be, used.

The process, briefly, is that of boiling down any fruit till it can be passed through a sieve, the skins and stones being thus removed. The pulp is then weighed and boiled again to get it as dry as possible. Sugar is then mixed in, twelve ounces for one pound of pulp being sufficient ; and the paste is let to boil till quite stiff. It is then spread out to dry on flat dishes, or is tightly pressed into pots. The test of a cheese or paste being sufficiently cooked is that it should come away in a solid mass from the sides of the preserving-pan ; and it should not make the fingers sticky when pressed.

The fruit pulp left over from jelly-making can be most advantageously utilised for fruit paste.

Weigh it *before* passing it through a sieve, boil it as dry as possible, and allow about seven ounces of castor sugar per pound. Boil till quite stiff—say about twenty-five to thirty minutes—stirring well.

Fruit drops, beloved of our great-grandmothers, are made by boiling thick fruit juice with eight ounces of sugar to each half-gill. It should simmer rather than boil until stiff, and then be just brought to boiling-point and removed. Drop it in minute pieces on an oiled plate or slab, and let set.

387. APPLE CHEESE (1815), No. 1

Pare and quarter your apples and take out the cores; put them into a deep pot or jar, and put the parings and cores at the top; let them bake in a moderate oven till quite soft; take off the parings, cores, and bits of apple which are at the top, if they are dry or hard; then put your apples into a stewpan, with fine powdered sugar to your taste, and boil them four hours till the cheese is quite stiff; put it in moulds or cups, and lay paper over it moistened with brandy; set it in a dry place, and in three weeks it will cut quite smooth.

N.B.—You may add a little of the rind of a lemon grated, or a few drops of essence of lemon, before you put it into the moulds, also a few blanched almonds cut into small pieces and mixed with it.

388. APPLE CHEESE, No. 2

Peel, core, and quarter apples sufficient to weigh half a pound, when prepared; add one pound of

sugar, and one grated lemon-rind; let boil slowly
for three hours, then stir in the juice of the lemon,
and boil and stir continually for ten minutes longer.

389. APRICOT CHEESE

Take an equal weight of just-ripe apricots and of
sugar. Cook the fruit until tender; take out the
stones, and pass it through a fine sieve. Return
it to heat through again, and gradually mix in the
sugar, stirring continuously. Let the paste become
just dry enough to leave the sides of the pan, then
remove and pot it.

390. BULLACE CHEESE (Eighteenth Century)

Take your bullaces when they are full ripe, and to
every quart of fruit put a quarter of a pound of loaf
sugar beat small. Put them in a jar in a moderate oven to bake till they are soft; then rub them
through a hair sieve, and to every pound of pulp
add half a pound of loaf sugar crushed fine; then
boil it four hours and a half over a slow fire, and
keep stirring it all the time. Put it into pots, and
tie brandy papers over them, and keep them in a
dry place. When the cheese has stood a few months,
it will cut out very bright and fine. You may make
sloe cheese the same way.

391. CHERRY CHEESE (1815), No. 1

Stone Kentish cherries; crack as many of the
stones as you choose, blanch the kernels in boiling
water, and mix them with the fruit; to every

twelve pounds of fruit add three pounds of sugar ; boil it to a thick paste, and when the fruit no longer cleaves to the pan, it is done enough.

392. CHERRY CHEESE, No. 2

Take good cooking cherries ; wash, stalk, stone, and boil till tender. Rub through a sieve, and weigh the pulp. Return it to the pan ; let boil fast till it becomes a stiff dry paste ; add twelve ounces of sugar to every pound of fruit ; mix it well in, (off the fire), and let it dissolve ; then return pan to fire and continue boiling and stirring till the fruit comes away dry from the sides of the pan ; then put it into pots and cover at once.

393. DAMSON CHEESE (1815), No. 1

Pick the damsons free from stalks, leaves, etc. ; put them into a jar and tie white paper over them ; bake them in a slow oven till quite soft ; rub them through a colander while hot ; put the pulp and juice which has passed through the colander into a stewpan, with fine powdered sugar to your taste ; boil it over a moderate fire till it is as stiff as you can possibly stir it, which will take three hours ; keep stirring it to prevent it burning to the pan ; and a few minutes before you take it off the fire, put the kernels of the damsons into the pan, and mix with it ; put it into pots or moulds. Let it stand a day, and cut some pieces of writing-paper the size of the tops of the pots or moulds, dip them

in brandy and put close over them ; put them in
a dry place, and they will keep for several years.

N.B.—You may make plum or bullace cheese
the same way ; it is necessary to take the shells off
the kernels before you put them into the pan.

394. DAMSON CHEESE, No. 2

Put your damsons in a large stone jar, and tie it
up tight and put it in the oven till the fruit is soft
and the juice running out ; rub it through the
sieve till you have got the pulp out ; add three-
quarters of a pound of sugar to every pound of pulp ;
boil it well. Try a little in a saucer, and if it sets,
it will be boiled enough. Break the stones, and
put in the kernels or some blanched bitter almonds
while boiling. Stir all the time, as it soon burns.

395. DAMSON CHEESE, No. 3

Take sound ripe damsons ; stew them (with no
water or sugar) till quite tender ; strain off the
juice, pass the pulp through a sieve, and remove the
stones and skins. Put back about half the juice
to the fruit-pulp, and having weighed, return it
to the pan and boil over a clear fire till it is a dry
paste ; add six ounces of sugar for each pound of
fruit, mix thoroughly, and go on stirring till the
paste comes right away from the sides of the pan.
Put into pots, and cover when cold.

396. GOOSEBERRY CHEESE

Take rough, ripe gooseberries ; cook in a double-
boiler, or in a stew-jar on the stove, till the fruit

is quite a pulp ; then rub it through a hair sieve, weigh, and place in a preserving-pan. Let simmer slowly for three to four hours. Allow three ounces of castor sugar to each pound of sieved pulp, and sprinkle it in gradually while the pulp boils. When the paste comes away quite dry from the sides of the pan, remove and press it into small pots. Cover when cold. Store in a dry place.

397. ALMACK'S PASTE, No. 1

Equal quantities of plums, pears, and apples, must be cut in slices, put into an earthen jar and baked ; when thoroughly done, squeeze them through a colander. To three pounds of fruit add one pound of sugar, and let it simmer gently for some time till it becomes a thick jam ; then put it into saucers or shallow pans, and let it stand on the kitchen rack for a day to stiffen and dry. When so, it will keep in paper.

398. ALMACK'S PASTE, No. 2

Take equal quantities of plums, pears, and apples ; stone the first and slice the two second, but they need not be peeled. Put them in alternate layers in an earthenware covered jar, and keep in a moderate oven till they are completely soft. Rub the pulp through a coarse sieve, weigh, and allow pound for pound of sugar. Place in a preserving-pan over a slow fire till very thick, stirring well ; then remove and pot.

399. APPLE PASTE

Peel some fine apples, take out the cores, and boil them in water. When quite soft, take them out and put them in cold water; having drained them, press them through a coarse cloth. Put this marmalade into a pan on the fire, stir it frequently with a wooden spoon, and when it is nearly dry, take it out and add an equal weight of sugar, mixing them well together; press the mixture flat, of the thickness of an ordinary piecrust, put it upon tins, and place to dry in a slack oven.

400. APPLE PASTE (WHITE)

Take some sound pippins; pare, halve, core, and place in a pan with just enough water to float them. Boil them to a pulp which can be strained through a sieve. Clarify two pounds of sugar with two whites of eggs; boil it with as little water as possible till it candies. Put in two and a half pounds of the apple pulp, and mix well. Let stand over a slow fire drying, and keep on stirring till the paste comes away clear from the bottom of the pan; then spread it upon large plates to finish drying in the oven or on the stove.

401. APPLE PASTE (GREEN)

Take juicy green pippins; place them with a very little water in a covered pan. Let stand over a slow fire five or six hours, or until thoroughly soft;

then pulp the fruit through a fine sieve. Boil two
pounds of sugar to candy, weigh, mix in two pounds
of pulp, and keep stirring over the fire. Proceed as
above.

For red apple paste, the sugar can be coloured
at pleasure with cochineal.

402. APPLE PASTE KNOTS (RED OR WHITE)

Pare some large apples, and cut them into a preserving-pan, with just water enough to come up
to the top of the apples ; let boil till the fruit is
pulped ; then pass it through a sieve into a flat
brown pan ; take some cochineal and mix it with
the fruit. Have another preserving-pan with as
much syrup in it as you have got apples, and
boil the syrup until it comes to "blow" ; take the
syrup off the fire, and mix the fruit with it in the
pan. Cover shallow baking-tins with the paste,
about an eighth of an inch deep, and put it into your
stove, which must be hot ; let them remain till next
day, then take another baking-tin, and, with a knife,
cut the paste round the edges and across the tin in
scores about a quarter of an inch wide ; then pull
it off, and if it comes off easily it is dried enough ;
when you have got it off in long strings, make them
into knots according to your fancy ; put them on
the other plate, then into the stove, and let them
stand in the stove two days, then take them
out ; when they are cold, put them into papered
boxes.

403. APRICOT PASTE

Set any quantity of the fruit you may require over the fire in a stewpan, and cook till it is quite soft ; then take out the stones, and pass the fruit through a sieve. Then take clarified sugar, equal in weight to the fruit, mix and dissolve it over the fire; turn out into shapes, and dry in a slow oven or in the sun.

404. BLACK CURRANT PASTE, No. 1

Dissolve an ounce of isinglass in about half a pint of the strained juice, and an equal weight of sugar ; put them in a stewpan, and let them simmer for at least an hour; then pour out the paste into a very shallow tin mould, and when it is cold and quite hard, cut it into pieces.

405. BLACK CURRANT PASTE, No. 2

Pick the stalks from four quarts of currants ; wash them, and boil them in one quart of water, mashing them with a wooden spoon. When quite soft, strain through a jelly-bag, and measure. To each pint of juice allow one pound and a half of sifted sugar ; put this to warm in the oven while the juice is boiled up ; then sprinkle in the sugar, stirring well. Replace on fire, and stir until the sugar is all melted, but do not let boil. Pour off on plates and dry in oven. Before it is quite hard, cut it in rounds or half-rounds.

406. BLACK CURRANT PASTE, No. 3

Pick and wash the currants, and proceed as for Black Currant Jelly (No. 57), but do not strain off all the juice. Rub the pulp through a sieve, weigh, and return it to the pan, and boil briskly till it is dry ; add eight ounces of castor sugar to each pound, mix well, and boil for twenty-five minutes. Be careful that it does not stick and burn. Pour off upon plates, and let dry thoroughly.

407. RED CURRANT PASTE

Proceed as for Black Currant Paste, No. 2, and be careful to put the sugar in at the moment the juice has boiled, and not to let it boil subsequently. The currants may be rubbed through a hair sieve instead of being strained through a jelly-bag.

408. DAMSON DROPS (1815)

Put some damsons in the oven to bake, but not so much as to break ; then skin and stone them, and pass them through a sieve. Sift some common loaf sugar through a fine sieve, and mix with them ; make it very thick ; drop them off the knife on paper. Put them in your stove to dry ; then when they are quite dry, turn them on a sieve, and wet the outside of the paper, and they will come off easily ; put them into the stove again till they are quite dry and hard, and then put them by in a papered tin box.

409. FIG CAKES OR PASTE

Peel ripe figs ; cook them in a double boiler, very slowly, with a very little sugar, a few chopped almonds, and any flavouring preferred. When they are quite thick and smooth, pour into shallow pans and let dry in the oven or the sun, quite slowly ; when absolutely dry, cut into squares or oblongs and keep in paper-lined tin boxes in a dry place.

410. GOOSEBERRY CHIPS OR PASTE

Take ripe gooseberries, and place in a large double boiler or in jars set in a fish-kettle. The water around them must boil till they are quite pulped. Remove and measure, and add half a pound of castor sugar to each pound of pulp ; mix thoroughly, and pour very thinly, just to cover the bottom of flat, shallow dish ; place in the sun to become perfectly dry ; then cut up into strips or chips.

411. GOOSEBERRY PASTE

Take some gooseberries from which you have extracted the juice for jelly, without drawing them very closely. Pass them through a sieve, weigh them, and boil the pulp for about an hour and a quarter, until it forms a dry paste in the pan ; lift it off the fire and stir in six ounces of good pounded sugar to each pound of fruit. When this is nearly dissolved, boil the mixture for twenty to twenty-five minutes ; stir it incessantly, or it will be likely to burn ; put it into moulds or shallow dishes, and use it as wanted for table.

412. GOOSEBERRY PASTE CAKES

Stew down green gooseberries (having topped and tailed them) in a double-boiler, or in a jar set in a pan of boiling water. When the fruit is soft, rub it through a sieve, weigh, and to every pound of pulp add one pound of castor sugar and the whites of two eggs, whisked fairly stiff. Beat all well together, form into small, flat, round cakes, and place them on paper in the oven to become dry. Keep in a dry place, stored in tin boxes.

413. GUAVA PASTE

Take unripe but well-filled-out guavas, and allow three-quarters of their weight in sugar, which must be cooked separately with its own amount in water, till reduced to a thick syrup. Slice but do not peel the guavas. Cook them in a little cold water till quite tender, pass them through a sieve, and put into a double-boiler. Cook slowly till the pulp is a thick paste, then add the boiling syrup. Let all boil till it sets hard like candy when dipped into cold water. Pour it into tin boxes lined with white or oiled paper, and keep in a dry place.

414. LEMON DROPS (1815)

Squeeze the juice of six lemons into a brown pan or basin ; take some double refined sugar, pound and sift it through a very fine sieve ; mix it with the lemon-juice and make it so thick that you can hardly stir it ; put it into a copper stewpan ; with a wooden spoon stir it over the fire five minutes ;

then take it off and let drop off the point of a knife, in bits about the size of a sixpence, on writing-paper, and let them stand till cold, and they will come off the paper.

415. ORANGE CHIPS OR PASTE

Take sweet oranges ; remove the rind in long thin strips ; for each pound of these allow one pound of sugar. Squeeze out the orange juice ; add the sugar to this, and let stand till next day. Meanwhile leave the peel soaking overnight in a bowl of fresh water. Next morning boil up the peel in the same water, and let simmer till quite tender but not broken. Cook the sugar and juice separately, till they become as syrup. Drain the peel and place it in the syrup ; let boil quietly till the syrup is quite thick and will candy if dropped into cold water ; then carefully lift up the chips, one at a time, out of the syrup, and place them on oiled paper on trays to dry and drain, putting them in the sun or in a fruit-dryer. Change the paper next day. The chips must remain in the sun until all moisture has evaporated : this may be a matter of weeks. Then put them in papered tin boxes in a dry place.

The syrup will be most useful for flavouring.

416. ORANGE DROPS (1815)

Rasp six China oranges very fine ; squeeze them in a small pan or basin with the rind ; squeeze two lemons with them, without rasping the rind ; sift

some powdered sugar and mix with the juice;
make it of a fine thickness; put it over the fire in a
small stewpan, and with a wooden spoon turn it
for five minutes; then take it off the fire, and drop
it off the point of a knife, as round as you can,
upon white paper, in pieces about the size of a silver
sixpence; let them stand till they are cold, and they
will come off; then put them in your box.

417. ORANGE PASTE CAKES (1815)

Cut one dozen of Seville oranges into halves, and
squeeze them into a brown pan; put the peels into
a pan of water and let them boil till they are quite
soft; take them out and scoop all the inside out of
them; pound the peels in a mortar. Then take one
dozen and a half of large apples, pare and cut
them in pieces into a preserving-pan; add to them
the juice of the oranges and water enough to cover
the apples, and let them boil till they come to
marmalade; pass it through a sieve with a spoon,
likewise pass the orange peels that are pounded
through a sieve; mix the apples and oranges together. Have as much syrup in another preserving-
pan as you have jam; boil the sugar till it is nearly
caramel; mix it with your jam; stir them well together; put it over the fire ten minutes, stir it all
the time with your spoon; put your heart-shaped
tin moulds, or any shape you like, on your oven-
sheets or plates; fill them with your paste; put
them into a hot stove, and let them stand till you
find the mould will come off easily and without
the jam running; take them off, place them in a

sieve, and put them into your stove till they are quite dry; then let them lie there one day.

418. PEACH CONSERVE OR PASTE

Make a marmalade of ripe peaches, with three-quarters of a pound of sugar to every pound of fruit; stir frequently, taking care they do not burn; dry the marmalade carefully on a hot plate, or in a slack oven; and when nearly dry, mix a quarter of a pound of the marmalade with a pound of very finely pounded sugar; press it into the form of a cake, drying thoroughly, and it will keep for almost any length of time. It cannot be dried too slowly.

419. PLUM PASTE, No. 1

Take juicy plums, not too sweet, and let cook in their own juice. When they are quite soft, take out the stones and pulp the rest through a sieve; weigh and return to pan; simmer slowly for an hour; add half the weight of fruit in warmed sugar; stir well till the sugar dissolves; let boil up one minute, then pour off the mixture into flat, shallow dishes, about a quarter of an inch thick, and place in a cool oven to dry. When quite dry, it may be cut into strips for better convenience of packing.

420. PLUM PASTE, No. 2

Cook some sharp but juicy plums in their own juice till quite tender; then take out stones and

pulp the fruit through a sieve; weigh the pulp,
return it to pan, and let simmer slowly for an hour;
then add half the original weight of pulp in sugar;
let it dissolve; boil for one minute, and pour off
into flat dishes, about a quarter of an inch deep,
and put in a very slow oven to dry. When completely dry, cut up and place in papered tin boxes.

421. RASPBERRY PASTE

Take one quart of ripe raspberries and mash them
to a pulp; strain half through a muslin or fine
sieve, and add the juice to the other half. Boil
this fifteen minutes; add one pint of red currant
juice; let boil till completely cooked. Place in a
separate pan one pound and a half of sugar, with
as much water as will dissolve it, and boil until it
candies. Put in the raspberries, mix, let just boil
up, and pour off on plates to dry in the oven.

422. VIOLET PASTE

Take the finest sweet violets you can get; pick
the petals off the stalks, beat them fine in a mortar,
with a little lemon-juice to moisten them, and
weigh; add twice their weight of sifted sugar, and
place in a preserving-pan over a slow fire. Stir
gently till all the sugar is dissolved, but do not
let it boil, or the violets will be discoloured. Pour
off on china plates to dry thoroughly, and afterwards pack in a box between layers of paper.

CHAPTER VI

FRUIT BUTTERS

NOTE.—These are scarcely known in England, but they are useful and economical concoctions. The Americans use them largely. Most of them require very little sugar. They are practically simple fruit pulp, boiled till thick, slightly flavoured and sweetened. In the case of apples, cider is usually added.

423. APPLE BUTTER, No. 1

Take a quantity of small apples; pare, quarter, and core them; add a little mixed spice, or a few cloves; place in preserving-pan, covered with cider, and let simmer slowly till the whole is of a thick, smooth consistency, and of a dark brown colour; a little Demerara sugar may be added. This will probably take seven hours, more or less.

424. APPLE BUTTER, No. 2

Fairly tart cooking-apples are required; peel, quarter, and core them; to every three pecks allow not less than nine pounds of brown sugar, and two gallons of cold water. Possibly more may be necessary, according to the tartness of the apples. Boil

214

the sugar and water; add the apples, and stir continually until the butter "sets" pretty firmly in a saucer, with no water showing. Flavour with cinnamon and nutmeg to taste; and put the butter into heated pots and cover immediately.

425. APPLE BUTTER, No. 3

Sour, tart apples should be used for this. Take a pailful of apples—about five pounds—wash them, dry thoroughly, and place in preserving-pan with one quart of cider; let simmer till they are reduced to a thick, smooth pulp; then pass them through a sieve, and add a little cinnamon, nutmeg, and cloves—say half a teaspoonful of each—before placing in jars.

426. APPLE AND GRAPE BUTTER

Take seven pounds of grapes; stem, and wash them in a colander; add ten pounds of apples, sliced and cored, but not peeled, and put all the fruit, with one quart of cold water, into a preserving-pan. Let boil till tender, and pass through a sieve; add four pounds of heated sugar, one teaspoonful of powdered cinnamon, and half a teaspoonful each of powdered cloves, ginger, and mace. Return to pan and let cook till the mixture thickens, stirring well. Place in jars, and cover.

427. GRAPE BUTTER

Weigh, skin, and seed grapes, ripe or unripe; let the pulp cook slowly till quite tender; put it through a sieve, return it to preserving-pan, and add the skins, which must also simmer till tender; add half a pound of sugar to each pound of fruit, and boil till the butter is quite thick; pour off and cover up.

428. PEACH BUTTER

Take four pounds of dried peaches; soak them overnight in enough water to cover them; boil them till tender in the same water next day. Mash them with a wooden spoon through a sieve; then take two tins of peaches and put them through the sieve. Place the fruit in preserving-pan with one pound and a half of sugar, and let it simmer carefully, well stirred, for two hours. Place in pots, and cover.

429. PRUNE BUTTER

Take four pounds of prunes, well wash, and leave overnight soaking in cold water. Next day, simmer them in the same water, and when they are tender, remove the stems and press the pulp through a sieve; add four pounds of sugar, and the juice and grated rind of one lemon; mix thoroughly, return to pan, and let cook gently till quite thick.

430. QUINCE BUTTER

Take some just-ripe quinces; wash, dry, and rub off the " fuzz " skin; peel and core. Put the pips, peels, and trimmings in a pan just covered with water; let simmer half an hour, and let strain through a fine sieve or doubled buttercloth. Slice the quinces quite small, and add them to the strained liquor from the peels, with a little extra water if need be; let simmer slowly till they are nearly tender, then add the same amount of peeled and cored cooking apples. When all the fruit has simmered till quite soft, press it through a sieve, and return it to the preserving-pan; let it cook till quite thick, stirring well; then add half its weight in granulated sugar, and go on cooking slowly for another hour and a half; place in pots, and cover.

431. RHUBARB BUTTER

Take one gallon of fresh red rhubarb; wash and wipe it, and chop small. Take one pound of stoned raisins, three oranges, and one lemon; chop them all as fine as can be, and mix with the rhubarb; add two pounds of sugar, and cook in a preserving-pan until the butter is thick and smooth—say an hour or so; place in pots, and cover.

432. TOMATO BUTTER

Take eight pounds of ripe but sound tomatoes; plunge them a minute into boiling water, remove skin, and slice them. Have ready two pounds of peeled and sliced apples, the juice of two lemons, two teaspoonfuls of ground ginger, and four pounds of Demerara sugar; mix well and leave overnight in an earthen bowl. Next day, place in preserving-pan and simmer for about four hours, or until the whole is thick and smooth.

433. MIXED DRIED-FRUIT BUTTER

Take equal parts of stoned raisins, figs, and dates; chop very fine, or put through a mincer; weigh, and add an equal weight of mixed shelled nuts—walnuts, almonds, hazels, Brazils, pea-nuts, etc. Chop or grind the latter; mix all thoroughly, and press tightly into a mould; put a heavy weight on the top.

CHAPTER VII

CANDIED, CRYSTALLISED, AND BRANDIED FRUITS

NOTE.—These, of course, are luxuries; but they are also very wholesome and nutritious when homemade, and their expensiveness or otherwise depends wholly on the price of sugar. They just devour sugar. When bought, they are dear out of all proportion to their original cost; when of private manufacture, they can be achieved quite reasonably.

You must study the notes on cooking of sugar (pp. 12 to 15) to make a success of these delightful dainties.

Our Elizabethan ancestors were great on candied edibles. All sorts of roots and fruits which we should never think of employing were called into service, merely as mediums for the attainment of sugared delight. The potato itself was only used at first for candying.

The process is in itself quite simple. It consists of cooking prepared fruits in syrup, for the most part making the syrup stronger for each coating; subsequently sprinkling them thickly with icing sugar. In a word, the fruits become thoroughly suffused and permeated with sugar.

219

Crystallised or glacés fruits are prepared, and then cooked till tender, before being immersed and boiled in clarified sugar.

434.   CANDIED CHERRIES, No. 1

Weigh pound for pound of sugar and of stoned cherries; make a syrup with the sugar and a little water (half a cupful per pound), and let simmer in preserving-pan till all is melted. When the syrup boils, put in the cherries; simmer them very slowly till quite clear. Pour off syrup, place fruit on flat dishes, and let dry in the sun or in a slow oven; it may take ten hours or more. When thoroughly dry, dust with sugar and put in papered tin box.

435.   CANDIED CHERRIES, No. 2

Make a thin syrup, allowing one pint of sugar to each half-pint of water; bring to a boil; let boil two minutes. Have the cherries in a deep bowl, and cover them with the syrup; leave for a day and night. Drain off the syrup; add to it half as much sugar as was used in making it; boil up till all is dissolved, and cover the cherries with it again. Leave for forty-eight hours, and repeat the previous boiling-up with extra sugar. Repeat the fourth time, and at last drain off all syrup, and wash the cherries in cold water; then dip in a syrup which is boiled to thread, and dry in a slow oven.

436.   CANDIED CHERRIES, No. 3

Take six pounds of the best Morella cherries, without blemish; cut the stalks short. Take three pounds of the best sugar, and a pint and a half of water ; boil it to a candy. Put the cherries into a new barrel ; when the sugar is cold, pour it upon the cherries and stop it close ; roll the barrel every day till it has done working ; but do not stop it too tight at first, or the barrel will burst.

437. CANDIED FIGS

Take one pound of good dried figs, and let soak one hour in cold water. Drain on a sieve, and place in a deep dish. Have ready a syrup made with one pound of sugar and half a pint of water; boil until it sets hard if dropped into cold water ; then add half a teaspoonful of lemon-juice or vinegar; stir, take off the fire, and pour over the figs. Let the figs absorb all the syrup, and, when quite dry, dust them with sugar and store in papered tin boxes.

438. CANDIED FILBERTS

Take sound filberts ; shell, blanch, and remove inner skins. Place them in very thin syrup to simmer for about an hour. Take off the pan, let cool, and then replace on fire, adding more sugar so as to thicken the syrup. Simmer for another hour, and then let cool. Repeat this process a third time, adding more sugar, until the syrup has become so thick as to candy when dropped into cold water. Take out the filberts before the syrup is cold; cover them well with powdered sugar; then dry in the sun or in a slow oven. The syrup may be used for any other purpose.

439. CANDIED GRAPEFRUIT PEEL

Take a large sound grapefruit ; wash, dry, and remove the rind, which should be cut into strips half an inch wide. Place them in a pan just covered with cold water, let boil, and continue to boil five minutes. Drain off the water, replace with cold, and repeat. Do this three times. In the fourth water, the rinds must go on boiling till they are tender ; then they must be drained and put into a fifth water, with one breakfastcupful of sugar to the same amount of rinds. Boil till the syrup is thick ; then drain, dry, and roll in sugar.

440. CANDIED LEMON OR ORANGE PEEL, No. 1

Remove the peel in halves or quarters ; let stand overnight in salted water. Next day, remove and wash thoroughly ; boil in fresh water, and change the water several times, till the peel is quite tender and does not taste of salt ; then remove as much as possible of the white lining of the peel. This latter can be left as it is, or cut into narrow strips. Have ready a syrup of one pound of sugar and one pint of water ; when boiling, put in one pound of peel ; let simmer till the syrup is almost absorbed, then boil fast until the peel is well coated with sugar ; stir carefully ; remove peel, dry it in a warm oven, and place in papered tin box.

441. CANDIED LEMON OR ORANGE PEEL, No. 2

Take twenty-four thoroughly good lemons ; halve them, and scoop out the pulp and white pith, leaving the yellow rinds intact. Leave in cold water for two days; drain in a sieve; plunge in boiling water for five minutes and drain again; put into preserving-pan with three pounds of granulated sugar and two quarts of cold water; mix lightly; let come to a brisk boil, then shift pan and simmer slowly for three hours; take off pan, let the contents cool slightly, then put into jars and cork tightly.

442. CANDIED LEMON OR ORANGE PEEL (1815), No. 3

Take some preserved lemon peels, wash them in warm water, and put them on a sieve to drain; boil some syrup on the fire till it comes to blow, and put your peels in; as soon as they are covered with sugar, take them out again, put them on wires for all the sugar to drop through; let them stand till cold, and put them in your boxes.

N.B.—Do orange peel in the same manner.

443. CANDIED ORANGE OR LEMON CHIPS (1815)

Take your preserved orange or lemon chips; wash them from the syrup with warm water, and the syrup you drain from them must boil till it comes to blow; put the chips in and rub the sugar all round till you see the syrup candy; then take the chips out with two forks, and put them on a wire for the sugar to drain off; let them stand till cold, and then put them in your boxes as before.

444. CANDIED MELON

Take sufficient citron melon to weigh five pounds when peeled, seeded, and sliced. Boil until tender in enough water to cover it, with a teaspoonful of powdered alum. Remove, drain, and rinse in cold water. In the meanwhile, prepare a syrup made with three pounds of sugar, the juice of eight lemons and grated rinds of three, and two ounces of green ginger root. Let boil till the syrup clears and thickens. Put the melon slices in, and cook till they are quite transparent. Remove, drain, and place them to dry in the oven or in the sun. Let stand twenty-four hours after they become dry. Reboil the syrup, replace the melon in it, just till it boils up again; drain and dry the fruit again. Repeat till the melon is completely candied. Store in air-tight boxes between layers of waxed paper.

445. CANDIED ORANGES

Peel the oranges, removing as much as possible of the white part; divide them, and boil in strong syrup for half an hour; let them stand till cold, and repeat the operation of boiling three or four times, until the syrup has become exceedingly thick; then take out the oranges, powder them with fine sugar, and put them into a very slack oven to dry.

446. CANDIED PEARS (1815)

Take the pears out of the syrup, and put them on wires or a large sieve; drain all the syrup from them; wash them in warm water to get the syrup off them; drain them quite dry. Then have a pan of syrup on the fire boiling, and let it boil till it comes to blow; take the pan off the fire, and take a spoon and rub it on the sides of the pan till you see the sugar turn white; then put your pears in. When you take them out, put them on a wire, and let them stand till cold; then put them in your box.

447. CANDIED PINEAPPLE

Take just-ripe pineapples; peel, slice thickly, remove eyes and cores, and halve the slices so that each half is a crescent. Weigh, add half a pint of water to each pound of fruit, and simmer slowly till the pineapple is clear and tender. Lift it out, and place in the water a pound of heated sugar for every pound of pineapple. When this syrup has boiled till reduced by one third, replace the fruit and let boil till it becomes quite transparent. Take it out with a skimmer, and put it on large flat dishes to dry in the sun. Boil the syrup till it candies, and pour it over the fruit. When completely dry, pack the pineapple in powdered sugar in large glass jars or tin boxes, and keep tightly covered.

448. CANDIED PINEAPPLE CHIPS (1815)

Take the top of the stalk of the pineapples; chip off the ends of the outsides and the bottoms of them; cut the pineapples in slices about the thickness of the fifth part of an inch. Take a deep earthen pan and one pound of sugar, lay some sugar at the bottom of the pan, then a layer of the pieces of pine, but not one piece over another ; then put another layer of sugar, then another of pine, and so on till the pan is almost full ; at the top put a good deal of sugar pretty deep ; cover them up with paper, and let them stand till you see the sugar is almost melted ; let them and the syrup boil half an hour, then put them in the same pan again. The next day give them another boil, and so continue eight days ; then drain all the syrup from them entirely, and lay them on your sieve to dry ; mind the sieve is quite dry. As you put them into the stove, dust a little very fine powdered sugar through a cloth bag over them ; put them in the stove, and let them remain there till you think they will not be sticky ; then put them in a tin box with clean white paper about them.

449. CANDIED PLUMS

Take four pounds of fine large plums, perfectly sound, and place in boiling water for ten minutes. Remove and drain. Have ready a syrup made with two pounds of sugar and two pints of water. Boil to " soft ball " (240°), and put in the plums. Place all in a slow oven, and leave overnight. Next day lift out the fruit, boil up the syrup, replace the fruit, remove from fire and place in oven overnight. This process must be repeated four times altogether. On the fifth day, make a fresh syrup in the same proportions as the first ; boil to " soft ball," place the plums in, and remove pan from fire. Let cool ; then lift out the plums and place them in a temperature of 65° till they are candied sufficiently hard. Keep in layers of paper in tin boxes in a dry place.

450. CANDIED SLICED QUINCE

Peel, core, thinly slice, and weigh the quinces; allow pound for pound of sugar. Scald the fruit, then place in a pan and let boil fast for eight or ten minutes. Drain off any liquor, place the fruit in a preserving-pan with the sugar and two table-spoonfuls of water, and let the sugar melt slowly, until the quinces are a deep clear red. Remove them carefully and drain them on a sieve. When they are dry, place them on dishes thickly powdered with icing sugar, and dust them well with sugar. Leave them in a dry place overnight, dust with more sugar, and pack in papered tin boxes.

The sugar which was used for them in the pre-serving-pan will come in very handy for preserving apples, etc.

CRYSTALLISED OR GLACÉ FRUITS

NOTE.—This process is not applicable to all fruits, only to those which are comparatively dry. Juicy moisture is fatal to it; and therefore, while nuts—walnuts, almonds, chestnuts, filberts, pea-nuts, etc.—are quite easy to prepare, there are but few fruits available. These chiefly consist of prunes, figs, cherries, lemon, orange, and grape-fruit peel.

General Rule.—Have ready a syrup, in the pro-portion of two parts sugar to one of water. Stir

well, and when the sugar is dissolved, add a small
saltspoonful of cream-of-tartar; then do not
touch it again until it boils to 290° or " crack,"
when you dip each fruit or nut separately into the
syrup, being careful to get it completely coated
all over. Put it on a buttered tin or slab to dry,
in a cool place, and when quite hard, store in
paper in a closed tin box. The dipping can be
repeated if it fails the first time.

451. CRYSTALLISED FRUITS, No. 1

Plums, greengages, cherries, pears, small oranges,
and green figs can be treated as under. They must
be sound, firm fruit, and under- rather than over-
ripe. Remove skins, stones, and stalks. Have
ready one pound of castor sugar mixed with one
saltspoonful of bi-carbonate of soda and the same
of cream of tartar (increase in proportion); roll
the fruit in this, then lay them on a flat dish, each
fruit separately, thickly covered with sugar; place
in a hot oven; and when the fruits are cooked quite
tender, take out the dish and set it in a cool place.
When the fruits are cool, but not cold, roll them
again in the mixture as above, leave on a coarse
sieve for twenty-four hours, and store in a papered
tin with butter-paper between the layers.

452. CRYSTALLISED FRUITS, No. 2

Pears, apricots, cherries, and pineapple can be
crystallised as under; peel thinly, or remove skins;
leave stalks on; place the fruits in boiling water,

CRYSTALLISED FRUIT 229

slightly salted, and bring to the boil, then stand the pan aside for twenty minutes; afterwards lift out fruits, and put them to drain on a coarse sieve. Make a syrup in preserving-pan, allowing one pound and a half of sugar and three-quarters of a pint of water for every pound of fruit; add the whisked white of an egg; let boil up twice, then move pan aside for fifteen minutes. At the end of that time, skim the syrup, pour it off carefully into another pan, not disturbing any sediment at bottom; put the fruit in and let boil for one minute; remove and drain fruits, coat them thickly with icing sugar, and place them on a coarse sieve or wire rack in a warm place to dry.

453. CHESTNUTS (*MARRONS GLACÉS*), No. 1

Take a quart of chestnuts; remove the outer shells, and place them in a pan just covered with lukewarm water. Simmer gently till soft, then drain on a sieve. Have ready a syrup made with half a breakfastcupful of water and one pound of sugar. Let it come to boiling-point, stir in one teaspoonful of glucose, and continue to boil until the syrup threads. Let it cool a little, then pour it over the chestnuts, and leave in a warm place for thirty-six hours. Next day remove and drain the nuts. Make a fresh syrup with the same proportions of sugar and water, but add a pinch of cream of tartar. Let it boil up to 250°, take off the fire, put the nuts in, and return to fire. Bring to boiling-point again, and, having carefully stirred the syrup, gently lift out the nuts and drain them.

Let them get dry. Then make a third syrup with one breakfastcupful of water, one pound of sugar, and one teaspoonful of glucose. Let boil to 235° or " feather." Then proceed as in last paragraph—*i.e.*, remove pan from fire, put in chestnuts, bring to boiling-point again. Remove from fire, stir gently; remove chestnuts, and place in buttered tin.

454. CHESTNUTS (*MARRONS GLACÉS*), No. 2

Take large sound nuts; shell, and blanch them in boiling water until a needle will go into them easily. Take off the skin, and place each nut in warm water with a little lemon-juice. Have ready a plain syrup made with two parts sugar to one of water. Drain the chestnuts, and put them into the syrup; let them boil very slowly till they are quite tender, but not broken. Remove and drain them on a sieve; boil the syrup to " crack," and let it grow nearly cold. Dip in the chestnuts one by one on a long packing-needle. Let them become thoroughly coated, and dry them off in the oven or on the rack.

455. CHESTNUTS (*MARRONS GLACÉS*), No. 3

Prepare the chestnuts by slitting each across one side with a sharp knife, plunging for a minute in boiling water, draining and drying. To each pint of nuts add one teaspoonful of butter, and shake them about over the fire for four or five minutes; you will then find the shell and skin come off easily together. Dry them, and dip them, one

by one, on a skewer, in sugar boiled to 310° F.
Remove and place them on buttered paper to cool.
Do not let the syrup exceed above weight ; take it
off the fire and stand it in a vessel of hot water.

456. CRYSTALLISED ORANGES AND GRAPES

Take some tangerine oranges, peel, and divide
them into sections, very carefully so as not to break
the skins ; leave them in a warm room for many
hours, to become thoroughly dry.   Take some sound
ripe grapes, and separate them, also with great
care not to break the skin, cutting the stems so
as to leave a small stalk to each grape ; wipe them
very dry with a clean soft rag.   Take one pound of
granulated cane sugar, and a quarter of a pint of
hot water, and make a syrup, which must be boiled
to "crack," *i.e.* when it will snap and crack like
glass if dropped into cold water (300° F. on sugar
thermometer).   Then place the syrup-pan in a
larger pan full of hot water, and drop the fruits in,
one at a time.   In lifting them out, be most careful
not to break the skins.   The grapes can be taken
by their stalks, with scissors or tweezers ; the oranges
with an oiled fork.   Place them separately on oiled
paper ; and when they are quite hard and cold, it
is advisable, but not actually necessary, to make
a fresh syrup and give them a second coating.

BRANDIED FRUIT

Note.—This is a *recherché* and expensive method
of preserving ; for certain purposes, however,
brandied fruits are invaluable.   There are three

chief methods : (1) Bottle the cooked fruit in
syrup (as per Chapter IV), and add brandy to
taste ; (2) bottle the fruit dry, uncooked, with
layers of sugar, and fill up with brandy ; (3) bottle
the prepared fruit with brandy only, and cork up
for a month ; then strain off the brandy, and for
each pint add four ounces of sugar candy, which
must be dissolved in the brandy ; strain liquor
through a jelly-bag and return to the bottled fruit.
The first and third of these are the best for keeping.
Other methods are indicated below.

457. BRANDIED CHERRIES, No. 1

White-heart cherries are most suitable for this.
Put them in deep jars and cover with brandy; leave
for two days. Then prepare a thick syrup; strain off
the brandy from the fruit, and measure it ; add an
equal quantity of boiling syrup to it, and strain it
over the cherries; let stand twelve hours, having
corked the bottles or jars. The following day, if
the syrup has shrunk, fill up with the rest of the
syrup and cover up.

458. BRANDIED CHERRIES, No. 2

Take five pounds of sound, fresh, sweet cherries ;
cut off half each stem with scissors ; place in a glass
jar ; fill up with brandy ; cork tightly, and put away
for three weeks. Then open ; add one pound of
castor sugar for every quart of brandy ; cork up
again ; shake smartly, and put away for two months
before using.

459. BRANDIED CHERRIES, No. 3

Take some fine, ripe, and large cherries; cut off half of the stalks, and put them into a large-mouthed bottle, with a few cloves and a little cinnamon. Prepare some very thick syrup, in the proportion of a quarter of a pound of sugar to one pound of cherries, and a quart of brandy; mix the brandy with the syrup, and when it is cold, pour it over the cherries; cork carefully, and tie over with parchment.

460. BRANDIED CHERRIES, No. 4

Take large, ripe, perfectly sound cherries; prick them with a darning-needle at the opposite side to the stalks (which can stay on); wash them in cold water, drain, wipe very gently in a folded cloth, and put into large sterilised glass jars. Have ready a rich syrup boiling (not less than four pounds of sugar to two pints of water), and pour it over them. Let stand overnight, then drain off and reboil the syrup; mix it with good brandy, in the proportion of one pint of syrup to two pints of brandy, and again pour over the cherries. Inside each jar, at the top, place, tied up in muslin, half an ounce each of coriander seeds and anise seeds, and half an ounce of cloves. Cork the jars closely, and let them stand in strong sunshine for a month; then take out the spices, recork, shake well so as to distribute the flavour of the spices, and store in a dry place.

461. BRANDIED CHERRIES, No. 5

Get some of the finest Morella cherries; cut the stalks and leaves from them about half an inch long, and put them into a glass jar; put ten ounces of powdered sugar to every quart of brandy; when the sugar is dissolved, pour it over the cherries, and cover close with bladder.

462. BRANDIED FIGS

Take about five pounds of fresh, ripe, green figs; shorten the stems by half; place them in a glass jar with one pound of sugar, and fill up with brandy; cork tightly; shake briskly, and put away for one month before using.

463. BRANDIED GRAPES

Take bunches of just-ripe grapes; carefully remove any unsound ones, and prick each remaining grape two or three times with a fine darning-needle. Take large jars, dust the inside bottom thickly with castor sugar, then fill up with alternate layers of grapes and sugar, nearly to the top of jars. Pour in brandy up to top, and cover at once.

464. BRANDIED GREENGAGES

Take six pounds of sound, fine greengages; wash and drain them; prick them with a darning-needle at the stalk side. Have ready boiling four pounds of sugar in half a pint of water; when it is clear, skim it, put in the fruit, let boil for ten minutes; then pour off all into a large earthen jar or pan, cover up closely, and leave for two days. The third day, drain off the syrup, and boil it up to "soft ball" (240°); take it from the fire and add three pints of brandy. Place the greengages neatly in large glass bottles, and fill right to the top with the brandied syrup. Cover immediately.

465. BRANDIED PEACHES, No. 1

Take eight pounds of peaches ; peel them carefully. Have ready a syrup of eight pounds of sugar and four pints of water. Let it boil eight minutes, then put in the peaches and boil for another five minutes. Remove the peaches and place in sterilised heated jars. Continue to boil the syrup. When it is thick, add two pints of brandy, and fill up the jars. Cover at once.

466. BRANDIED PEACHES, No. 2

Take five pounds of sound ripe peaches ; peel, halve, and remove stones ; place the fruit in a glass jar ; break the stones and add the kernels to the peaches ; add one pound of castor or crushed loaf sugar ; fill up with brandy ; cork tightly, shake well, and put away for thirty days before using.

467. BRANDIED PEARS

Peel, core, and weigh small pears ; allow pound for pound of sugar ; to every four pounds each of fruit and sugar allow one pint of brandy. Make a syrup in the proportion of four pounds of sugar to one quart of water ; boil, then simmer two minutes, and add the pears; boil all for five minutes; then place the pears in jars, and boil the syrup till it thickens. Put the brandy to it, take off at once; pour the syrup and brandy over the pears, and cover at once.

468. BRANDIED PLUMS

Take fully grown but under-ripe greengages; arrange them nicely in jars, and cover them with brandy. For each pint of brandy add two and a half ounces of granulated sugar; cover closely.

469. RASPBERRY ROYAL

Take four quarts of, very good, ripe red raspberries; pick off all stalks, and add one quart of cider vinegar and one pound of white sugar; crush and mix all into a paste, and place in hot sunshine for four hours; pulp through a sieve; add one pint of brandy, and bottle.

470. TUTTI-FRUTTI, OR RAW FRUIT COMPÔTE, No. 1

Take a large stoneware seven-pound jar, and put one pint of brandy into it; add a quart of any ripe fruit which is in season, with one pound of castor sugar to each quart. You can continue to add fruit and sugar in this proportion until the jar is full, only each time you must stir the mixture, right from the bottom, with a wooden spoon. Small fruits must be stalked and picked; apples, pears, plums, bananas, oranges, pineapples, and

peaches must be peeled, cored, and cut small. Of
course it is not necessary to add a quart of the
same kind of fruit—*i.e.* you could have half a quart
of raspberries and half of strawberries, etc. ; but
the more variety you put in the better. The jar
must be kept very closely covered, with a bladder
or otherwise.

The best fruits for the above purpose are red
currants, raspberries, strawberries, cherries, and
the large fruit mentioned above. Gooseberries are
not suitable.

471. TUTTI-FRUTTI, No. 2

Remove stalks from two pounds of strawberries
(only just ripe), and from two pounds of sound ripe
raspberries. Take two pounds of sweet cherries,
shorten the stems by half, and place the fruit in a
large jar in layers, in the following order : cherries
at the bottom, sprinkled with half a pound of
castor sugar ; strawberries over them with another
half-pound of sugar ; raspberries on top, with
another half-pound of sugar. Fill up with brandy ;
cork tightly ; put away, and do not use for thirty
days.

472. BRANDIED WALNUTS

Take rather under-ripe walnuts ; shell and peel
carefully, so as not to break, and plunge them
into cold water to blanch and harden them.
Have ready a pan of fast-boiling water ; put the
nuts in this, long enough to scald them, but not

long enough for the water to boil up again. Drain
them and replace in cold water, which, this second
time, should have some lemon-juice in, enough to
be perceptible to the taste. Have a syrup boiled
to " thread," and when you have drained the walnuts
again, put them in a vessel and pour the boiling
syrup on them, and let stand overnight. The
following day drain off and boil up the syrup to
the same point ; again pour it over the walnuts and
leave overnight. Repeat this a third day. After
the fourth night boil the syrup to a strong thread ;
put the nuts into another pan, and add to them
the syrup and an equal amount of brandy. Bring
to boiling-point, then pour into bottles or jars, and
cork up.

CHAPTER VIII

SPICED FRUITS

NOTE.—These are a sort of cross between preserves and pickles. They are not much known in Britain, but are gradually coming into favour. You might define them as pickles made with fruit (only they are not salt), or as jam made with vinegar. In any case, they are very nice and a welcome novelty; especially as they need but little sugar, and do not require first-class fruit. In many cases the fruit is employed whole.

Correctly speaking, the vinegar and sugar should first be boiled till the syrup thickens a little, the spices then added and mixed, and the fruit put in to simmer for two to three hours, then removed. Subsequently the syrup is boiled up and poured upon the fruit. According to some authorities, one boiling-up of the syrup is enough; according to others, it should be drained off, reboiled, and repoured nine days running. As I do not think any fruit is worth while making into a nine-days' wonder, I should suggest (if need be) a compromise, of three days' reboiling, as for many preserved fruits in syrup. But most people will probably content themselves with a one-day job.

It is best to tie up the respective spices in little

muslin bags, or all, well mixed, in one bag; but
when they are in a ground or powdered form, this
is not absolutely necessary.
The best white wine vinegar should be used.

473. SPICED APPLES, No. 1

Make a syrup with three to four pounds of sugar
and from a pint to a pint and a half of vinegar; when
it thickens, add two teaspoonfuls each of cinnamon,
cloves, and allspice (ginger may be added at discretion), and put in four pounds of apples, pared,
halved, and çored; let simmer gently till tender;
put into heated jars, and boil the syrup till quite
thick; fill up the jars with it, and cover at once.

474. SPICED APPLES, No. 2

Unripe and tasteless apples will serve for this.
Peel thinly and core; weigh eight pounds. Have
ready a boiling syrup made with four pounds of
sugar, half an ounce each of ground nutmeg and
cloves, one ounce of powdered cinnamon. Put in
the apples, and cook gently till they are tender
enough to pierce with a wooden splinter. Place
them in jars, pour the syrup over, and cover at
once.

475. SPICED APPLES, No. 3

Peel, core, and halve four pounds of apples. Have
ready a boiling syrup made with three pounds of
sugar, one quart of vinegar, and one teaspoonful
each of cinnamon, cloves, and allspice. Simmer

the fruit till tender, remove it into jars ; boil down
the syrup, and when it thickens, pour it over the
fruit, and cover up.

476. SPICED CRANBERRIES

Take one pint of vinegar, three pounds and a half
of Demerara sugar, one tablespoonful each of
(ground) cloves, cinnamon, and allspice ; mix well,
and let boil for twenty minutes ; add five pounds
of just-ripe cranberries, well picked, and let boil
gently for about two hours ; bottle at once.

477. SPICED CURRANTS

Take four pounds of sugar, one pint of vinegar,
one tablespoonful each of (ground) ginger, cinnamon, cloves, and allspice, one teaspoonful of salt ;
mix thoroughly, and boil for twenty minutes ; then
add five pounds of well-picked red currants, and
simmer slowly for about two hours and a half ;
bottle at once.

478. SPICED FIGS

Take two pounds of loose dried figs, steep them
overnight in cold water, and next day drain them.
Prepare the following : half a pint of vinegar and
twenty ounces of Demerara sugar, boiled till thick ;
add one tablespoonful each of (ground) cloves and
cinnamon, one teaspoonful each of (ground) mace
and allspice ; put in the figs ; simmer gently for an
hour and a quarter ; bottle and cover at once.

479. SPICED GRAPES, No. 1

Take sound grapes and skin them ; measure, and to every five quarts allow three pounds of Demerara sugar and half a pint of vinegar ; add one tablespoonful each of powdered cloves and mace with two tablespoonfuls of powdered cinnamon, and simmer gently, skins and all, for an hour and a half; rub the mixture through a sieve. Have ready the pulps, which must be seeded and boiled till tender in a quarter of a pint of vinegar ; mix thoroughly with the rest, and bottle at once.

480. SPICED GRAPES, No. 2

Take eight pounds of picked and washed grapes, and let boil fast in one quart of water for ten minutes, or until the grapes are soft enough to put through a sieve ; weigh the pulp, and add sugar in equal quantity if the grapes are green, or at the rate of three breakfastcupfuls to every four of pulp if for ripe grapes ; boil till quite thick ; then add one heaped teaspoonful each of ground ginger, cloves, nutmeg, and cinnamon ; let simmer and stir for a minute or two till the spices are well blended ; then pour into pots, and cover.

481. SPICED MELONS

Citron melons not too ripe should be selected. Peel, slice, and seed them, leaving only the firm flesh ; cut into pieces of required size, and place in large jars. Make a syrup in the following proportions : to one pound and a half of sugar add

one pint and a half of vinegar, one teaspoonful each
of ground cloves, ginger, and cinnamon, half a teaspoonful of white pepper, one grated lemon-rind.
Boil, let cool, and pour over fruit in jars. Leave
for twenty-four hours; drain off syrup, reboil it
(adding more sugar if need be) till it thickens; pour
back on fruit. Repeat three or four times.

482. SPICED PEACHES

Take seven pounds of peaches just ripe; you can
halve and stone them at discretion—some people
prefer them peeled only. Put into a pan three
pounds of sugar, one pint of vinegar, half an ounce
of ground cloves and allspice, two ounces of powdered cinnamon. Bring just to the boil; then pour
over the peaches in an earthen pan. Let stand for
twenty-four hours, then drain off the liquid; bring
it again to boiling-point, pour over the peaches, and
again leave overnight. The third day place all
in the preserving-pan, and let boil until the peaches
are tender, but not broken. Remove the fruit into
large jars; boil down the syrup till it thickens, fill
up the jars with it, and cover at once.

483. SPICED PEARS, No. 1

Take one pint of wine or cider vinegar, three
pounds of sugar, and one teaspoonful each of
ginger, cloves, and cinnamon; boil up all these
together. Have ready six pounds of peeled pears
(smallish) and add them gradually to syrup; let
simmer till tender; remove pears carefully to an

earthen pan; pour the syrup over them; leave for three days; then drain off and boil up the syrup, place the pears in jars, and fill up with the syrup; cover at once.

484. SPICED PEARS, No. 2

Take nine pounds of just-ripe pears; peel thinly, halve, and core them; rinse quickly in cold water. Have ready a boiling syrup, made with three pounds of sugar, one quart of vinegar, one grated lemon-rind, a quarter of an ounce of cinnamon. Place the pears in it, and boil till tender, but not broken. Remove them carefully into jars with a skimmer, and place the flat sides downwards. Pour the syrup over them, leave overnight; next day drain off and boil up syrup, pour it back over pears; the third day let the syrup reduce and thicken before you finally pour it back into the jars. Cover at once.

485. SPICED PLUMS

The fruit for this should be fresh, ripe, and sweet. Place some of it in enough water to cover it, and simmer slowly till it is reduced to a pulp. Strain, and to a quart of the juice add one pint of vinegar, one pound of sugar, one teaspoonful of allspice, and half a teaspoonful each of powdered cinnamon, cloves, and mace. Boil for half an hour. Have ready the rest of the plums, each well pricked with a darning-needle, in large heated jars. Pour the boiling syrup over them, cover them (but not finally), and leave overnight. Next day drain off and reheat the syrup, pour it back upon the plums, and let stand for twelve hours. The third time boil down the syrup to half, and fill jars. Cover at once. The fruit juice in above may be replaced by more vinegar, but the result will be nothing like so good.

486. SPICED QUINCES

Take seven pounds of quinces ; peel and core, but do not slice them. Have ready boiling a syrup made with four pounds of sugar and one pint of vinegar, seasoned with the following : two teaspoonfuls each of ground cinnamon and allspice ; one teaspoonful each of ground cloves and ground ginger ; half a teaspoonful of powdered mace (all well mixed before putting in). Add the quinces, let boil, and pour off all into earthen jar. Proceed next day and subsequently as for spiced peaches ; but some people continue to boil the syrup and pour it over the fruit for nine days running. I imagine that three to five days would be ample for the purpose.

487. SPICED RHUBARB, No. 1

Take five quarts of rhubarb (washed, peeled, and sliced rather small), and let simmer till quite tender in as little water as possible ; add one pint of vinegar, one pound of Demerara sugar, one teaspoonful of each of ground allspice, ginger, cloves, cinnamon, and salt, and half a teaspoonful of nutmeg (grated) ; mix thoroughly and boil till thick,

stirring now and then ; pour off and cover at once.
[It might be as well to boil the vinegar, sugar, and
spices separately, as in other recipes. It would
certainly save time subsequently.—*Ed.*]

488. SPICED RHUBARB, No. 2

Take six pounds of rhubarb, wipe, and cut into
one-inch pieces ; place it in an earthen pan, with
one pound and a half of sugar. Allow one quart
of vinegar, and one teaspoonful each of ground allspice, cloves, cinnamon, and ginger ; boil up together and pour off upon the fruit and sugar. Let
stand twenty-four hours ; strain off the liquor, boil
up for five minutes, and set aside. Next day, boil
up the liquor for ten minutes, and add the rhubarb
to it ; let simmer till quite tender, but do not
allow to boil ; pour off when cold.

CHAPTER IX

VARIOUS

NOTE.—In this section will be found such preserves as cannot well be classed with the others, but are useful and unusual. They make a pleasing variety from the more well-known fruit jams and jellies; and as "variety is the salt of life," they can be recommended to anybody in search of something at once nice and new.

489. ANGELICA PRESERVED IN SYRUP

Cut the stalks of the angelica about a foot long; put them in a pan of water and boil them till they are quite salt; then string the outsides of them, and put them into a tub of cold water, till they are all done; drain all the water off; lay them in an earthen pan till it is three parts full; pour some boiling syrup over them and fill the pan with it, always keeping the angelica covered with syrup, and let it stand till next day; drain the syrup from the angelica without disturbing it; boil the syrup, and put it to the angelica. Do this for several days successively, and bottle.

490. CARROT JAM

Take six breakfastcupfuls of grated carrots
which have been well washed and scraped ; add an
equal amount of sugar, the grated rind of two lemons,
and the juice of six, also the juice of two oranges ;
mix thoroughly ; place in preserving-pan, and simmer
slowly till the jam thickens and sets—say two hours
and a half.

491. CELERY PRESERVED IN IMITATION OF GINGER

Cut the blanched part of the celery in pieces,
and boil it in water with a large quantity of ginger
until it is quite tender; then throw it into cold
water and allow it to remain an hour. At the end
of this time put it over a slow fire in good syrup,
with some pieces of ginger, and let it remain simmering for an hour. Cool it again, and in the
meantime thicken the syrup by further evapora-
tion. Put the celery in again, and repeat the same
process. After a third simmering in this way,
taking care to keep the syrup thick, put the celery
into pots, and cover with a syrup. The stalks of
lettuce, taking off the outside, may be prepared in
the same way.

492. CHESTNUT JAM

Take four pounds of Spanish chestnuts ; make a
small incision in each, and boil till tender ; peel
them, put through a sieve, weigh, and allow pound
for pound of crushed or powdered sugar ; put all

into preserving-pan; flavour to taste with essence
of vanilla; simmer slowly for forty-five minutes,
stirring continually; put into pots, and let cool
before covering.

COCOANUT

NOTE.—This unparalleled nut has its name spelt
in three different ways, "and every single one of
them is right." (1) As above, the same as cocoa
the powdered bean, which itself is a corruption of
cacao (Spanish, from the Mexican *caca-natl*, cocoa-
tree). (2) Coco, from the Spanish word signify-
ing a grimace; the reason for this nomenclature
is not evident. (3) Coker; this is the usual commercial term, employed to avoid confusion with
cocoa the powdered bean.

Only those who can eat the cocoanut in its native
air are really aware of its virtues, when the half-
ripe kernel can be eaten with a spoon, and the milk
is transparent and refreshing. By the time it is in
our hands, the kernel is very hard, the milk opaque
and not too attractive except to children. The
only form in which we can well preserve it, therefore, is in cocoanut candy and similar sweetmeats;
but the following recipe presents an alternative
method.

493. COCOANUT JAM

Take four good-sized shelled cocoanuts; grate the
" meat," and put it into a pan with the cocoanut
milk and a breakfastcupful of cold water. Let
cook till quite tender. Have ready in another pan

one pound of sugar and two breakfastcupfuls of water, with a teaspoonful of salt. Let boil for five or six minutes, then put it to the cocoanut. Let all cook gently for about an hour, then pour off into jars, and cover.

HAWTHORN

NOTE.—The large variety of lovely berries, which are borne by the different species of thorn or Cratægus, and which are of the apple type (and hence of the vast Rose family), are nearly all edible in some form or other; and, as such, they are employed in countries less wasteful than our own. Owing to the extraordinary neglect of them in this kingdom, I have only been able to obtain one recipe : for jelly made from ordinary wild " haws." It is probable that these might be also successfully treated like wild-rose hips (which see). The service-berry, which grows in our gardens, is also used extensively abroad ; and a variety of it, the sorb, is said to be a regular commodity in the London market, forwarded from English country towns ; but I am not able to confirm this statement.

494. HAWTHORN JELLY

Take ripe red hawthorn berries; pick off the stalks ; wash and put them in preserving-pan with about a breakfastcupful of cold water to every two pounds of berries; let simmer till they are quite soft, mashing the fruit occasionally with a wooden spoon ; strain through a jelly-bag, but do not

squeeze; measure fruit, and return to pan and boil
up; add one pound of sugar to every pint, and boil
until the jelly sets.

GINGER

NOTE.—It is the root, not the fruit, of the ginger
plant, *Zingiber officinalis*, which is used for culinary
or medicinal purposes. What one usually buys is
the dried root, which has been dug when about a
year old and prepared for market—often losing half
its goodness *en route* between the ground and the
grocer, by methods which it were unkind to mention. But the young, green, tender roots are also
procurable; and these are what one should take for
preserving or candying. They are exceedingly
delectable when so dealt with; and (to most people)
extremely comforting and wholesome. Ever since
the spacious days of great Elizabeth we have employed that ginger which is "hot i' the mouth.'
Ginger, however, is chiefly used for preserves in
conjunction with some fruit ingredient.

495. GINGER CONSERVE

Make a syrup with two pounds of sugar and one
pint of water. Boil till it reaches "thread." Have
ready half a pound of green ginger root, which has
been cut small, boiled for an hour in water to cover
it, and drained. Put this in a separate pan, pour
over it syrup to cover it, and simmer for an hour
and a half. Remove and drain; let grow cold;
dust with powdered sugar. Put it into the syrup

again ; let cool again ; thoroughly coat with sugar,
and pack, in sugar, in pots or jars.

496. GINGER MARMALADE, No. 1

Two pounds of crystallised ginger, one teaspoonful of ground ginger, four pounds of preserving
sugar, three pints of water. Having boiled the
sugar and water to a syrup, add the ground ginger,
and the other ginger cut into very small pieces ;
let the whole boil until it will " set " upon a cold
slab or plate.

497. GINGER MARMALADE, No. 2

Make a syrup with two pounds of sugar and one
pint and a half of water. When it is boiling fast,
add half a teaspoonful of ground ginger, and one
pound of crystallised ginger cut up very small ;
boil till the marmalade will set.

498. GINGER PRESERVED

Take some young green roots, scrape and weigh
them ; weigh pound for pound of sugar. Boil the
ginger till it is tender enough to be pierced with a
splinter ; boil the sugar separately (adding to each
pound half a pint of water and half a teaspoonful of
cream of tartar) till it becomes a syrup : it must
be skimmed while boiling. Now put the ginger
into the syrup, and let it well boil up ; put it in jars
and cover them. To flavour the above, you can
add the thinly-pared rind and juice of one lemon

to every three pounds of ginger. For each additional half-pint of lemon juice, add half a pound more sugar.

ROSE

NOTE.—The queen of flowers is liberally invoked for a culinary purpose in Eastern countries. Here we have forgotten most of its old usages in this respect, and crystallised rose-petals represent, as a rule, our sum-total. But while the garden rose should never be allowed to shed its leaves, " angry and brave," when sweet and pleasant preparations can be so easily made from them; neither should the wild or dog-rose's millions of edible berries be left to rot upon the bough. Not now can it be said of rose-hips that " cookes and gentlewomen make tartes and such-like dishes for pleasure thereof." The bristly silk in which the seeds are wrapped is curiously irritant both to fingers and throat; therefore, in making conserve of rose-hips (a very popular thing in continental market-places), it is advisable to remove this silk before cooking—a somewhat tedious operation—and to pulp the berries, when soft, through a fine sieve.

Dark-red garden roses—sweet-scented—are the best for preserving in any form, especially as regards the petals. I do not know if experiment has been made with the huge apple-like hips of the Rugosas or Japanese roses ; they should be well worth while to attempt.

Medicinally speaking, the rose has a remarkable and a unique value. But for " pleasant meates and

banketting dishes " the rose-fruit, beaten up with
sugar, was long esteemed superlatively choice.
And when you reflect that the rose is the original
parent, so to speak, of nearly every fruit that grows
in Britain, as has been frequently stated before in
this book, it seems exceedingly odd that we ignore
it so much at present; apples, pears, quinces,
medlars, plums, peaches, apricots, nectarines,
almonds, cherries, strawberries, raspberries, blackberries, dewberries, being all derivative from or
relative to the Rose tribe! The commingled beauty
and utility, in leafage, blossom, and fruit, which
are combined in the uncountable members of the
Rosaceœ, present a theme for much surprise and
admiration.

499. RED ROSE CONSERVE, No. 1

Take some fresh, sweet, dark-red rose-petals;
weigh; plunge a moment into boiling water; drain
and dry; pound in a mortar; and place in a pan with
sugar, one pound to every eight ounces of petals. Let
cook very slowly till the roses have absorbed all moisture from the sugar; then add a little good rose-
water, enough to moisten the conserve so that it
will pour out upon a large flat dish; let it become
thoroughly dry (in the sun if possible); cut it into
strips, and keep in papered tins in a dry place.

500. RED ROSE CONSERVE, No. 2

Take one pound of red-rose petals of the sweet-
scented kind; dry them out of the sun; plunge them
in boiling water just for a moment or two; drain

and dry them. Have ready a syrup made with
one pound of fine white sugar and a very little
rose-water; add one teaspoonful of orange flowers,
put in the rose-leaves, and let simmer till the preserve is quite soft and thick.

501. RED ROSE CONSERVE, No. 3

Gather roses in full bloom, pull out the petals, and
dry them on a tray, but not in full sun; place in
an enamelled pan, with only just enough water to
cover them; cover and let simmer gently till
tender, when add pound for pound of sugar, and
boil slowly till the whole is a thick syrup.

502. RED ROSE CONSERVE, No. 4 (Seventeenth Century)

Take a quart of red rose-water, and a quart of
fair (fresh) water, and boil in it a pound of red
rose-leaves, the whites cut off. The leaves must
be boiled very tender. Then take three pounds of
sugar, and put it to the roses, a pound at a time,
and let it boil a little between every pound; and
so put it up in your pots.

503. RED ROSE CONSERVE, No. 5

Spread the rose-leaves on a tray to dry (out of
the sun), and when they are dried, weigh two pounds
of them. Wash them quickly in boiling water,
drain and dry them. Have ready a syrup, made
with two pounds of loaf sugar and a very little water;
put in the rose-leaves, with six teaspoonfuls of
orange-flower water; stir, and simmer till the conserve thickens.

504. RED ROSE LOZENGES (Seventeenth Century)

(Proportions not given.)   Boil your sugar to sugar again (*i.e.* till it candies) ; then put in your red roses, being finely beaten and made moist with the juice of a lemon.   Let it not boil after the roses are in, but pour it upon a pie plate and cut it into what form you please.

505. ROSE-HIP JELLY, No. 1

Take a large quantity of well-ripened rose-hips ; wash them in a colander and dry them.   Slit them lengthwise; remove the hairs and pips with a sharp penknife ;   weigh the fruit, and place in a pan with enough water to float it, and a pint of sugar to every pint of fruit.   Boil all together till quite soft, and strain off the liquor, which must be boiled up again for a few minutes and then poured into pots.

506. ROSE-HIP JELLY, No. 2

Proceed as above, but, having prepared the fruit, cook it till tender in a very little water, then strain off the juice and measure it, as for other jellies. Boil it up again for ten minutes, add one pint of warmed sugar for every pint of juice, and cook until the jelly sets.

507. ROSE-HIP MARMALADE, No. 1

Take ripe wild-rose hips, cut off the tops, slit them down, and carefully remove all seeds and hairs (it is well to wear gloves while doing this, as the hairs get under the nails and are curiously irritating). Then boil down the berries in a preserving-pan, with as little water as possible; and when they are quite tender, pulp them through a sieve; add sugar, the proportion being at least three-quarters of a pound to each pound of pulped berries, and let the mixture boil up quickly till the sugar is dissolved; then remove it from the fire and bottle it as soon as coolish.

508. ROSE-HIP MARMALADE, No. 2

To every pound of ripe rose-hips, add half a pint of water, and simmer together in a preserving-pan. When thoroughly soft, pulp them through a fine sieve, so that the seeds are kept back; weigh the pulp; add pound for pound of sugar, and boil until it sets—about half an hour.

509. ROSE-HIP MARMALADE, No. 3

Prepare some ripe rose-hips by washing, drying, slitting open lengthways, and taking out the pips and small hairs; weigh the rest; place in a preserving-pan, just barely covered with water; cover up and cook slowly till tender. Add an equal weight of vegetable-marrow chopped very small, and sugar equal, or almost equal, to the weight of both together—i.e. for four pounds of rose-hips and four pounds of marrow, seven pounds of sugar would be ample. Boil for half an hour.

510. ROSE LEAVES CRYSTALLISED

Take two pounds of freshly gathered red rose-petals (picked off separately); rinse in cold water

and place on clean paper to dry, out of the sun.
Make a syrup with one pint of water and two pounds
of loaf sugar. Stir till the sugar is thoroughly
dissolved, add a pinch of cream of tartar, and let
boil to " soft ball " (or 240° by sugar thermometer).
Take the pan from the fire, and put in the rose-
leaves, pushing them right under the syrup. Boil
up, and immediately pour off upon a cold dish.
Leave overnight, and next day drain the rose-leaves
on a sieve, and boil up the syrup again, with half a
pound more sugar. Cook to the " soft ball " stage
again, but do not stir it. Put in the flowers, and
lift the pan off ; let stand overnight. The following
day repeat the process of draining, heating syrup
(to boiling-point this time), and replacing flowers in
it. Lift off the pan and continue to stir gently.
When the syrup " grains," pour it off upon white
paper, separate the petals, and let dry ; they can
then be removed from the sugar.

511. PARSLEY JELLY, No. 1

Take at least two pounds of freshly gathered
parsley ; wash well ; place in preserving-pan covered
with cold water, and simmer for at least thirty
minutes ; strain twice ; measure the juice, and add
one pound of sugar for each pint. Boil up the juice
again, add the sugar, stir well while it is dissolving ;
then boil fast for twenty to twenty-five minutes, or
until the jelly sets.

512. PARSLEY JELLY, No. 2

Take fresh parsley in large quantity ; wash it,
and place in preserving-pan, covering it with water

and pressing it well down. Let boil slowly for not
less than half an hour ; strain twice through a muslin,
measure, and for each pint allow twelve ounces of
sugar. Put the sugar to warm in the oven, while
the juice is boiled up for twenty minutes. Stir in
the sugar, and when it is quite dissolved, boil up
for ten minutes.

513. POTATO JELLY

Peel, slice small, and weigh some sound potatoes ;
allow pound for pound of sugar. Make a strong
syrup with the sugar and as little water as possible ;
when it boils, add the potatoes ; continue to boil
until all the moisture has evaporated, and the jelly
is smooth and thick.

CHAPTER X

FRUITS BOTTLED WITHOUT SUGAR

NOTE.—This is a most important province of preserving—from an economical view, *the* most important. It provides practically fresh fruit against
the days of dearth; it entails not much more trouble
than the ordinary methods of jam-making; and it
supplies a means to "rescue the perishing," which
often, for want of sugar, money, or enterprise, are
left to rot upon the trees. I sincerely commend the
methods following to all country-people with plenty
of fruit. And especially as regards apples. I wish
to reiterate the statement before made, that no apple
need ever go to waste : it can be dried, if not bottled,
and you will prize in March what you disdained in
October.

The purchases of a sterilising apparatus (for
bottling), and of an evaporator (for drying)—even
small ones—will pay for themselves the first year.
Where several neighbours combine to procure and
use these, and so larger ones can be afforded, the
saving in fruit will be incalculable. I have said
this before in Chapter I, but it is so novel a
proposition to most people that it cannot be said
too often.

Much of the following advice is adapted from

the excellent leaflets on the subject published by the experts of the Board of Agriculture.

I would call special attention to the making of fruit pulp. This, if properly prepared, can be used at any time for the basis of jam (inordinate quantities of foreign fruit pulp are imported for that purpose), or for other culinary purposes. It is so cheap, so easy, and so obvious a means of saving fruit, that we have literally no excuse for neglecting it.

For fruit-bottling, it is absolutely essential that the bottles should be air-tight. If rubber rings are used, they must fit perfectly; so must the screw top, glass top, spring-clip top, or whatever is used. White rubber is not so good as black, which is more durable. New rubbers must be used every season, and must be boiled for at least twenty minutes before you use them.

For simple, ordinary use many people proceed as follows: Choose dry, firm fruit, not too ripe. Fill your bottles up to the neck with it; wrap each bottle in several thicknesses of newspaper, and stand them in a large fish-kettle, which should have a thick layer of hay or paper at bottom. Fill the kettle with cold water up to the necks of bottles, set it on the fire, and let it come *very gradually* to the boil. When it boils, fill each bottle separately with boiling water from a kettle. Remove each bottle one at a time, and tie it down with bladder *while still at boiling-point*: this is essential. Three-pound glass jam-jars, or sweet-bottles, do very well for this. It is most important not to hurry the boiling, as the bottles may crack.

Melted fat or oil may be poured on, instead of the
bladder cover, but does not always answer. Patent
screw-top bottles are very good; but the above
method is extremely simple and successful. Plums,
apples, currants, blackberries, damsons, or indeed
any fruit large or small, may be preserved as above.

Various other simple methods are stated below.
But if you do not want to take any risks, and wish
to make absolutely certain of your bottled fruit
turning out all right, it is best to procure a proper
sterilising apparatus and outfit. This can be
obtained from about £1 5s., while air-tight quart
bottles cost about 4s. a dozen (normal prices).

If apples and pears are peeled and quartered
before being bottled (in water), it is well to drop each
piece into cold water, as it is cut, or it will quickly
become discoloured.

Gooseberries should be topped-and-tailed;
rhubarb peeled and cut into pieces of equal size;
currants picked carefully from the stalks; cherries
stalked; raspberries hulled; damsons, greengages,
and plums stalked; very large plums halved;
peaches and nectarines skinned, stoned, and halved.

The fruit should be gently pressed into position
in regular layers. A little shaking is necessary for
soft fruits like gooseberries and currants. Rhubarb
should be placed, if possible, in upright rows.

If bubbles should appear in a bottle during the
process of sterilisation (while it stands in the slowly
boiling water), air must have got in somehow, and
that bottle is no good. Refill it with water, and see
if the stopper or cover is all right : another may be
required.

The following formulas should be very closely studied, and in particular the fact that the water in which the bottles are placed must be brought to boiling-point very, very slowly. It cannot be done too slowly : it should take one and a half to two hours. 160° F. is the ideal temperature to attain ; but anywhere between 150° and 180° will suffice.

514. TO BOTTLE FRUIT WITHOUT SUGAR, No. 1

Stone fruit of any kind may be preserved whole as follows : Take perfectly sound fruit, unblemished and unbroken ; pack it in wide-mouthed bottles, which must be absolutely clean and dry. Fill the bottles with fruit nearly up to the neck ; then pour in boiling water, which must reach to an inch above the fruit. On the top of this pour in melted mutton suet an inch deep, and cover the whole tightly with brown paper.

515. TO BOTTLE FRUIT WITHOUT SUGAR, No. 2

Plums, damsons, cherries, and similar fruits are the best for this method. They must be absolutely sound and unbroken, and not soft or over-ripe.

Have wide-mouthed bottles, which must be perfectly clean and dry, with soft new corks. Take each bottle separately ; have the fruit ready to hand. Light a wax match or gas taper, and hold it burning in the bottle for a few seconds—this will exhaust the air ; then, as quickly as you possibly can, pack in the fruit, cork the bottle, and go on with the next. Having filled and corked all as above described, place them in a very cool oven for six

hours or more. When the fruit has shrunk down
by about a quarter, take out the bottles, firmly press
down the corks, cover them with hot sealing-wax,
and put away in a cool dry place.

516. TO BOTTLE FRUIT WITHOUT SUGAR, No. 3

Choose sound ripe fruit; arrange it carefully in
wide-mouthed bottles. Moisten some bladder in
warm water (do not let it get wet at both sides) and
tie up each bottle-mouth, moist side outwards,
using fine twine very firmly tied. On no account
open the bottles again. Stand them in pots and
pans of cold water with straw, hay, grass, or folds
of newspaper underneath and between them. Let
stand on the hot stove till the juice has run sufficiently to cover the top layer of fruit; then remove
from the water, tie an extra string round each
bladder, and, when the bottles are cold, store in a
dry place. This is an excellent method for retaining
the full flavour of the fresh fruit. Of course it will
sink considerably in the bottle, so pack it as fully
as possible to begin with.

517. FRUIT PULP, No. 1

Take sound, ripe fruit, gathered in dry weather;
stalk, stone, or top-and-tail it; remove skins if
large fruit; pass it through a clean, dry sieve; put
it into well-sterilised, dry bottles, and cork tightly;
cover the bottles with bladder, set them in a pan of
cold water, and let it come slowly to the boil; let
boil twenty minutes, then remove pan from stove,

but leave the bottles in it overnight. The following day, take them out, wipe, and keep in a dry cupboard.

518. FRUIT PULP, No. 2

Any kind of fruit may be preserved this way, almost indefinitely, so long as it is gathered on a dry day, and is perfectly sound and not over-ripe, and all the utensils employed are absolutely clean.

Rub the fruit (having wiped it clean) through a fine sieve, and place the pulp in wide-mouthed bottles which have been thoroughly scalded, dried, and allowed to get quite cold. Cork tightly and cover with bladder. Place the bottles in a fish-kettle, with cold water up to their shoulders. Let the water heat very gradually till it boils ; then let boil for twenty minutes, without cessation. Remove pan from fire, leave bottles in it overnight, and the following day wipe the bottles dry and put them away in a dry place. Fruit pulp made as above can be kept until it is wanted for any cooking purpose ; or it can be made into jam when convenient, as follows : weigh the pulp, place in a pan, and bring to boiling-point; add equal weight of cooked syrup, also boiling. Then boil both together for twenty-five or thirty minutes ; this will ensure a better and a better-keeping jam than if sugar were added to the pulp.

519. BOTTLED RHUBARB

Take fresh red rhubarb ; wash, string, and cut it into even pieces, not more than two inches long.

Arrange it firmly in glass jars, fix rubber rings in the necks, and place each jar under the cold water tap. Let the water go on running hard into it for twenty minutes, then remove it (it must be quite full of water), and put the top on at once. Screw tightly.

Another method is to stand the jars, filled with the rhubarb, in a pan of warm water, and pour boiling water into them. When full, cover up and leave for ten minutes ; then drain off the water, refill with boiling water, and screw the lid on at once.

CHAPTER XI

DRIED FRUITS, WITH AND WITHOUT SUGAR

NOTE.—In this climate it is not easy to dry fruits in the sun, which is undoubtedly the best and most natural method. They must be either dried by absorption of the juice, aided by heat and sugar ; or by a very slow process, in cool ovens, or other similar places, on shallow trays, without sugar ; or sliced and strung, like apples.

A better flavour is obtained by sun-drying ; but a better colour is obtained by rapid artificial drying. Sun-dried fruit must be taken indoors the moment that the sun goes off it.

I have placed the sugared fruits first, but those dried or evaporated without sugar will be found infinitely more important.

FRUITS DRIED WITH SUGAR

520. GENERAL RULE FOR FRUITS SUN-DRIED WITH SUGAR

Allow one pint of crushed or powdered sugar to every pound of fruit, picked free of stalks. Place the fruit on large shallow dishes overnight, sprinkled with sufficient sugar to cover it; put a small quantity of water with the rest of the sugar, just enough to dissolve it slowly. Next morning put on the sugar and water to boil up, and then boil the fruit in it for ten minutes. Remove and drain the fruit; boil down the syrup till it thickens, put back the fruit in it, and let it stand for half an hour at the side of the range, simmering slowly. Then skim out the fruit, lay it on buttered dishes, and stand it in strong sunlight till perfectly dry.

The above method is best suited for raspberries, cherries, and other small fruit; but apples, pears, and peaches may be used in the same way.

521. CHERRIES DRIED WITH SUGAR, No. 1

Take sound, ripe cherries; stone, weigh, and place in preserving-pan, with six ounces of castor sugar to every pound of fruit; let simmer slowly over the fire for twenty minutes, or until the juice is well absorbed; remove from fire, but leave in pan till slightly cool; place in a large dish and dry slowly.

522. CHERRIES DRIED WITH SUGAR, No. 2

Stew some cooking cherries with a little sugar, but no water; put them to dry in plates in a slow oven. Boil down the syrup, and pour it over the cherries when they are dry; return them again to oven, and when dry, pour a little more syrup over, and dry again. Repeat this process every day till no syrup is left.

523. CHERRIES DRIED WITH SUGAR, No. 3

Stone the cherries, crushing them as little as possible, and having made some very strong syrup, give them one boil in it; then take them off the fire, and let them stand for several hours. Repeat this process twice, then take out the cherries, powder them with white sugar, and put them on a tin, or on plates, to dry. When dry, put in boxes. The syrup may be used for making cherry jelly, or for fruit tarts.

524. CURRANTS DRIED WITH SUGAR

The currants should be not quite ripe, though on the verge of ripeness. Simmer them with a little sugar, but if possible do not let them break. Lay them on plates, thickly dusted with sugar, and let dry in the sun. To be cooked, they should be soaked overnight in a little water, and stewed in the same water.

525. MELONS DRIED WITH SUGAR

Take just-ripe citron melons; peel, quarter, and core them; slice them into pieces the size and shape required. Weigh, and allow twelve ounces of sugar to every pound of fruit; put all together in a deep jar overnight, with a weight on top sufficient to help press out the juice. Next day drain off all liquid, bring it to boiling-point, and let boil for five minutes. Put in the fruit, with grated lemon-peel and a little root ginger to taste. Simmer till the syrup becomes very thick and the fruit transparent.

Place on buttered dishes, and let stand for three days running in hot sunlight. Store in wide glass jars, tightly corked.

526. MULBERRIES DRIED WITH SUGAR

Gather them when not quite ripe, and give them a boil in syrup; then let them stand for twenty-four hours near the fire, so as just to keep warm; at the end of this time take them out, drain them, and put them upon tins, powdering them well with fine sugar, and exposing them to the sun; when they are dry on one side, turn them, powder them in the same way, and finish the drying.

527. PEACHES DRIED WITH SUGAR

Take ripe peaches; peel and slice thinly, lay out on dishes, sprinkle with granulated sugar, and place in a moderate oven till the fruit is thoroughly heated and has absorbed the sugar. Subsequently let the peaches become slowly dried in a coolish oven or in the sun.

528. PEARS DRIED WITH SUGAR

Put the fruit whole into an earthen jar, with two pounds of sugar to a peck of pears; put *no* water, but lay the parings on top of the fruit; cover and tie up the jar closely, and set it in the oven, at a temperature that would suffice for baking bread. When the pears are thoroughly baked, lay them in a clean dripping-pan, flattening them down a little; and put them thus into a slow oven every day until they are thoroughly dry.

529. PLUMS DRIED WITH SUGAR

Take sweet plums, open them, but leave the stones in; spread them on plates and sprinkle them thickly with sugar; put them in a slow oven till all the sugar is absorbed; sprinkle more, and continue the process as long as the plums will absorb it; then place in large jars, and cover tightly.

530. PINEAPPLES DRIED WITH SUGAR

Take sound pineapples; thinly slice them, peel, and remove the " eyes." Spread the slices on dishes, thickly covered with powdered sugar, and place in a slow oven. They must be kept there, and turned every day for ten days; then put them into a sharp oven for ten minutes, no more; take them out, let cool, and place between layers of wax paper, strewing them well with fine powdered sugar.

531. POWDERED DRIED FRUIT

Take any kind of fruit: if small fruit, remove stalks, tops-and-tails, etc.; if stone fruit, remove stones. Mash and crush in a bowl, until the juice is completely out; strain the juice through a sieve (it can be squeezed a little), and for every cupful of juice allow five cupfuls of castor sugar; mix thoroughly, till the juice is quite absorbed into a sugary paste; let dry very slowly in the oven; crush into powder, and place in thoroughly sterilised and dry bottles; cork tightly.

532. TO SUGAR ANY SORT OF SMALL FRUIT
(Seventeenth Century)

Beat the white of an egg, and dip the fruit in it;
let it lie on a dry cloth. Take some fine sifted sugar
and gently roll the fruit in it till it is quite covered
and coated with sugar. Lay it in a sieve on the
stove, or before a fire, to dry it well; it will keep
well for a week.

FRUITS DRIED WITHOUT SUGAR

NOTE.—It is hardly necessary to remind the
reader what an immense amount of these are
exported into Britain, especially in the shape of
dried apples, pears, plums (prunes), peaches, and
apricots. Why we let our own fruit (much better
fruit) go to waste, and buy the inferior article from
overseas, is " one of those things no fellah can
understand." There are many ways of drying our
own fruit, for where there's a will there's a way; but
undoubtedly the quickest and simplest, and therefore cheapest method in the long run, is to purchase
an evaporator, costing from 30s. to £3, for use on an
ordinary kitchen stove; or a large one with inde-
pendent stove, costing from £4 to £20. By this
means you can desiccate and save, not only apples,
pears, peaches, apricots, plums, damsons, cherries,
etc., but a number of most valuable vegetables.

A special apparatus for prune-making can also be
had, for use in an ordinary oven, by means of which
plums can be economically preserved instead of
rotting by tons on the trees.

Apples, pears, etc., should be prepared by washing, drying, and thinly peeling. For sun-drying (which, as before observed, is difficult in this country) spread the fruit on wooden trays, or as indicated below ; if to be dried over the fire or in an oven, spread on wire racks. Store in a dry place, in boxes or muslin bags.

533. DRIED APPLES, No. 1

Tart cooking-apples keep their flavour best. Peel, core, and slice in rings ; string, or place loose on shallow trays ; dry in a cool oven, in the sun, or in an evaporater. Elderflowers, placed between the layers of apples when stored, are said to impart a peculiarly delicate taste.

534. DRIED APPLES, No. 2

Take ripe cooking-apples, pare, and slice them about three inches long ; string them with twine and a clean darning-needle, and hang them over a warm kitchen range or in a similarly warm place until they are perfectly dry : this may take weeks. When quite ready, store them in tin or wooden boxes in a cool, dry place.

535. DRIED APPLES, No. 3

Procure a round cutter for coring the apples, and peel them thinly. Remove any specks or bruises, and, having cored the fruit, cut each apple across in four or five rings. Thread them on strings, and hang them out to dry in the sun. Bring them in directly the sun goes off them. It may take several

days to dry them thus. If no sunshine be available,
they may be strung over the rack of the kitchen
stove. When quite dry, they must be packed in
air-tight tins.

Windfalls can be successfully utilised as above.

536. DRIED CHERRIES, No. 1

Select sound ripe cherries; wipe them clean, leaving the stalks on; place in a moderate oven and
leave till thoroughly dried; tie in bunches, and
keep in dry glasses or tins in a dry place.

537. DRIED CHERRIES, No. 2 (Seventeenth Century)

Stone the cherries and set them in a pan over
the fire, with only what liquor comes out of them;
shake them as they boil; then put them in an
earthen pot. The next day scald them, and when
they are cold, lay them on sieves to dry in an oven
not too hot. Twice heating in an oven will dry
any sort of cherries.

538. DRIED CHERRIES, No. 3

Take sound just-ripe cherries; place them on
dishes in a moderate oven, and let them get
thoroughly dried right through before they have
time to change colour. Tie them in bunches, and
store in a dry place in paper bags. Soak overnight
in a little water before cooking.

539. DRIED DAMSONS

Damsons, gathered fully ripe, should be spread
on a coarse cloth and set in a very cool oven for a

day or two. If they are not by then as dry as fresh prunes, put them in again for a day or two longer. Then keep them in a dry place.

540. DRIED PEACHES

Take very ripe peaches; peel, stone, and crush them. Spread out the pulp on plates, and let dry in a slow oven until it looks like leather. It can be rolled up and kept in boxes or bags, and should be soaked overnight, before using, in a very small quantity of water.

541. DRIED PLUMS

For these there are three requisites : an ordinary oven, a thermometer registering up to 250° F., and a few shallow trays—I should recommend good enamel ones which will stand heat, or, failing these, fireproof shallow dishes.

The fruit must be just ripe and perfectly sound in all respects. It must be put into an oven at a temperature of 100° F. and kept at that heat for eight hours. It will swell in the course of that time, and must be taken out and let to subside before replacing ; the skin must not burst. This means that you must watch and examine it frequently.

After the first eight hours are up, take out the trays and let the fruit cool off in them ; then replace them in a temperature of 130° F. for another eight hours, and again remove and cool off. Put an empty tray on top of each full one, and turn them together upside down, so as to reverse the fruit, and place for the third eight-hour shift in a temperature of 170° F. At the end of that time the fruit should be dried; if not, the process must continue. But it cannot be hurried in any way, and as some plums dry much faster than others, no hard-and-fast rule as to time is possible.

When the fruit is dry, store it in air-tight boxes in a very dry place.

542. DRIED QUINCES

Peel, core, and slice the quinces; string them and hang them to dry, the same as apples and pears. They must be washed and soaked overnight when you wish to use them, and stewed in a syrup made with the water in which they were soaked.

543. DRIED RASPBERRIES

Take sound ripe raspberries; shake them gently in a clean cloth, but do not wipe, rub, or squeeze them; spread them on fireproof dishes to a depth of three berries, and put them in the oven till they come to scalding-point; then place in a warm but not hot place, such as the side of the range, and stir now and then to turn the berries about well. It will take about forty-eight hours before the moisture has all evaporated; then put the fruit back in the oven, let them heat up once more as at first, and place them in clean, dry jars; cover at once.

A CATALOGUE OF SELECTED DOVER BOOKS
IN ALL FIELDS OF INTEREST

A CATALOGUE OF SELECTED DOVER
BOOKS IN ALL FIELDS OF INTEREST

CONDITIONED REFLEXES, Ivan P. Pavlov. Full translation of most complete statement of Pavlov's work; cerebral damage, conditioned reflex, experiments with dogs, sleep, similar topics of great importance. 430pp. 5⅜ x 8½. 60614-7 Pa. $4.50

NOTES ON NURSING: WHAT IT IS, AND WHAT IT IS NOT, Florence Nightingale. Outspoken writings by founder of modern nursing. When first published (1860) it played an important role in much needed revolution in nursing. Still stimulating. 140pp. 5⅜ x 8½. 22340-X Pa. $2.50

HARTER'S PICTURE ARCHIVE FOR COLLAGE AND ILLUSTRATION, Jim Harter. Over 300 authentic, rare 19th-century engravings selected by noted collagist for artists, designers, decoupeurs, etc. Machines, people, animals, etc., printed one side of page. 25 scene plates for backgrounds. 6 collages by Harter, Satty, Singer, Evans. Introduction. 192pp. 8⅞ x 11¾. 23659-5 Pa. $5.00

MANUAL OF TRADITIONAL WOOD CARVING, edited by Paul N. Hasluck. Possibly the best book in English on the craft of wood carving. Practical instructions, along with 1,146 working drawings and photographic illustrations. Formerly titled Cassell's Wood Carving. 576pp. 6½ x 9¼. 23489-4 Pa. $7.95

THE PRINCIPLES AND PRACTICE OF HAND OR SIMPLE TURNING, John Jacob Holtzapffel. Full coverage of basic lathe techniques—history and development, special apparatus, softwood turning, hardwood turning, metal turning. Many projects—billiard ball, works formed within a sphere, egg cups, ash trays, vases, jardiniers, others—included. 1881 edition. 800 illustrations. 592pp. 6⅛ x 9¼. 23365-0 Clothbd. $15.00

THE JOY OF HANDWEAVING, Osma Tod. Only book you need for hand weaving. Fundamentals, threads, weaves, plus numerous projects for small board-loom, two-harness, tapestry, laid-in, four-harness weaving and more. Over 160 illustrations. 2nd revised edition. 352pp. 6½ x 9¼. 23458-4 Pa. $5.00

THE BOOK OF WOOD CARVING, Charles Marshall Sayers. Still finest book for beginning student in wood sculpture. Noted teacher, craftsman discusses fundamentals, technique; gives 34 designs, over 34 projects for panels, bookends, mirrors, etc. "Absolutely first-rate"—E. J. Tangerman. 33 photos. 118pp. 7¾ x 10⅝. 23654-4 Pa. $3.50

THE SENSE OF BEAUTY, George Santayana. Masterfully written discussion of nature of beauty, materials of beauty, form, expression; art, literature, social sciences all involved. 168pp. 5⅜ x 8½.   20238-0 Pa. $2.50

ON THE IMPROVEMENT OF THE UNDERSTANDING, Benedict Spinoza. Also contains *Ethics, Correspondence,* all in excellent R. Elwes translation. Basic works on entry to philosophy, pantheism, exchange of ideas with great contemporaries. 402pp. 5⅜ x 8½.   20250-X Pa. $4.50

THE TRAGIC SENSE OF LIFE, Miguel de Unamuno. Acknowledged masterpiece of existential literature, one of most important books of 20th century. Introduction by Madariaga. 367pp. 5⅜ x 8½.
20257-7 Pa. $4.50

THE GUIDE FOR THE PERPLEXED, Moses Maimonides. Great classic of medieval Judaism attempts to reconcile revealed religion (Pentateuch, commentaries) with Aristotelian philosophy. Important historically, still relevant in problems. Unabridged Friedlander translation. Total of 473pp. 5⅜ x 8½.   20351-4 Pa. $6.00

THE I CHING (THE BOOK OF CHANGES), translated by James Legge. Complete translation of basic text plus appendices by Confucius, and Chinese commentary of most penetrating divination manual ever prepared. Indispensable to study of early Oriental civilizations, to modern inquiring reader. 448pp. 5⅜ x 8½.   21062-6 Pa. $4.00

THE EGYPTIAN BOOK OF THE DEAD, E. A. Wallis Budge. Complete reproduction of Ani's papyrus, finest ever found. Full hieroglyphic text, interlinear transliteration, word for word translation, smooth translation. Basic work, for Egyptology, for modern study of psychic matters. Total of 533pp. 6½ x 9¼. (Available in U.S. only)   21866-X Pa. $5.95

THE GODS OF THE EGYPTIANS, E. A. Wallis Budge. Never excelled for richness, fullness: all gods, goddesses, demons, mythical figures of Ancient Egypt; their legends, rites, incarnations, variations, powers, etc. Many hieroglyphic texts cited. Over 225 illustrations, plus 6 color plates. Total of 988pp. 6⅛ x 9¼. (Available in U.S. only)
22055-9, 22056-7 Pa., Two-vol. set $12.00

THE ENGLISH AND SCOTTISH POPULAR BALLADS, Francis J. Child. Monumental, still unsuperseded; all known variants of Child ballads, commentary on origins, literary references, Continental parallels, other features. Added: papers by G. L. Kittredge, W. M. Hart. Total of 2761pp. 6½ x 9¼.
21409-5, 21410-9, 21411-7, 21412-5, 21413-3 Pa., Five-vol. set $37.50

CORAL GARDENS AND THEIR MAGIC, Bronsilaw Malinowski. Classic study of the methods of tilling the soil and of agricultural rites in the Trobriand Islands of Melanesia. Author is one of the most important figures in the field of modern social anthropology. 143 illustrations. Indexes. Total of 911pp. of text. 5⅝ x 8¼. (Available in U.S. only)
23597-1 Pa. $12.95

CATALOGUE OF DOVER BOOKS

THE PHILOSOPHY OF HISTORY, Georg W. Hegel. Great classic of Western thought develops concept that history is not chance but a rational process, the evolution of freedom. 457pp. 5⅜ x 8½. 20112-0 Pa. $4.50

LANGUAGE, TRUTH AND LOGIC, Alfred J. Ayer. Famous, clear introduction to Vienna, Cambridge schools of Logical Positivism. Role of philosophy, elimination of metaphysics, nature of analysis, etc. 160pp. 5⅜ x 8½. (Available in U.S. only) 20010-8 Pa. $2.00

A PREFACE TO LOGIC, Morris R. Cohen. Great City College teacher in renowned, easily followed exposition of formal logic, probability, values, logic and world order and similar topics; no previous background needed. 209pp. 5⅜ x 8½. 23517-3 Pa. $3.50

REASON AND NATURE, Morris R. Cohen. Brilliant analysis of reason and its multitudinous ramifications by charismatic teacher. Interdisciplinary, synthesizing work widely praised when it first appeared in 1931. Second (1953) edition. Indexes. 496pp. 5⅜ x 8½. 23633-1 Pa. $6.50

AN ESSAY CONCERNING HUMAN UNDERSTANDING, John Locke. The only complete edition of enormously important classic, with authoritative editorial material by A. C. Fraser. Total of 1176pp. 5⅜ x 8½. 20530-4, 20531-2 Pa., Two-vol. set $14.00

HANDBOOK OF MATHEMATICAL FUNCTIONS WITH FORMULAS, GRAPHS, AND MATHEMATICAL TABLES, edited by Milton Abramowitz and Irene A. Stegun. Vast compendium: 29 sets of tables, some to as high as 20 places. 1,046pp. 8 x 10½. 61272-4 Pa. $14.95

MATHEMATICS FOR THE PHYSICAL SCIENCES, Herbert S. Wilf. Highly acclaimed work offers clear presentations of vector spaces and matrices, orthogonal functions, roots of polynomial equations, conformal mapping, calculus of variations, etc. Knowledge of theory of functions of real and complex variables is assumed. Exercises and solutions. Index. 284pp. 5⅝ x 8¼. 63635-6 Pa. $5.00

THE PRINCIPLE OF RELATIVITY, Albert Einstein et al. Eleven most important original papers on special and general theories. Seven by Einstein, two by Lorentz, one each by Minkowski and Weyl. All translated, unabridged. 216pp. 5⅜ x 8½. 60081-5 Pa. $3.00

THERMODYNAMICS, Enrico Fermi. A classic of modern science. Clear, organized treatment of systems, first and second laws, entropy, thermodynamic potentials, gaseous reactions, dilute solutions, entropy constant. No math beyond calculus required. Problems. 160pp. 5⅜ x 8½. 60361-X Pa. $3.00

ELEMENTARY MECHANICS OF FLUIDS, Hunter Rouse. Classic undergraduate text widely considered to be far better than many later books. Ranges from fluid velocity and acceleration to role of compressibility in fluid motion. Numerous examples, questions, problems. 224 illustrations. 376pp. 5⅝ x 8¼. 63699-2 Pa. $5.00

THE COMPLETE BOOK OF DOLL MAKING AND COLLECTING, Catherine Christopher. Instructions, patterns for dozens of dolls, from rag doll on up to elaborate, historically accurate figures. Mould faces, sew clothing, make doll houses, etc. Also collecting information. Many illustrations. 288pp. 6 x 9. 22066-4 Pa. $4.50

THE DAGUERREOTYPE IN AMERICA, Beaumont Newhall. Wonderful portraits, 1850's townscapes, landscapes; full text plus 104 photographs. The basic book. Enlarged 1976 edition. 272pp. 8¼ x 11¼.
23322-7 Pa. $7.95

CRAFTSMAN HOMES, Gustav Stickley. 296 architectural drawings, floor plans, and photographs illustrate 40 different kinds of "Mission-style" homes from *The Craftsman* (1901-16), voice of American style of simplicity and organic harmony. Thorough coverage of Craftsman idea in text and picture, now collector's item. 224pp. 8⅛ x 11. 23791-5 Pa. $6.00

PEWTER-WORKING: INSTRUCTIONS AND PROJECTS, Burl N. Osborn. & Gordon O. Wilber. Introduction to pewter-working for amateur craftsman. History and characteristics of pewter; tools, materials, step-by-step instructions. Photos, line drawings, diagrams. Total of 160pp. 7⅞ x 10¾. 23786-9 Pa. $3.50

THE GREAT CHICAGO FIRE, edited by David Lowe. 10 dramatic, eyewitness accounts of the 1871 disaster, including one of the aftermath and rebuilding, plus 70 contemporary photographs and illustrations of the ruins—courthouse, Palmer House, Great Central Depot, etc. Introduction by David Lowe. 87pp. 8¼ x 11. 23771-0 Pa. $4.00

SILHOUETTES: A PICTORIAL ARCHIVE OF VARIED ILLUSTRATIONS, edited by Carol Belanger Grafton. Over 600 silhouettes from the 18th to 20th centuries include profiles and full figures of men and women, children, birds and animals, groups and scenes, nature, ships, an alphabet. Dozens of uses for commercial artists and craftspeople. 144pp. 8⅜ x 11¼. 23781-8 Pa. $4.00

ANIMALS: 1,419 COPYRIGHT-FREE ILLUSTRATIONS OF MAMMALS, BIRDS, FISH, INSECTS, ETC., edited by Jim Harter. Clear wood engravings present, in extremely lifelike poses, over 1,000 species of animals. One of the most extensive copyright-free pictorial sourcebooks of its kind. Captions. Index. 284pp. 9 x 12. 23766-4 Pa. $7.95

INDIAN DESIGNS FROM ANCIENT ECUADOR, Frederick W. Shaffer. 282 original designs by pre-Columbian Indians of Ecuador (500-1500 A.D.). Designs include people, mammals, birds, reptiles, fish, plants, heads, geometric designs. Use as is or alter for advertising, textiles, leathercraft, etc. Introduction. 95pp. 8¾ x 11¼. 23764-8 Pa. $3.50

SZIGETI ON THE VIOLIN, Joseph Szigeti. Genial, loosely structured tour by premier violinist, featuring a pleasant mixture of reminiscenes, insights into great music and musicians, innumerable tips for practicing violinists. 385 musical passages. 256pp. 5⅝ x 8¼. 23763-X Pa. $3.50

TONE POEMS, SERIES II: TILL EULENSPIEGELS LUSTIGE STREICHE, ALSO SPRACH ZARATHUSTRA, AND EIN HELDEN-LEBEN, Richard Strauss. Three important orchestral works, including very popular *Till Eulenspiegel's Marry Pranks*, reproduced in full score from original editions. Study score. 315pp. 9⅜ x 12¼. (Available in U.S. only)
23755-9 Pa. $7.50

TONE POEMS, SERIES I: DON JUAN, TOD UND VERKLARUNG AND DON QUIXOTE, Richard Strauss. Three of the most often performed and recorded works in entire orchestral repertoire, reproduced in full score from original editions. Study score. 286pp. 9⅜ x 12¼. (Available in U.S. only)
23754-0 Pa. $7.50

11 LATE STRING QUARTETS, Franz Joseph Haydn. The form which Haydn defined and "brought to perfection." *(Grove's).* 11 string quartets in complete score, his last and his best. The first in a projected series of the complete Haydn string quartets. Reliable modern Eulenberg edition, otherwise difficult to obtain. 320pp. 8⅜ x 11¼. (Available in U.S. only)
23753-2 Pa. $6.95

FOURTH, FIFTH AND SIXTH SYMPHONIES IN FULL SCORE, Peter Ilyitch Tchaikovsky. Complete orchestral scores of Symphony No. 4 in F Minor, Op. 36; Symphony No. 5 in E Minor, Op. 64; Symphony No. 6 in B Minor, "Pathetique," Op. 74. Bretikopf & Hartel eds. Study score. 480pp. 9⅜ x 12¼.
23861-X Pa. $10.95

THE MARRIAGE OF FIGARO: COMPLETE SCORE, Wolfgang A. Mozart. Finest comic opera ever written. Full score, not to be confused with piano renderings. Peters edition. Study score. 448pp. 9⅜ x 12¼. (Available in U.S. only)
23751-6 Pa. $11.95

"IMAGE" ON THE ART AND EVOLUTION OF THE FILM, edited by Marshall Deutelbaum. Pioneering book brings together for first time 38 groundbreaking articles on early silent films from *Image* and 263 illustrations newly shot from rare prints in the collection of the International Museum of Photography. A landmark work. Index. 256pp. 8¼ x 11.
23777-X Pa. $8.95

AROUND-THE-WORLD COOKY BOOK, Lois Lintner Sumption and Marguerite Lintner Ashbrook. 373 cooky and frosting recipes from 28 countries (America, Austria, China, Russia, Italy, etc.) include Viennese kisses, rice wafers, London strips, lady fingers, hony, sugar spice, maple cookies, etc. Clear instructions. All tested. 38 drawings. 182pp. 5⅜ x 8.
23802-4 Pa. $2.50

THE ART NOUVEAU STYLE, edited by Roberta Waddell. 579 rare photographs, not available elsewhere, of works in jewelry, metalwork, glass, ceramics, textiles, architecture and furniture by 175 artists—Mucha, Seguy, Lalique, Tiffany, Gaudin, Hohlwein, Saarinen, and many others. 288pp. 8⅜ x 11¼.
23515-7 Pa. $6.95

SECOND PIATIGORSKY CUP, edited by Isaac Kashdan. One of the greatest tournament books ever produced in the English language. All 90 games of the 1966 tournament, annotated by players, most annotated by both players. Features Petrosian, Spassky, Fischer, Larsen, six others. 228pp. 5⅜ x 8½.   23572-6 Pa. $3.50

ENCYCLOPEDIA OF CARD TRICKS, revised and edited by Jean Hugard. How to perform over 600 card tricks, devised by the world's greatest magicians: impromptus, spelling tricks, key cards, using special packs, much, much more. Additional chapter on card technique. 66 illustrations. 402pp. 5⅜ x 8½. (Available in U.S. only)   21252-1 Pa. $3.95

MAGIC: STAGE ILLUSIONS, SPECIAL EFFECTS AND TRICK PHO-TOGRAPHY, Albert A. Hopkins, Henry R. Evans. One of the great classics; fullest, most authorive explanation of vanishing lady, levitations, scores of other great stage effects. Also small magic, automata, stunts. 446 illustrations. 556pp. 5⅜ x 8½.   23344-8 Pa. $6.95

THE SECRETS OF HOUDINI, J. C. Cannell. Classic study of Houdini's incredible magic, exposing closely-kept professional secrets and revealing, in general terms, the whole art of stage magic. 67 illustrations. 279pp. 5⅜ x 8½.   22913-0 Pa. $3.00

HOFFMANN'S MODERN MAGIC, Professor Hoffmann. One of the best, and best-known, magicians' manuals of the past century. Hundreds of tricks from card tricks and simple sleight of hand to elaborate illusions involving construction of complicated machinery. 332 illustrations. 563pp. 5⅜ x 8½.   23623-4 Pa. $6.00

MADAME PRUNIER'S FISH COOKERY BOOK, Mme. S. B. Prunier. More than 1000 recipes from world famous Prunier's of Paris and London, specially adapted here for American kitchen. Grilled tournedos with anchovy butter, Lobster a la Bordelaise, Prunier's prized desserts, more. Glossary. 340pp. 5⅜ x 8½. (Available in U.S. only)   22679-4 Pa. $3.00

FRENCH COUNTRY COOKING FOR AMERICANS, Louis Diat. 500 easy-to-make, authentic provincial recipes compiled by former head chef at New York's Fitz-Carlton Hotel: onion soup, lamb stew, potato pie, more. 309pp. 5⅜ x 8½.   23665-X Pa. $3.95

SAUCES, FRENCH AND FAMOUS, Louis Diat. Complete book gives over 200 specific recipes: bechamel, Bordelaise, hollandaise, Cumberland, apricot, etc. Author was one of this century's finest chefs, originator of vichyssoise and many other dishes. Index. 156pp. 5⅜ x 8.

23663-3 Pa. $2.50

TOLL HOUSE TRIED AND TRUE RECIPES, Ruth Graves Wakefield. Authentic recipes from the famous Mass. restaurant: popovers, veal and ham loaf, Toll House baked beans, chocolate cake crumb pudding, much more. Many helpful hints. Nearly 700 recipes. Index. 376pp. 5⅜ x 8½.

23560-2 Pa. $4.50

"OSCAR" OF THE WALDORF'S COOKBOOK, Oscar Tschirky. Famous American chef reveals 3455 recipes that made Waldorf great; cream of French, German, American cooking, in all categories. Full instructions, easy home use. 1896 edition. 907pp. 6⅝ x 9⅜. 20790-0 Clothbd. $15.00

COOKING WITH BEER, Carole Fahy. Beer has as superb an effect on food as wine, and at fraction of cost. Over 250 recipes for appetizers, soups, main dishes, desserts, breads, etc. Index. 144pp. 5⅜ x 8½. (Available in U.S. only) 23661-7 Pa. $2.50

STEWS AND RAGOUTS, Kay Shaw Nelson. This international cookbook offers wide range of 108 recipes perfect for everyday, special occasions, meals-in-themselves, main dishes. Economical, nutritious, easy-to-prepare: goulash, Irish stew, boeuf bourguignon, etc. Index. 134pp. 5⅜ x 8½. 23662-5 Pa. $2.50

DELICIOUS MAIN COURSE DISHES, Marian Tracy. Main courses are the most important part of any meal. These 200 nutritious, economical recipes from around the world make every meal a delight. "I . . . have found it so useful in my own household,"—N.Y. Times. Index. 219pp. 5⅜ x 8½. 23664-1 Pa. $3.00

FIVE ACRES AND INDEPENDENCE, Maurice G. Kains. Great back-to-the-land classic explains basics of self-sufficient farming: economics, plants, crops, animals, orchards, soils, land selection, host of other necessary things. Do not confuse with skimpy faddist literature; Kains was one of America's greatest agriculturalists. 95 illustrations. 397pp. 5⅜ x 8½. 20974-1 Pa. $3.95

A PRACTICAL GUIDE FOR THE BEGINNING FARMER, Herbert Jacobs. Basic, extremely useful first book for anyone thinking about moving to the country and starting a farm. Simpler than Kains, with greater emphasis on country living in general. 246pp. 5⅜ x 8½. 23675-7 Pa. $3.50

A GARDEN OF PLEASANT FLOWERS (PARADISI IN SOLE: PARADISUS TERRESTRIS), John Parkinson. Complete, unabridged reprint of first (1629) edition of earliest great English book on gardens and gardening. More than 1000 plants & flowers of Elizabethan, Jacobean garden fully described, most with woodcut illustrations. Botanically very reliable, a "speaking garden" of exceeding charm. 812 illustrations. 628pp. 8½ x 12¼. 23392-8 Clothbd. $25.00

ACKERMANN'S COSTUME PLATES, Rudolph Ackermann. Selection of 96 plates from the Repository of Arts, best published source of costume for English fashion during the early 19th century. 12 plates also in color. Captions, glossary and introduction by editor Stella Blum. Total of 120pp. 8⅜ x 11¼. 23690-0 Pa. $4.50

HOUSEHOLD STORIES BY THE BROTHERS GRIMM. All the great Grimm stories: "Rumpelstiltskin," "Snow White," "Hansel and Gretel," etc., with 114 illustrations by Walter Crane. 269pp. 5⅜ x 8½.
21080-4 Pa. $3.00

SLEEPING BEAUTY, illustrated by Arthur Rackham. Perhaps the fullest, most delightful version ever, told by C. S. Evans. Rackham's best work. 49 illustrations. 110pp. 7⅞ x 10¾. 22756-1 Pa. $2.50

AMERICAN FAIRY TALES, L. Frank Baum. Young cowboy lassoes Father Time; dummy in Mr. Floman's department store window comes to life; and 10 other fairy tales. 41 illustrations by N. P. Hall, Harry Kennedy, Ike Morgan, and Ralph Gardner. 209pp. 5⅜ x 8½. 23643-9 Pa. $3.00

THE WONDERFUL WIZARD OF OZ, L. Frank Baum. Facsimile in full color of America's finest children's classic. Introduction by Martin Gardner. 143 illustrations by W. W. Denslow. 267pp. 5⅜ x 8½.
20691-2 Pa. $3.50

THE TALE OF PETER RABBIT, Beatrix Potter. The inimitable Peter's terrifying adventure in Mr. McGregor's garden, with all 27 wonderful, full-color Potter illustrations. 55pp. 4¼ x 5½. (Available in U.S. only)
22827-4 Pa. $1.25

THE STORY OF KING ARTHUR AND HIS KNIGHTS, Howard Pyle. Finest children's version of life of King Arthur. 48 illustrations by Pyle. 131pp. 6⅛ x 9¼. 21445-1 Pa. $4.95

CARUSO'S CARICATURES, Enrico Caruso. Great tenor's remarkable caricatures of self, fellow musicians, composers, others. Toscanini, Puccini, Farrar, etc. Impish, cutting, insightful. 473 illustrations. Preface by M. Sisca. 217pp. 8⅜ x 11¼. 23528-9 Pa. $6.95

PERSONAL NARRATIVE OF A PILGRIMAGE TO ALMADINAH AND MECCAH, Richard Burton. Great travel classic by remarkably colorful personality. Burton, disguised as a Moroccan, visited sacred shrines of Islam, narrowly escaping death. Wonderful observations of Islamic life, customs, personalities. 47 illustrations. Total of 959pp. 5⅜ x 8½.
21217-3, 21218-1 Pa., Two-vol. set $12.00

INCIDENTS OF TRAVEL IN YUCATAN, John L. Stephens. Classic (1843) exploration of jungles of Yucatan, looking for evidences of Maya civilization. Travel adventures, Mexican and Indian culture, etc. Total of 669pp. 5⅜ x 8½. 20926-1, 20927-X Pa., Two-vol. set $7.90

AMERICAN LITERARY AUTOGRAPHS FROM WASHINGTON IRVING TO HENRY JAMES, Herbert Cahoon, et al. Letters, poems, manuscripts of Hawthorne, Thoreau, Twain, Alcott, Whitman, 67 other prominent American authors. Reproductions, full transcripts and commentary. Plus checklist of all American Literary Autographs in The Pierpont Morgan Library. Printed on exceptionally high-quality paper. 136 illustrations. 212pp. 9⅛ x 12¼. 23548-3 Pa. $7.95

UNCLE SILAS, J. Sheridan LeFanu. Victorian Gothic mystery novel, considered by many best of period, even better than Collins or Dickens. Wonderful psychological terror. Introduction by Frederick Shroyer. 436pp. 5⅜ x 8½. 21715-9 Pa. $6.00

JURGEN, James Branch Cabell. The great erotic fantasy of the 1920's that delighted thousands, shocked thousands more. Full final text, Lane edition with 13 plates by Frank Pape. 346pp. 5⅜ x 8½. 23507-6 Pa. $4.50

THE CLAVERINGS, Anthony Trollope. Major novel, chronicling aspects of British Victorian society, personalities. Reprint of Cornhill serialization, 16 plates by M. Edwards; first reprint of full text. Introduction by Norman Donaldson. 412pp. 5⅜ x 8½. 23464-9 Pa. $5.00

KEPT IN THE DARK, Anthony Trollope. Unusual short novel about Victorian morality and abnormal psychology by the great English author. Probably the first American publication. Frontispiece by Sir John Millais. 92pp. 6½ x 9¼. 23609-9 Pa. $2.50

RALPH THE HEIR, Anthony Trollope. Forgotten tale of illegitimacy, inheritance. Master novel of Trollope's later years. Victorian country estates, clubs, Parliament, fox hunting, world of fully realized characters. Reprint of 1871 edition. 12 illustrations by F. A. Faser. 434pp. of text. 5⅜ x 8½. 23642-0 Pa. $5.00

YEKL and THE IMPORTED BRIDEGROOM AND OTHER STORIES OF THE NEW YORK GHETTO, Abraham Cahan. Film Hester Street based on Yekl (1896). Novel, other stories among first about Jewish immigrants of N.Y.'s East Side. Highly praised by W. D. Howells—Cahan "a new star of realism." New introduction by Bernard G. Richards. 240pp. 5⅜ x 8½. 22427-9 Pa. $3.50

THE HIGH PLACE, James Branch Cabell. Great fantasy writer's enchanting comedy of disenchantment set in 18th-century France. Considered by some critics to be even better than his famous Jurgen. 10 illustrations and numerous vignettes by noted fantasy artist Frank C. Pape. 320pp. 5⅜ x 8½. 23670-6 Pa. $4.00

ALICE'S ADVENTURES UNDER GROUND, Lewis Carroll. Facsimile of ms. Carroll gave Alice Liddell in 1864. Different in many ways from final Alice. Handlettered, illustrated by Carroll. Introduction by Martin Gardner. 128pp. 5⅜ x 8½. 21482-6 Pa. $2.00

FAVORITE ANDREW LANG FAIRY TALE BOOKS IN MANY COLORS, Andrew Lang. The four Lang favorites in a boxed set—the complete Red, Green, Yellow and Blue Fairy Books. 164 stories; 439 illustrations by Lancelot Speed, Henry Ford and G. P. Jacomb Hood. Total of about 1500pp. 5⅜ x 8½. 23407-X Boxed set, Pa. $14.95

CATALOGUE OF DOVER BOOKS

THE COMPLETE WOODCUTS OF ALBRECHT DURER, edited by Dr. W. Kurth. 346 in all: "Old Testament," "St. Jerome," "Passion," "Life of Virgin," Apocalypse," many others. Introduction by Campbell Dodgson. 285pp. 8½ x 12¼. 21097-9 Pa. $7.50

DRAWINGS OF ALBRECHT DURER, edited by Heinrich Wolfflin. 81 plates show development from youth to full style. Many favorites; many new. Introduction by Alfred Werner. 96pp. 8⅛ x 11. 22352-3 Pa. $5.00

THE HUMAN FIGURE, Albrecht Dürer. Experiments in various techniques—stereometric, progressive proportional, and others. Also life studies that rank among finest ever done. Complete reprinting of *Dresden Sketchbook*. 170 plates. 355pp. 8⅜ x 11¼. 21042-1 Pa. $7.95

OF THE JUST SHAPING OF LETTERS, Albrecht Dürer. Renaissance artist explains design of Roman majuscules by geometry, also Gothic lower and capitals. Grolier Club edition. 43pp. 7⅞ x 10¾ 21306-4 Pa. $8.00

TEN BOOKS ON ARCHITECTURE, Vitruvius. The most important book ever written on architecture. Early Roman aesthetics, technology, classical orders, site selection, all other aspects. Stands behind everything since. Morgan translation. 331pp. 5⅜ x 8½. 20645-9 Pa. $4.00

THE FOUR BOOKS OF ARCHITECTURE, Andrea Palladio. 16th-century classic responsible for Palladian movement and style. Covers classical architectural remains, Renaissance revivals, classical orders, etc. 1738 Ware English edition. Introduction by A. Placzek. 216 plates. 110pp. of text. 9½ x 12¾. 21308-0 Pa. $8.95

HORIZONS, Norman Bel Geddes. Great industrialist stage designer, "father of streamlining," on application of aesthetics to transportation, amusement, architecture, etc. 1932 prophetic account; function, theory, specific projects. 222 illustrations. 312pp. 7⅞ x 10¾. 23514-9 Pa. $6.95

FRANK LLOYD WRIGHT'S FALLINGWATER, Donald Hoffmann. Full, illustrated story of conception and building of Wright's masterwork at Bear Run, Pa. 100 photographs of site, construction, and details of completed structure. 112pp. 9¼ x 10. 23671-4 Pa. $5.50

THE ELEMENTS OF DRAWING, John Ruskin. Timeless classic by great Viltorian; starts with basic ideas, works through more difficult. Many practical exercises. 48 illustrations. Introduction by Lawrence Campbell. 228pp. 5⅜ x 8½. 22730-8 Pa. $2.75

GIST OF ART, John Sloan. Greatest modern American teacher, Art Students League, offers innumerable hints, instructions, guided comments to help you in painting. Not a formal course. 46 illustrations. Introduction by Helen Sloan. 200pp. 5⅜ x 8½. 23435-5 Pa. $4.00

THE EARLY WORK OF AUBREY BEARDSLEY, Aubrey Beardsley. 157 plates, 2 in color: *Manon Lescaut, Madame Bovary, Morte Darthur, Salome,* other. Introduction by H. Marillier. 182pp. 8⅛ x 11. 21816-3 Pa. $4.50

THE LATER WORK OF AUBREY BEARDSLEY, Aubrey Beardsley. Exotic masterpieces of full maturity: *Venus and Tannhauser, Lysistrata, Rape of the Lock, Volpone,* Savoy material, etc. 174 plates, 2 in color. 186pp. 8⅛ x 11. 21817-1 Pa. $4.50

THOMAS NAST'S CHRISTMAS DRAWINGS, Thomas Nast. Almost all Christmas drawings by creator of image of Santa Claus as we know it, and one of America's foremost illustrators and political cartoonists. 66 illustrations. 3 illustrations in color on covers. 96pp. 8⅜ x 11¼. 23660-9 Pa. $3.50

THE DORÉ ILLUSTRATIONS FOR DANTE'S DIVINE COMEDY, Gustave Doré. All 135 plates from Inferno, Purgatory, Paradise; fantastic tortures, infernal landscapes, celestial wonders. Each plate with appropriate (translated) verses. 141pp. 9 x 12. 23231-X Pa. $4.50

DORÉ'S ILLUSTRATIONS FOR RABELAIS, Gustave Doré. 252 striking illustrations of *Gargantua and Pantagruel* books by foremost 19th-century illustrator. Including 60 plates, 192 delightful smaller illustrations. 153pp. 9 x 12. 23656-0 Pa. $5.00

LONDON: A PILGRIMAGE, Gustave Doré, Blanchard Jerrold. Squalor, riches, misery, beauty of mid-Victorian metropolis; 55 wonderful plates, 125 other illustrations, full social, cultural text by Jerrold. 191pp. of text. 9⅜ x 12¼. 22306-X Pa. $6.00

THE RIME OF THE ANCIENT MARINER, Gustave Doré, S. T. Coleridge. Dore's finest work, 34 plates capture moods, subtleties of poem. Full text. Introduction by Millicent Rose. 77pp. 9¼ x 12. 22305-1 Pa. $3.50

THE DORE BIBLE ILLUSTRATIONS, Gustave Doré. All wonderful, detailed plates: Adam and Eve, Flood, Babylon, Life of Jesus, etc. Brief King James text with each plate. Introduction by Millicent Rose. 241 plates. 241pp. 9 x 12. 23004-X Pa. $6.00

THE COMPLETE ENGRAVINGS, ETCHINGS AND DRYPOINTS OF ALBRECHT DURER. "Knight, Death and Devil"; "Melencolia," and more—all Dürer's known works in all three media, including 6 works formerly attributed to him. 120 plates. 235pp. 8⅜ x 11¼. 22851-7 Pa. $6.50

MAXIMILIAN'S TRIUMPHAL ARCH, Albrecht Dürer and others. Incredible monument of woodcut art: 8 foot high elaborate arch—heraldic figures, humans, battle scenes, fantastic elements—that you can assemble yourself. Printed on one side, layout for assembly. 143pp. 11 x 16. 21451-6 Pa. $5.00

AMERICAN ANTIQUE FURNITURE, Edgar G. Miller, Jr. The basic coverage of all American furniture before 1840: chapters per item chronologically cover all types of furniture, with more than 2100 photos. Total of 1106pp. 7⅞ x 10¾. 21599-7, 21600-4 Pa., Two-vol. set $17.90

ILLUSTRATED GUIDE TO SHAKER FURNITURE, Robert Meader. Director, Shaker Museum, Old Chatham, presents up-to-date coverage of all furniture and appurtenances, with much on local styles not available elsewhere. 235 photos. 146pp. 9 x 12. 22819-3 Pa. $5.00

ORIENTAL RUGS, ANTIQUE AND MODERN, Walter A. Hawley. Persia, Turkey, Caucasus, Central Asia, China, other traditions. Best general survey of all aspects: styles and periods, manufacture, uses, symbols and their interpretation, and identification. 96 illustrations, 11 in color. 320pp. 6⅛ x 9¼. 22366-3 Pa. $6.95

CHINESE POTTERY AND PORCELAIN, R. L. Hobson. Detailed descriptions and analyses by former Keeper of the Department of Oriental Antiquities and Ethnography at the British Museum. Covers hundreds of pieces from primitive times to 1915. Still the standard text for most periods. 136 plates, 40 in full color. Total of 750pp. 5⅜ x 8½. 23253-0 Pa. $10.00

THE WARES OF THE MING DYNASTY, R. L. Hobson. Foremost scholar examines and illustrates many varieties of Ming (1368-1644). Famous blue and white, polychrome, lesser-known styles and shapes. 117 illustrations, 9 full color, of outstanding pieces. Total of 263pp. 6⅛ x 9¼. (Available in U.S. only) 23652-8 Pa. $6.00

Prices subject to change without notice.